The Story of the World
Activity Book One

Ancient Times

From the Earliest Nomads to the Last Roman Emperor

Edited by Susan Wise Bauer

With activities, maps, and drawings by:
Joyce Crandell, Sheila Graves, Terri Johnson, Lisa Logue,
Karla Middleton, Tiffany Moore, Matthew and Katie Moore,
Kimberly Shaw, Jeff West, and Sharon Wilson

WELL-TRAINED MIND PRESS

www.welltrainedmind.com

Address requests for permissions to make copies to support@welltrainedmind.com

Designed by Charlie Park. Composed in Adobe Garamond Pro.
Printed in the United States of America.

ISBN-10:   1-933339-05-5
ISBN-13:   978-1-933339-05-4

ALSO BY SUSAN WISE BAUER

The Complete Writer: Writing With Ease
(WELL-TRAINED MIND PRESS, 2008)

The History of the Ancient World
From the Earliest Accounts to the Fall of Rome
(W.W. NORTON, 2007)

The History of the Medieval World
From the Conversion of Constantine to the First Crusade
(W.W. NORTON, 2010)

The History of the Renaissance World
From the Rediscovery of Aristotle to the Conquest of Constantinople
(W.W. NORTON, 2013)

The Story of the World
History for the Classical Child
(WELL-TRAINED MIND PRESS)

Volume 1: Ancient Times (revised edition, 2006)
Volume 2: The Middle Ages (revised edition, 2007)
Volume 3: Early Modern Times (2004)
Volume 4: The Modern Age (2005)

The Well-Educated Mind
A Guide to the Classical Education You Never Had
(REVISED EDITION, W.W. NORTON, 2016)

WITH JESSIE WISE

The Well-Trained Mind
A Guide to Classical Education at Home
(REVISED EDITION, W.W. NORTON, 2016)

For more on Susan Wise Bauer, visit www.susanwisebauer.com

Table of Contents

Chapters

How to Use This Activity Book

History is the most absorbing and enthralling story you can tell a young child, because it's true. A good history narrative is as strange and wondrous as a good fairy tale. Kings, queens, mummies, wooden horses, knights, and castles can be as fascinating as giants and elves—but they *really existed*!

In classical education, history lies at the center of the curriculum. The chronological study of history allows even small children to learn about the past in an orderly way; after all, the "best way to tell a story," as the King tells Alice in *Alice in Wonderland*, "is to begin at the beginning and go on to the end." When the study of literature is linked to history, children have an opportunity to hear the stories of each country as they learn more about that country's past and its people. History teaches comprehension; young students learn to listen carefully, to pick out and remember the central facts in each story. History even becomes the training ground for beginning writers. When you ask a young student to narrate, to tell back to you the information he's just heard in his own words, you are giving him invaluable practice in the first and most difficult step of writing: putting an idea into words.

This activity guide is designed to go along with Volume One of Susan Wise Bauer's *The Story of the World: History for the Classical Child*. Think of each section in *The Story of the World* as a "springboard" into the study of world history. This book provides you with a simple, chronological overview of the progression of history. It isn't intended to be complete, but when you do history with young students, you're not aiming for a "complete" grasp of what happened in the Modern Age. Instead, you want to give the child an enthusiasm for history, a basic understanding of major cultures and an idea of the chronological order of historical events.

Using This Activity Book at Home

The Activity Book has two sections: a parents' guide in the front, and consumable Student Pages in the back. (Note the page numbers at the bottom of each page to see what section you're in.) For each section in *The Story of the World*, follow this pattern:

1) Read the child one section from *The Story of the World*. Longer chapters are divided into several sections; each section is appropriate for one session of history. Good readers can read the section to you instead.

2) **Review Questions:** These test the student's comprehension. When he has thoroughly studied the chapter, he should answer these questions orally without looking at the book. Encourage him to answer in complete sentences when possible. This is training in reading comprehension (and it will help you evaluate whether the child is listening with attention and whether he's really understanding what he's reading). Answers given are approximate; accept any reasonable answer. You can also make up your own questions.

3) **Narration Exercise:** Have the child tell you in two to five sentences what the history lesson was about. You can prompt the child with the Review Questions. Encourage the child to include the major facts from the history reading, but not EVERY fact. We have supplied sample narrations simply to give some idea of acceptable answers, not to imply that you child's narration should match word for word!

   Write down the child's narration if the child is not writing independently. Good writers can be asked to write the narration down themselves. To help with this process, listen carefully to the child's narration and repeat it back to her while she writes; this will help with "writer's block." For any given section, you can instead ask the child to draw a picture of her favorite part of the history lesson and then describe the picture to you. Write the description at the bottom of the picture. Put the narration or the picture in a History Notebook—a looseleaf notebook that will serve as the child's record of her history study.

4) When you have finished both sections of a chapter, stop and do **additional reading** and **activities** on the topic covered by that chapter. This Activity Book provides titles of books that you can find at your library for additional history reading, as well as maps, hands-on activities, and other projects. Some topics have many more resources available than others. Ask your local librarian for further suggestions.

When you reach a topic that has a wealth of interesting books and activities connected to it, stop and enjoy yourself; don't feel undue pressure to move on. Check your local library for titles before buying. The recommended titles range in difficulty from books for reading aloud to first graders to advanced books appropriate for fourth graders to read independently. When appropriate, ask the child to draw pictures, to narrate, or to complete brief outlines about the additional reading as well. Put these pictures and narrations into a three-ring History Notebook. This should begin to resemble the child's own one-volume history of the world. Don't ask the child to narrate every book or she'll grow frustrated; use this as occasional reinforcement for a topic she finds particularly interesting.

Because students from a wide range of grades will be using this Activity Book, we have tried to provide a range of activities, appropriate for different levels. Some are more appropriate for younger students; others will require more in-depth thought. We encourage you to select the projects are most appropriate for you and your students.

5) **Maps:** Almost every section in Volume One of *The Story of the World* has an accompanying map activity. A blank map is in the Student Pages; an answer key-showing the correct, completed maps begins on page 168.

6) We have provided **encyclopedia cross-references** to the appropriate pages in *The Kingfisher Illustrated History of the World*, *The Kingfisher History Encyclopedia* (revised), *The Usborne Book of World History*, and *The Usborne Internet-Linked Encyclopedia of World History*. Use these books for additional supplemental reading, especially for those topics that don't have extensive lists of age-appropriate library books.

7) Choose appropriate titles from the recommended **literature lists** and read these with your child. Classical philosophy discourages the use of "reading textbooks" which contain little snippets of a number of different works. These textbooks tend to turn reading into a chore—an assignment that has to be finished—rather than a wonderful way to learn more about the world. Instead of following a "reading program," consider using the "real books" from these literature lists. Following each title is a range of grades showing the appropriate reading level. (RA=read aloud, IR=independent read)

8) Every four chapters, you should take one history class to prepare your history review cards. Photocopy the history cards (use stiff cardstock for longer-lasting cards) and cut them out; have the student color the picture. After the cards are completed, use them once or twice a week to review material already covered.

9) Optional: You can administer written tests (available separately from Well-Trained Mind Press) if you desire a more formal evaluation or wish to develop your child's test-taking ability.

Multilevel Teaching

The Story of the World series is intended for children in grades 1–4, but is often used by older students: Volume One is written primarily for grades 1–4; Volume Two for grades 2–5; Volume Three for grade 3–6; Volume Four for grades 4–8. The maps and many of the activities in this book are also appropriate for children in grades 4–8. To use *The Story of the World* as the center of a multilevel history program, have your older child independently do the following: Read *The Story of the World*; follow this with the appropriate pages from the *Kingfisher History Encyclopedia*; place all important dates on a timeline; do additional reading on his or her own level. For more book lists and detailed directions on classical education methods for both elementary and middle-grade students, see *The Well-Trained Mind: A Guide to Classical Education at Home*, by Jessie Wise and Susan Wise Bauer (revised edition, W.W. Norton, 2016), available from Well-Trained Mind Press (www.welltrainedmind.com) or anywhere books are sold.

An Important Note for Parents

Families differ in their attitudes towards teaching myths, in their willingness to view partially-clothed people in ancient art, and in their sensitivity towards the (inevitable) violence of ancient times. We suggest that you skim through the activities in this book, glance through the literature that we recommend, and skip anything that might be inappropriate for your own family. In addition, both the *Kingfisher History Encyclopedia* and the *Usborne Internet-Linked Encyclopedia of World History* contain a number of pages on prehistoric peoples that may not agree with your family's convictions about humankind's beginnings. If this might pose a problem for you, preview these books before purchasing or using them.

Additionally, we recommend that you **preview** the coloring pages for Chapters 17, 20, and 28 (Student Pages 50, 58, and 87), to make sure that they are appropriate for your family.

Using This Book in the Classroom

Although this Activity Book was initially designed to be used by homeschooling families, it adapts well to the classroom. On the next page is a sample of how each chapter may be taught:

1) The teacher reads aloud a chapter section while the students follow along in their own books. When you reach the end of a section, ask the review questions provided in this book to selected students. Depending upon the length of a chapter, you may read the entire chapter in one day or break it up over two days.

2) Using the review questions and chapter tests as a guide, type up a list of facts that the students should memorize, perhaps employing a fill-in-the-blank format. Give one to each student to help her prepare for the upcoming test. If you would like to administer formal tests, you can purchase them separately from Well-Trained Mind Press.

3) Have the students do the map exercises in the Student Pages.

4) Select one or two activities, found in the Student Pages. Some are more appropriate for classroom use than others.

5) Each day there should be an oral or written review. You can make it fun by playing oral quizzing games such as "Around the World," "Last One Standing," or "Jeopardy!"

6) On the last day before the test, have the students color their chapter review cards.

7) Test the students.

8) Periodically review past lessons so your students will remember history chronologically.

Pronunciation Guide

Abram – AY bram

Aegeus – EE jus or EE jee us

Ahmose – AH mos

Akhenaten – ah ken AH ten

Akkad – AH kad

Akkadia – ah KAY dee uh

Alaric – ah LAR ic

Alcibiades – al sih BYE uh deez

Amenemhet – AH men EM het

Amenhotep – AH men HO tep

Amon-Ra – AH men RAH or AY men RAY

Amun – AH men or AY men

Amytis – uh MYE tis

Anansi – ah NAN see

Anu – AY noo

Anubis – uh NOO bis

Aphrodite – A fro DITE ee or AH fro DITE ee

Appian – AP ee un

Ariadne – AIR ree ADD nee

Ashurbanipal – ash ur BAN ih pal

Asia Minor – AY zhuh MY nor

Asoka – uh SO kuh

Assur – AH sur

Assyria – uh SEE ree uh

Astyges – uh STIH jeez or uh STEE uh jeez

Aten – AH tun

Athena – ath EE nuh

Attila the Hun – uh TILL uh the HUN

Augustus Caesar – uh GUS tus SEE zer

Belshazzar – bel SHAZ er

Bhagiratha – bah gih RAH thuh

Boadicea – BO uh dih SEE uh

brahmin – BRAH min

Brutus – BROOT us

Bucephalas – byoo SEH fuh lus
     or byoo SHE fuh lus

Caesar – SEE zer

canopic – kuh NO pick or kuh NAW pick

Carthage – CAR thij

Carthaginian – CAR thuh JIN ee un

Cassius – CASS ee us

Ceres – SEER eez

Cheops – KEE ops

Cincinnatus – sin sih NAH tus

Claudius Pulcher – CLAW dee us PULL care

Cleopatra – clee o PAT ruh

Confucius – con FYU shis

Constantinople – CON stan tih NO pul

Cyclops – SIGH clops

Cyrus – SIGH rus

Diocletian – DIE o CLEE shun

Dorians – DOOR ee un

E pluribus unum – EE PLUR ih bus OO num

Enkidu – en KEE doo or en KIE doo

Eris – AIR ris

Et tu, Brute? – Et TOO, BROO tay?

Euphrates – you FRATE eez

familia – fah MEE lee ah

floris – FLO ris

frigidarium – frih gih DAR ee um
          or frih jih DAYR ee um

Ganga – GANG guh

Gautama – GOW tuh muh

Gilgamesh – GILL guh mesh

Gordian – GORE dee un

Gutians – GOO tee ANS

Hammurabi – hah mu RA bee

Hannibal – HAN ih bel

Haran – hah RAN

Harappan – huh RAP uh

Harpagus – har PAG us

Hatshepsut – hat SHEP soot

Hera – HEER uh or HAIR uh

Hieroglyphs – HIGH ro glifs

Honoria — on or EE uh	Minotaur — MIN uh tar or MY nuh tar
Horus — HORE us	Momyllus — muh MILL us
Huang Di — hwang DEE	murex — MYUR eks
Hyksos — HICK sos	Mycenaeans — MY suh NEE uns
imperator — im PEAR uh tor	Narmer — NAR mare
Indus — IN dus	navis — NAH vis
Ishtar — ish TAR	Nazca — NAZ kuh
Isis — EYE sis	Nebuchadnezzar — NEH buh kud NEH zer
Jakata — ja KA tah	Nefertiti — NEH fer TEE tee
Janus — YAH nus	Nero — NEER o
Jericho — JAYR ih ko	Nineveh — NIN uh vuh
Jove — JOHV	Ningal — NING gul
Judah — JOO duh	Nubia — NOO bee uh
Judea — joo DEE uh or joo DAY uh	Numitor — NOO mih tor
Julius Caesar — JOO lee us SEE zer	Octavian — ock TAY vee un
Juno — JOO no	Odysseus — o DIS ee us
Khufu — KOO foo	Olmecs — OLE mecs
Kish — KISH	Olympus — o LIM pus
Knossos — NAW sus	Orestes — o REST eez
Kush — KUSH (the "u" sounds like the "oo" in "foot")	Osiris — o SYE rus
Lei Zu — lay TZU	Parthenon — PAR thuh non
liber — LEE bear	Pax Romana — PACKS ro MAH nah
Londinium — lon din EE um	Peloponnesian — pel uh puh NEE zhun
Macedonians — mah suh DO nee unz	Pericles — PEAR ih cleez
Mahayana — MAH high yah nuh	Pheidippides — fih DIP uh deez or fie DIP uh deez
Marduk — MAR duke	Pictograms — PICK toe gramz
Mari — MAH ree	Plato — PLAY toe
mastaba tombs — MAH stuh buh toomz	Pompey — POM pee
Mauryan — MAR ee un	Poseidon — po SYE din
Maximian — mack SIH mee un	Potiphar — PAH tih far
Mayans — MY unz	princeps — PRIN keps or PRIN seps
Medes — MEEDZ	Proserpine — PRO ser PEE nuh
Media — MEE dee uh	Ptolemy — TALL uh mee
Menelaus — men uh LAY us or men uh LOUSE	Purusha — POO ruh shuh
Menes — MEN eez	Qin — CHIN
Mesopotamia — MESS uh puh TAY mee uh	Qin Zheng — chin ZHUNG
Milvian — MILL vee un	Ra — RAH or RAY
Min Lai — min LIE	Remus — REE mus
Minos — MY nus or MY nos or MEE nos	Romulus — ROM you lus

Rubicon – ROO bih con

Sakka – SACK uh

Sarai – SAIR eye

Sargon – SAR gone

Scipio – SKIP ee o   or   SIP ee o

scriptum – SKRIP tum

secutor – sec YOO tur

Seleucids – seh LOO sidz

Seleucus – seh LOO cuss

shaduf – sha DOOF

Shamshi-Adad – SHAM shee   ah DAD

Shang – SHANG

Shi Huangdi – SHIH   hwang DEE

Shiva – SHEE vuh

Siddhartha – sid ARE thuh   or   sih DART uh

Sparta – SPAR tuh

sphinx – SFINKS

Stilicho – STILL ih ko

Suddhodana – SUD ho DAN uh

Suetonius – soo TOE nee us

Sumer – SOO mer

Sumerian – soo MARE ee un

Sutra – SOO truh

Syrians – SEER ee enz

T'ang – TANG

Terah – TARE uh

Thebes – THEEBZ

Theodosius – thee uh DO shus

Thera – THAYR uh

Theseus – THEE see us

Thutmose – THUT mohs

Tiber – TIE ber

Tiberius – tie BEER ee us

Tiglathpileser – TIG lath pih LAY zer

Tigris – TIE gris

Tiye – TIE ee

Tripitaka – TRIP ee TAK uh

Tutankhamen – toot ang KAH men

Tutankhaten – toot ang COT en

Tyre – TIRE

Ulysses – you LIS eez

Uruk – OO rook

Utnapishtim – ut nah PISH tim

Veni, Vidi, Vici – VAYN ee, VEE dee, VEE chee
              or WAYN ee, WEE dee, WEE kee

Visigoth – VIZ ih gawth

Xi'an – SHYAN

Xiling Ji – SHEE ling   JEE

Yangtze – YANG see   or   YANG dzu

INTRODUCTION
How Do We Know What Happened?

Encyclopedia Cross-References

Usborne Book of World History: 2–3
Usborne Internet-Linked Encyclopedia: 104–105

Kingfisher Illustrated History of the World: 1–8
Kingfisher History Encyclopedia: viii–ix

Review Questions — What is History?

What do we call someone who reads letters, journals and monuments to find out about the past? *A historian.*

What do we call the story that historians write about the past? *History.*

Narration Exercise — What is History?

Ask the child to tell you in his own words about two ways that historians learn about the past. Acceptable narrations might include, "Historians read letters and look at monuments," or "People wrote letters and kings told people to write down stories. Historians can read them."

Review Questions — What is Archaeology?

What do *archaeologists* do? *Dig objects out of the ground and learn about them*

What kinds of things did people leave behind them, in the story we read? *Dishes, tools, toys*

Narration Exercise — What is Archaeology?

Ask the child to tell you in his own words about the kinds of things that archaeologists dig out of the ground. An acceptable narration might be, "Archaeologists dig things like dishes and toys out of the ground." You can prompt the child to add, "They find out about the past from these things."

Additional History Reading

Me and My Family Tree, by Joan Sweeney, illus. Annette Cable (Dragonfly, 2000). A picture-intensive book that explains a family tree in very simple terms. (RA [read-aloud])

Archaeologists Dig for Clues, by Kate Duke (HarperCollins, 1997). Explains archaeological work using a cartoon format. (RA)

The Magic School Bus Shows and Tells: A Book About Archaeology, by Jackie Posner (Scholastic, 1997). The Magic School Bus goes on a dig; also available on video. (RA)

I Can Be an Archaeologist, by Robert Pickering (Children's Press, 1987). Explains archaeology with simple text and real pictures. **Out of print; check your library.** (RA)

Writing Down the Days: 365 Creative Journaling Ideas for Young People, by Lorraine M. Dahlstrom (Free Spirit Publishing, 2000). For children who enjoy writing. (RA)

Activity Projects

Writing/Craft Project: Make a History of My Family Book
Materials:
- History of My Family cover and Family History page (Student Pages 1–2)
- crayons, pencils, and pens

- photographs of family members
- double stick tape or glue
- hole punch
- brass plated fasteners
- tape recorder (optional)

Directions:

1. Color the cover page for your *History of My Family* book and write your name where it says "taken by."

2. Make a copy of the Family History page for each member of your family.

3. Interview family members using the questions on each person's history page. Use a tape recorder if one is available. Paste or tape their picture on the page.

4. Punch holes and fasten book together with brass fasteners.

Writing / Craft Project: Make a "This is My Life" Timeline
Materials:
- timeline (Student Page 3)
- photographs
- double stick tape or glue

Directions:

Use the timeline sheet to record the important dates in your history. Each number on the timeline represents a year in your life so this timeline will last until your tenth birthday. You can leave the timeline in one piece or cut it on the dotted line and cover it with contact paper for durability.

1. Start at zero and write in your birthday and paste your first picture close to the date. You can draw a line or glue a piece of string from the date to your picture.

2. Add as many dates and pictures as you can. You can even draw pictures and glue souvenirs like theater tickets on your timeline.

Some ideas for things to include on your timeline are when you got your first tooth, when you first sat up, crawled, or ate with a spoon, your birthdays, and when your brothers and sisters were born.

Activity: A Dirty Dig!
(a simulation of an archaeological dig)
Materials:
- items from your household that represent our civilization
- a place to bury the above items
- a small shovel or garden trowel
- small brushes (old toothbrushes work well ... but don't plan on using them again!)
- bucket and containers
- a screen or sieve for sifting dirt
- plastic bags, string, paper, pencil

Setup Directions:

1. Assemble items to bury. Try to find things that would answer these kinds of questions: What did these people eat? What kind of transportation did they have? What kind of houses did they live in? What did they do for entertainment? Did they read and write? Think of some questions of your own.

2. Make a list of the "artifacts" and then bury them in a sandbox. If you can, spray the site with water and let it sit for a few days.

3. You will pretend you are an archaeologist digging up the ruins of an ancient civilization.

Activity Directions:

1. Use the string to mark off sections of the dig area (make a "grid" with the string across the surface of the ground). For elementary students, you should probably use only two strings to divide the ground into quarters; older children can use three or more pieces of string to divide the "dig" area into six or nine spaces.

2. Excavate one section at a time using the small shovel. Work carefully so the artifacts don't get damaged.

3. Use the small brushes to gently brush dirt from the artifacts.

4. Sift the dirt you remove from the hole so the smaller artifacts aren't missed.

5. As you remove the artifacts write down what you found and what square of the "grid" you found it in. Use plastic bags and containers to hold the artifacts.

6. Tell what you learned about this "ancient civilization."

CHAPTER ONE
The Earliest People

Encyclopedia Cross-References

Usborne Book of World History: 4–7

Usborne Internet-Linked Encyclopedia: 108–109

Kingfisher Illustrated History of the World: 18–19

Kingfisher History Encyclopedia: 8

Review Questions — The First Nomads

What sort of food did nomads eat? *Plants such as grasses, leaves, grain, roots, berries; large animals such as elk, deer, reindeer, bison; other foods such as eggs, honey, lizards, snakes, and fish.* See if your child can remember one type of food from each of the three categories. Prompt her by asking, "What kinds of growing things did they eat? What kinds of large animals did they hunt? What other kinds of food could they find?"

Where did nomads sleep? *In caves or tents*

Why did nomads move from place to place? *Because they hunted all the game and ate all the plants in one place, and had to move to another to find food*

What does "nomad" mean? *One who wanders or roams around*

Narration Exercise — The First Nomads

"Nomads moved around a lot. They lived in tents. They gathered grasses and berries and hunted animals for food."
OR
"Some people in olden times didn't have homes. They slept outside. They ate food that they picked and hunted, and they went from place to place."

Review Questions — The First Nomads Become Farmers

Why was the Fertile Crescent a good place to live? *Because there was water, good soil, and plenty of grass and plants*

Why was it called "fertile"? *Because lots of plants grew there*

What was it shaped like? *A crescent* OR *The new moon*

What did the first farmers grow? *Wheat and barley*

Did farmers move from place to place like nomads? *No.* Why? *Because they had to stay in one place long enough to tend their crops, water them, and harvest them*

How did farmers water their crops? *They dug canals from the river and built* shadufs.

Did the farmers still hunt wild animals? *They kept their own tame animals.*

What did the farmers build their houses out of? *Mud bricks and reeds*

How did they protect their villages? *They built stone walls around them.*

Narration Exercise — The First Nomads Become Farmers

"Some nomads settled down and grew crops. They watered the crops and built houses. They built walls around the houses. They lived in the Fertile Crescent"
OR

"Some people in olden times didn't have homes. They slept outside. They ate food that they picked and hunted, and they went from place to place. Farmers grew wheat and barley. They dug canals to water their plants. They lived in villages."

Additional History Reading

It's Disgusting and We Ate It! True Food Facts from Around the World and Throughout History, by James Solheim, illus. Eric Brace (Aladdin, 2001). Includes the foods that prehistoric peoples ate. (Possible IR [independent read])

Prehistoric World: Usborne World History (EDC Publications, 2000). Assumes evolution of humans as a fact. (RA)

Ancient Agriculture, by Michael Woods (Runestone Press, 2000). Chapters are divided into sections, each appropriate for reading aloud, covering the food-raising and food-gathering techniques of several different eras. The first chapter covers the nomadic lifestyle. (RA 1–3, IR 4–6)

Corresponding Literature Suggestions

One Small Blue Bead, by Byrd Baylor (Atheneum, 1992). A boy makes it possible for an old man in their primitive tribe to go in search of other men in far-off places. (RA)

The First Dog, by Jan Brett (Harcourt Brace, 1998). A cave boy makes friends with a wolf who saves him from danger. (RA)

Tonka, the Cave Boy, by Ross Hutchins (Rand McNally, 1973). The adventures of a boy living 8,000 years ago in an Alabama cave. **Out of print; check your library.** (RA)

Little Grunt and the Big Egg, by Tomie dePaola (Putnam, 2006). A light-hearted story about a nomadic family; no historical accuracy, but fun reading for beginners. Not appropriate for parents who wish to avoid "prehistoric man." (IR for most first graders)

Map Work

Chapter 1: The Earliest People (Student Page 4)

1. Find and circle the town of **Jericho**.

2. Trace the **Tigris** and **Euphrates Rivers** in blue. Lightly shade the seas blue.

3. Use a green crayon or colored pencil to color in the area between and around the Tigris and Euphrates Rivers. (If you need help, look at page 10 in *The Story of the World, Volume 1 revised* [page 20 in the first edition of *Volume 1*].) This area is known as the **Fertile Crescent**, and some nomads moved here because it was so easy to find food.

Coloring Page

A Farmer Using a Shaduf (Student Page 5)

Activity Projects

Art Project: Make a Cave Painting
Materials:
- Brown paper grocery bag or other paper
- Acrylic paints in black, beige, and reddish-brown
- Thick paintbrush

Directions:

1. Cut the paper bag open so that you have a large surface area to paint on. Next, crumple the paper, and then smooth it flat. This is to add irregularities to the painting surface to simulate painting on a cave wall.

2. To simulate the charcoal used by prehistoric man to draw pictures, use the black paint and draw a simple outline of an animal. Draw the animal's most obvious feature (e.g. tusks or antlers) in an exaggerated way. You can also add several stick figures carrying spears to depict a hunt.

3. After the animal outlines have dried, use the beige paint to fill in the design. Next use the reddish-brown paint to add highlights. This color resembles the red-ochre used by early man.

4. Let the entire piece dry completely, then hang it up to admire.

Craft Project: Make a Prehistoric Hunter's "Game Bag"

Materials:
- 18" x 22" animal print material
- 1 yard of thin rope or drawstring cord

Directions:

1. Fold right sides together so the piece measures 18 inches by 11 inches. Sew a ⅝-inch seam along the bottom and side edges. Be sure to leave the top of the bag open for turning.

2. Turn the bag right side out. Fold down a 2-inch hem towards the inside of the bag and top stitch 1 inch down from the folded edge. This will make the casing for the drawstring.

3. Next, with a sharp pair of scissors snip a small opening on one side of the casing. Make sure that you only cut through the top layer.

4. Finally, use a bodkin or a safety pin to thread the rope or cord around the bag and out the same opening. Tie the ends together and push the fabric down the cord to gather the material and close the bag.

Activity Project: Build Your Own Hut

After reading the chapter, go out in your backyard and try to construct a shelter from whatever materials are available in the yard. The hut can be for your favorite stuffed animal or, if you are more adventuresome, for yourself. Use sticks or branches to make the support structures then cover them using leaves, grass, fabric (an animal print would be nice) or an old blanket.

If you built a hut large enough for yourself, why not spend the night in it with another family member? When you're done, make a "What We Did" narration page that talks about what you think it was like for prehistoric man to live outside. What materials did he use to make his home? What did he have to worry about when he made it (like weather, wild animals, other hostile people)? Was it an easy way to live? Be sure to include a drawing or picture of the hut you made, so that it can be added to your history notebook.

CHAPTER TWO
Egyptians Lived on the Nile River

Encyclopedia Cross-References

Usborne Book of World History: 14–15 *Kingfisher Illustrated History of the World*: 26–27
Usborne Internet-Linked Encyclopedia: 114–115 *Kingfisher History Encyclopedia*: 10–11

Review Questions — Two Kingdoms Become One

Where is the Nile River? *In Africa*

What country did the Nile run through? *Egypt*. You may have to explain the difference between a continent—a huge land mass—and a country—a certain group of people who live on the land mass.

What did the Nile do every year? *It flooded.*

Why was this important? *Because it watered the land and brought silt up onto the riverbanks*

What were the two tribes who lived in Egypt called? *Upper Egyptians and Lower Egyptians*

Who ruled them? *The King with the Red Crown and the King with the White Crown*

Were they friends? *No, they fought constantly.*

Who won the battle between the White Crown and Red Crown Kings? *The White Crown King*

What kind of crown did the new king wear? *The Double Crown*

Narration Exercise — Two Kingdoms Become One

"The Nile is in Africa. Farmers liked for it to flood because it watered their land. The Egyptians fought each other until one king conquered the other and ruled the whole country. He wore both crowns."

OR

"The Upper Egyptians lived along the straight part of the Nile. The Lower Egyptians lived up in the delta. The Nile flooded every year. They grew crops in the soil."

Review Questions — Gods of Ancient Egypt

Did the Egyptians worship one god or many gods? *Many gods*

Can you name any of them? *Ra, Horus, Isis, Osiris, the pharaoh*

Do you remember the name of Osiris' evil brother? *Set*

How did Set get Osiris to lie down in the coffin? *He said that he would give it to whoever fitted it best.*

Did Osiris stay dead? *No, he came back to life again.*

Narration Exercise — Gods of Ancient Egypt

"The Egyptians believed in many different gods. Osiris was the king of the gods. His brother tried to kill him, but he came back to life."

OR

"Set wanted to kill his brother. He got him to lie down in a coffin and then threw it into the river. But Osiris didn't stay dead. That's why the Nile fills up every year."

Additional History Reading

The Nile River, by Alan Fowler (Children's Press, 2000). Pictures and descriptions of the land along the Nile. (RA)

Egyptian Gods and Goddesses, by Henry Barker (Grossett & Dunlap, 1999). Describes each Egyptian god briefly, along with pictures. (RA)

The Ancient Egyptians (History Opens Windows), by Jane Shuter (Steck-Vaughn, 2000). Good colorful illustrations of ancient Egyptian life. (RA)

Ancient Egyptian Jobs, by John Malam (Heinemann, 2002). Fairly detailed descriptions of the daily lives of ancient Egyptians in a variety of professions, including doctors, merchants, jewelers, coffin makers, pyramid builders, embalmers, and many more. (RA 1–3, IR 4–5)

Eyewitness: Ancient Egypt, by George Hart (DK Eyewitness, 2000). Very detailed two-page spreads on Egyptian history and customs; text fourth-grade level and up, but photographs are appropriate for all age levels. The first four pages deal with the earliest days of Egypt. (RA 1–4, IR 4–6)

Corresponding Literature Suggestions

Bill and Pete Go Down the Nile, by Tomie dePaola (Putnam, 1996). Bill and Pete (a little crocodile and his toothbrush) go on a class trip to the museum where they attempt to save the Sacred Eye of Isis. Will they succeed? You'll have to read to find out! (Possible IR)

Croco'nile, by Roy Gerrard (Farrar, Straus and Giroux, 2001). A young boy and his sister journey down the Nile River where they find a baby crocodile. (Possible IR)

Egyptian Myths, by Jacqueline Morley (Peter Bedrick Books, 1999). Legends include tales of creation, life after death, good and evil and the search for knowledge. (RA)

Tales of the Dead: Ancient Egypt, by Stewart Ross (DK Children, 2003). This well-illustrated book combines factual information and illustrations with an ongoing, graphic-novel-format mystery tale starring two young Egyptians from ancient times. Layout of factual information is similar to the Eyewitness book listed above, but text is simpler and shorter. (RA 1–3, IR 3–5)

Corresponding Audiobook Suggestions

Egyptian Treasures: Mummies and Myths, read by Jim Weiss (Greathall Productions). The central stories on which the Egyptian culture was based for thousands of years. In addition to these myths, the recording tells a true, modern story of scientists seeking a lost pharoah's tomb which includes information on the pyramids and the valley of kings. Available at www.greathall.com.

Map Work

Chapter 2: Egyptians Lived on the Nile River (Student Page 6)

1. Find the **Nile River** and trace its course in blue.

2. Draw a blue triangle around the **Nile Delta**, where the river breaks into several smaller rivers and empties into the Mediterranean Sea.

3. Draw a **red crown** in the area of **Lower Egypt**. Then, draw a **white crown** in the area of **Upper Egypt**. Remember, the Lower Egyptians lived in the area of the Nile Delta, and the Upper Egyptians lived along the straight part of the river.

4. When King Narmer conquered the Red Crown King, he wore the red crown over his own white crown. He made Egypt into one country. To show this on your map, shade all of **Egypt** lightly in red, even coloring lightly over the white crown in Upper Egypt.

Coloring Page

Osiris and Set (Student Page 7)

Using your colored pencils, crayons or markers, color the picture of Osiris in the coffin he won from Set. Everyone wouldn't look so happy, if they knew Set was going to throw Osiris into the Nile River!

Projects

Craft Project: Make a Model of the Nile

Materials:
- grass seed, potting soil, rocks and pebbles
- large waterproof pan (such as a disposable aluminium roasting pan), about 3" deep.
- tin foil
- water

Directions:
1. Fill the container ⅔-full with soil.

2. Push the soil away from the area of the Nile River to make the riverbed. Look at your map to see what shape the Nile should be. It should run through the center of the container, just as the Nile River runs through the center of ancient Egypt. Don't forget to make a triangle or Y-shape at one end, where the delta will be located.

3. Using a double layer of aluminium foil, line the riverbed. Ensure the foil is long enough to reach over the top of the container at each end, otherwise your river might drain into the surrounding soil. To make the Y shape for the delta, just cut the foil into the same shape and mould into the riverbed you created in Step 2.

4. Spread some pebbles into the river to weigh down the foil.

5. Sprinkle grass seed along the banks of the Nile.

6. Place some larger rocks along the right side of the container, to imitate the mountains in ancient Egypt.

7. Fill the river with water, letting it flood over the banks to water the seeds. This is the first method used for watering the crops.

8. Each week, water your model by flooding the Nile. Watch the grass flourish!

9. For added realism, make clay replicas of the pyramids and place them on your model of ancient Egypt, and float some grass boats (gather fresh or dry grass, and tie off each end, spread out grass in the center to make a boat shape) in your river, just like the ancient Egyptians would have floated their reed boats.

Craft Project: Make the White Crown of Upper Egypt

Materials:
- tape
- paper (one sheet of 8½" x 11")
- waxed paper (or a large sheet of white paper)

Directions:
1. Wrap the waxed paper around your head to make a cone shape. Tape the edges to hold the shape, then cut off any excess paper.

2. Scrunch the 8½" x 11" sheet of paper into an egg shape.

3. Push the ball of paper into the peak of the cone, and gently mould the waxed paper around it. This should result in a cone with a flattened top and an indent at the bottom of the egg-shaped top.

4. Cut the bottom edge of the cone so it fits nicely onto your head. Then, cut out the area around the ear.

5. Wear the White Crown on its own to be King of the Upper Egyptians.

Craft Project: Make the Shepherd's Crook of the Pharaohs

Materials:
- masking tape (wider is better)
- newspaper
- paint and brushes

Directions:
1. Twist the newspaper into a cylindrical shape, and bend to form a hook or C shape, leaving a straight tail at one end to insert into the tube. The hook should be about 5 to 6 inches from top to bottom, at most.

2. Insert the tail into the tube. Using masking tape, cover the hook, attaching it firmly to the tube. The entire hook should be covered with masking tape, to make painting possible (alternately, use your favorite paste and cover the hook with papier maché. Be sure it dries entirely before painting, if you do this).

3. Paint the tube to decorate as you think a pharaoh would see fit. Let it dry completely.

4. Wear your double crown, and carry your crook as the pharaohs did years ago. If you want to be even more like the ancient pharaohs, tie a swatch of yarn to one end of another tube, decorate, and you'll have your own switch, too.

CHAPTER THREE
The First Writing

Encyclopedia Cross-References

Usborne Book of World History: 10–122, 15

Usborne Internet-Linked Encyclopedia: 110–111

Kingfisher Illustrated History of the World: 28–29

Kingfisher History Encyclopedia: 9–10

Review Questions — The First Writing

What two types of writing did we talk about? *Cuneiform and hieroglyphics*

What two countries wrote in cuneiform and hieroglyphics? *Egypt and Sumer*

What three things did the Egyptians and Sumerians write on? *Stone, clay, and paper (or papyrus)*

Which is easiest to write on? *Paper*

Which ones lasted the longest? *Stone and clay*

Which one fell apart? *Paper*

What does "Mesopotamia" mean? *Between the rivers*

Do you remember what "hippopotamus" means? *River-horse*

Narration Exercise — The First Writing

Have the child tell you in three to five sentences what the history lesson was about. You can prompt the child with the questions listed above. The child's narration should include something about both cuneiform and hieroglyphics; you should prompt him for these names. Acceptable narrations might include:

"The Egyptians wrote on stone. These were called hieroglyphics. The Sumerians wrote on clay. These were called cuneiform."

OR

"Writing on stone was called hieroglyphics. Writing on clay was called cuneiform. This writing lasted a long time. Writing on paper didn't."

Additional History Reading

Ancient Egyptian Jobs, by John Malam (Heinemann, 2002). Fairly detailed descriptions of the daily lives of ancient Egyptians in a variety of professions, including doctors, merchants, jewelers, coffin-makers, pyramid builders, embalmers, and many more. (RA 1–3, IR 4–5)

Footsteps in Time: The Egyptians, by Ruth Thompson (Watts Books, 1995). An informative book with several fun activities which can be completed by the child, with minimal assistance from an adult or older sibling. (RA)

100 Things You Should Know About Ancient Egypt, by Jane Walker (Mason Crest Publishers, 2003). Has a write-your-name-in-hieroglyphs activity. (RA)

Corresponding Literature Suggestions

Seeker of Knowledge: The Man Who Deciphered Egyptian Hieroglyphs, by James Rumford (Houghton Mifflin, 2003). The story of the quest to understand Egyptian writing. (RA)

The Everyday Life of An Egyptian Craftsman, by Giovanni Caselli (Macdonald & Co., 1986). Information about various crafts from ancient Egypt, told by a school-aged Egyptian boy whose father has just been promoted to be a scribe. **Out of print; check your library.** (RA)

Casting the Gods Adrift, by Geraldine McCaughrean (Cricket Books, 2002). Suspenseful story about Tutmose, an apprentice who must decide between obeying his father or the king. Set in ancient Egypt and written by a great storyteller. (IR 4–6)

Map Work

Chapter 3: The First Writing (Student Page 8)

1. Find **Egypt** and shade it lightly in red. Remember, the White Crown King united Egypt into one country. He wore the red crown over his own white crown.

2. Find the **Nile River**. Trace it in blue. Many people in Egypt lived along the Nile River and near the Nile Delta.

3. Find **Sumer** and shade it lightly in green. Egypt and Sumer are the two countries where people first learned to write.

Coloring Page

Carving Hieroglyphs (Student Page 9)

This Egyptian scribe is carving hieroglyphs into stone.

Projects

Craft Project: Make Cuneiform Tablets
Materials:
- clay
- cuneiform alphabet guide (Student Page 10)
- scrap of paper
- small wedge (a thick screwdriver would work well)
- drinking straw and heavy string (optional)

Directions:
1. On the scrap of paper, write the message you will be translating and carving into the clay tablet. You could write your name to make a door plaque or a simple message to a friend or relative. Use your mind and imagination to determine what you would like to carve.

2. Roll the clay so it is a flattened rectangle, about ½-inch to ¾-inch thick. Trim the edges to make them neat.

3. Using your wedge, and following the cuneiform alphabet guide, carve your message into the clay tablet. The further you dig the wedge into the clay, the wider the mark will be. This is how the triangle shapes in the cuneiform alphabet were made by Sumerians. To make a narrower mark, press the wedge in the clay with less pressure. Alternately, if you are using a screwdriver, press the edge into the clay, wiggle it a little bit from side-to-side to get the triangle shape, then drag it straight through the clay to get the straight line. You might want to practise this before beginning your message. Once you are comfortable making the marks, re-roll the clay and begin carving your message.

4. If you want to hang your tablet, use a straw to punch a hole in both top corners.

5. Let the clay tablet dry according to package directions. If you are using clay gathered from outside, you can let it dry in the sun, or bake in the oven at a low temperature until the tablet is hardened and completely dry.

6. If you punched holes into your tablet in order to hang it you will need to thread some heavy string through the holes, and hang.

Craft Project: Make a Hieroglyphic Scroll

Materials:

- firm bristled paint brush
- hieroglyphic letter guide (Student Page 10)
- ink OR paint OR purple berry juice
- ribbon (yarn or string would also work)
- tape, thumb tacks
- lightweight paper (several sheets—computer banner paper would also work well) OR for more historical realism, buy some sheets of papyrus paper from a craft/art supply store
- 2 wooden dowels or sticks (slightly longer than the paper)

Directions:

1. On a piece of paper, plan the hieroglyphs you will use on your scroll. Remember to use the sounds in the words, not the actual letters (that means "Christopher" would be spelled "Kristofer"). You don't need to include silent letters (that means "night" would be spelled "nit"). If you really want to be authentic, search the Internet for "Egyptian hieroglyphs."

2. Tape several sheets of paper together, side to side, to make one long strip (you can skip this step if you are using computer banner paper, since it is already one long piece).

3. Using a stiff brush (the Egyptians used reeds with one end crushed into a brush) and the ink, paint, or berry juice, paint the hieroglyphs onto your scroll.

4. Let the ink dry completely, which shouldn't take very long.

5. Tack each end of the scroll onto a piece of dowel, or a stick.

6. Roll the scroll toward the center, ensuring roughly half the paper ends up on each pole. The two dowels or sticks should meet in the center.

7. Tie the scroll with a ribbon.

Activity Project: Why Do Clay Tablets Last Longer Than Paper?

Materials:

- Hieroglyphic scroll (use directions above; if you use paint or ink, make sure it is water-soluble)
- clay tablet (use directions for "cuneiform tablet" above)

Directions:

1. Place the clay tablet and the hieroglyphic scrolls outside. Leave them there for several days.

2. After a week, look at the tablet and the scroll. Are they the same as when you first put them outside? How are they different? Open the scroll and look at the print. Is it changed at all? Depending on the weather, they may have been rained or snowed on, or they may have sat under the hot sun's rays or in damp fog. The weather will determine how they have changed. If it rained, snowed (which is wet like rain), or was foggy (also wet), the paper scroll is likely soggy. Maybe it is even torn. The print is likely hard to read as well. If it was sitting in the hot sun for many days, the scroll might not look very different. The clay tablet, though, will be the same as the day you set it outside to weather. Even if it is wet, the print will still be easy to read. You won't see any changes in it unless you had a big wind storm, earthquake, or other phenomena that would cause it to fall, and possibly break—even then, you could piece it back together to read it.

3. Next, we will simulate a flood (the Egyptians did live next to the Nile, remember). If you haven't already, roll up the scroll. Take it and the tablet inside. Fill the kitchen sink with water. Put the clay tablet in. Now, put the paper scroll in. Let them sit for 5 minutes (it was a really quick flood—if you leave it longer, the

paper might fall apart!) How is the tablet? Wet, but doing OK, right? What about the scroll? Unroll it and look at the print. Can you still make it out? Good for you, if you can.

4. Now, roll up the scroll, if you haven't already. Have an adult put them in the oven for you, at a low temperature (not more than 200 degrees F). This part of the experiment is simulating the hot, dry conditions of ancient Egypt and Mesopotamia. The paper scrolls and clay tablets of long ago spent many years in hot, dry weather. To speed up the process, we're using the oven (after all, we can't wait years for this experiment!).

5. In half an hour, peek into the oven. If the paper starts to char, turn the oven off immediately (the scroll can remain inside the hot oven, though). In another half an hour, have an adult remove the tablet and scroll from the oven. Does the tablet look any different? Can you still read it as easily as before? What about the scroll? Unroll the scroll and look at the print. Is it any different? Did the paper tear or break at all when it was opened? The hot, dry air in the oven caused any changes you might see. Hot air outside will do the same thing over long periods of time.

6. The clay tablet will be very hot, so let it cool for an hour.

7. While you are waiting for the tablet to cool, re-roll the scroll. Show it to someone (your family pet, baby sibling or parent is fine). Make sure you unroll it when you show it to them. Then roll it up again. Show it to someone else, making sure you unroll it, then roll it up again. Keep showing it to other people (if you run out of live people or animals to show it to, stuffed animals would like to see it, too), making sure you unroll it to show them the hieroglyphs, and re-rolling it after looking. Remember how many times you showed the scroll. After an hour of unrolling and rolling the scroll, take a look at it. Has it changed in any way? The unrolling and rolling of the scroll simulated the use it might get if it were a real ancient Egyptian document. Did the paper tear or break from all this use?

7. The clay tablet should be cooled by now. If it isn't, use oven mitts to handle it. Now you will simulate the use it might get if it were a real Sumerian clay tablet in ancient Mesopotamia. Show it to the same number of family, friends and stuffed pals as you did with the scroll. (Lucky for you, this won't take as long, since there is no rolling and unrolling involved.) Has the clay tablet changed in any way after showing it so many times? Not at all. Your clay tablet sure is sturdy!

Results:

Likely by this point, your paper scroll isn't looking very healthy (How many pieces is it in?). The clay tablet, on the other hand, is looking pretty much the same way it did before we began this experiment.

If you wanted to test if further, have an adult build a campfire, and put the clay tablet in the fire. Even after burning for a several hours, it would still be in good shape. It might be black and sooty, but that can easily be wiped off (at least enough to read the print).

If you put the scroll in the fire, I think you know it would burn within minutes. While a real ancient scroll and tablet wouldn't be dunked in the water or baked in the oven, they would be exposed to the weather, including floods and the hot, dry air of the Middle East. The experiments you did simulated these elements of the weather, and reduced the waiting time (it might takes years for nature to do this much damage to a paper scroll).

Now, you know why the ancient clay tablets lasted much longer than the ancient paper scrolls.

CHAPTER FOUR
The Old Kingdom of Egypt

Encyclopedia Cross-References

Usborne Book of World History: 18–21
Usborne Internet-Linked Encyclopedia: 116–117
Kingfisher Illustrated History of the World: 26, 45
Kingfisher History Encyclopedia: 10–11

Review Questions — Making Mummies

What does *embalming* do? *It preserves a body.*

What did priests do to a body to make a mummy? *They took the insides out, preserved the body with salt and spices, wrapped it in linen and put it into a coffin.*

Why did the Egyptians think it was important to preserve dead bodies? *So that dead people could go on to the next world*

What did the Egyptians bury with their mummies? *Everything a dead person would need: food, clothes, toys, games, jewelry, furniture*

What was this time in Egyptian history called? *The Old Kingdom*

What do "BC" and "BCE" mean? *"Before Christ" and "Before the Common Era"*

What do "AD" and "CE" mean? *"Anno Domini" ("The Year of Our Lord" in Latin) and "Common Era"*

Narration Exercise — Making Mummies

"The Egyptians thought that people couldn't go to heaven if they didn't have their bodies. So they made mummies out of the bodies. They did this during the Old Kingdom."
OR
"The Old Kingdom was when the Egyptians made mummies out of dead bodies. They put all their insides into jars and put the mummies in special coffins."

Review Questions — Egyptian Pyramids

What kinds of tombs did pharaohs have? *Pyramids*

What were they made out of? *Stone.* [The child can also add that they were covered with white stone and capped with gold.]

What was Cheops's pyramid called? *The Great Pyramid*

How long did it take to build it? *Twenty years*

How did the Egyptians build the pyramids? *Thousands of workers built them by hand.*

What does the Great Sphinx look like? *It is half lion, half man.*

Did the Great Pyramid keep robbers out? *No, Cheops's mummy and treasures were still stolen.*

Narration Exercise — Egyptian Pyramids

"Cheops built the Great Pyramid out of stone. It was supposed to keep him safe, but robbers stole his treasure anyway."
OR
"The Egyptians built pyramids for their pharaohs. They thought pharaohs were gods."

Additional History Reading

Who Built the Pyramids?, by Jane Chisholm (Usborne, 2003). An Usborne guide to life in ancient Egypt, written for first through third grade. (RA for all but the most advanced readers)

Mummies Made in Egypt, by Aliki (HarperTrophy, 1985). A very simple guide to the mummy-making process. (RA)

Mummies: A Strange Science Book, by Sylvia Funston (Maple Tree Books, 2000). A book about mummies around the world; includes illustrations, photographs, a game, and an activity to complete. (RA)

Look Inside: An Egyptian Tomb, by Brian Moses (Raintree, 2000). Everything a child might want to know about an Egyptian tomb, illustrated with photographs of real objects and paintings. (RA)

Cat Mummies, by Kelly Temple (Clarion, 1999). Why were cats important to the ancient Egyptians? This illustrated guide explains. (RA)

The Best Book of Mummies, by Philip Steele (Kingfisher, 2005). Two-page spreads with colorful drawings and simple text explain how mummies were made and also add details about Egyptian daily life, history, and the discovery of the tombs in modern times. (RA 1–2, IR 2–4)

Curse of the Pharaohs: My Adventures with Mummies, by Zahi Hawass (National Geographic, 2004). A long but relatively simple book, written by an archaeologist and illustrated with many photos, describing his own experiences excavating in Egypt and also discussing the mythical "curse" of the mummies. An interesting appendix on "How to Become an Archaeologist," aimed at an elementary-school audience. (RA 1–3, IR 4–6)

Corresponding Literature Suggestions

I Am the Mummy Heb Nefert, by Eve Bunting (Voyager, 2000). An Egyptian mummy looks back on her days as a queen. (IR for many children; RA for beginners)

Easy to Read Mummy Riddles, by Katie Hill (Sagebrush, 1999). Nothing but mummy humor in this book of kid's jokes. (IR for many children; RA for beginners)

Magic Tree House: Mummies in the Morning, by Mary Pope Osborne (Random House, 1993). Jack and Annie find themselves whisked away to ancient Egypt, where they come face to face with a dead queen—and her 1,000–year-old mummy! (RA)

Magic Tree House Research Guide #3: Mummies and Pyramids, by Mary Pope Osborne and Will Osborne (Random House, 2001). Jack and Annie's very own guide to the secrets of ancient Egypt. Includes information on hieroglyphics, how mummies were made, tomb treasures and robbers, Egyptian gods and goddesses, and much more! (RA)

Map Work

Chapter 4: The Old Kingdom of Egypt (Student Page 11)

1. Find **Egypt**. Cheops's pyramid was located to the west, or on the left side, of the Nile River. On your map, draw a **golden pyramid** where Cheops's Great Pyramid and Sphinx were located.

Coloring Page

The Pyramids of Egypt (Student Page 12)

Projects

Activity Project: Make a Chicken Mummy

Materials:

- baking powder (3 cans)
- baking soda (3 boxes)
- chicken (small is good)
- freezer bags (large and lots)
- paper towels
- plastic gloves (chicken harbors nasty germs)
- rubbing alcohol (or any alcohol you may have—the Egyptians used wine)
- salt (several boxes)
- scented oil (recipe below—you can use unscented, if you prefer, and just rub the chicken with the spices when the oil is used)
- various spices (cinnamon, allspice, cloves, nutmeg, etc.)—optional
- water, white glue
- white linen fabric (or other fabric you have on hand)

Directions:

1. Put on your gloves! Chicken (and other poultry) can harbor bacteria that can make you sick.

2. Remove the neck and package of liver, heart, gizzard, etc. You can mummify these, but they continue to smell, even after being dried. It's your choice. If you do mummify them, the heart is usually wrapped in linen, and stuffed back inside the body. The other parts are put in canopic jars. Dry them following the same method as for the chicken.

3. Wash the chicken well in hot running water. Pat dry with paper towels. Wash again with the alcohol and pat dry. Don't forget to wash inside the cavity of the chicken as well. This helps to reduce the amount of bacteria that will grow on the bird. Dry the bird as much as possible before continuing with step 4.

4. Mix ½ a box of baking soda with ½ a can of baking powder and 2 boxes of salt. The addition of baking soda and powder will increase the acidity of the salt mixture, reducing the amount of bacteria that grows … the salt mixture will also be more similar to the *natron* salt that the ancient Egyptians used (which consisted of the three salts we are using, plus sodium sulfate). If you like, you can add spices to the mixture as well, to make it smell a bit nicer.

5. Pour some of this mixture into the cavity of the chicken until it is full. Then, pour some into a large freezer bag. Put the chicken in the bag, and add the rest of the salt mixture. The chicken should be completely covered. If it isn't, add more salt. Seal the bag. Put the sealed bag into a second freezer bag and seal.

6. Check the chicken every day for the first week. If the salt is wet, put on some gloves, remove the chicken from the bag, dust off the salt, and repeat step 4. You will likely need to do this after one day, then again two days later, and two to four days after that.

7. After the first week, check the chicken only once per week. If the salt is wet, put on some gloves, remove the chicken from the bag, dust off the salt, and repeat step 4. Likely you will need to do this at the end of the second and fourth weeks (usually every 5–10 days).

8. At the end of the sixth week, put on your gloves, remove the chicken from the bag, dust off the salt as completely as you can. Wet a paper towel and wipe any remaining salt off the bird. Be sure to dry it immediately afterwards with paper towels.

9. Rub the fragrance oil into the chicken, inside and out. If you are using unscented oil, you may rub spices into the chicken before rubbing in the oil.

10. Stuff the inside of the bird with fabric (or sawdust) and spices, if you like.

11. Now we begin the wrapping process. Tear the linen into 1-inch strips. Mix white glue and water (1–2 parts water to 1 part glue).

12. Dip the strips of linen into the glue, then begin wrapping. Wrap the wings and legs separately from the body. Once that is complete, wrap the body. It should be wrapped in at least 2–3 layers. If you like, wrap a few amulets into the mummy like the Egyptians did. Let it dry completely.

Craft Project: Scented Oil
Materials:
- jar with lid
- oil (any cooking or baby oil is suitable)
- spices (any that you like—a combination of 3 or 4 is good)

Directions:
1. Fill a jar to the top with spices.

2. Add oil to fill the jar.

3. Set it in a sunny location for a week. Shake the jar well 2–3 times per day.

4. Drain the oil. Repeat steps 1–4 for a stronger scent.

5. Use as a perfume as the Egyptians did, and in the mummy-making process.

Craft Project: Canopic Jars
Materials:
- 4 jars with screw top lids
- paints and brushes
- paper (any scraps will do; newspaper strips work well)
- water
- white glue

Alternately: instead of paper, water, and glue, you could purchase ready-made papier maché mixture or "paper clay" (a premixed papier maché mix) at a local art or craft supply store.

Directions:
1. Clean the labels off the jars, using hot, soapy water. If they are set well, try soaking overnight.

2. Put the paper and water into a blender and puree. If you are using a premixed pulp, follow package directions. Once mixed, continue with step 4.

3. Remove, drain excess water, mix in glue by hand or with a spoon.

4. Mould pulp onto jar lids into the shapes of the head's of Horus's four sons: human (Imsety, who protected the liver), jackal (Duamutef, who looked after the stomach), baboon (Hapy, who cared for the lungs) and falcon (Qebhsemuf, who tended the intestines). Let your creations dry completely.

5. Paint details onto the heads and let the paint dry. Decorate the jars, if you wish, with hieroglyphics or pictures.

6. Fill your jars with anything you like and enjoy.

Art Project: Sand-Cube Step Pyramid
Materials:
- cardboard
- plastic cling wrap
- sand
- white glue

(Alternatively, you could use 55 square sugar cubes OR 55 square LEGO blocks)

Directions:

1. Mix the sand with the glue, until it forms a thick, firm, moldable mixture. If you would rather, you can use sugar cubes or square LEGOS instead of home-made sand cubes (more realistic, and bugs won't try to eat them). If you choose this route, you can jump to step 5.

2. Spread the sand-glue mixture onto the cling wrap. It should be flat, and a little less than an inch thick. Let it set for 30–45 minutes—don't let it dry completely, or the next step will be more difficult.

3. Cut the slightly dried sand mixture into ¾-inch squares. A ruler could be used to do this, by pressing into the sand with the long, thin edge. You don't need to separate the blocks at this point. In total, you will need 55 cubes. Let the cubes dry another 24 hours.

4. Check to see if the cubes are dry. If they are, cut them apart again and continue with step 5. If they are not yet dry, re-cut the cubes, following the same cut marks from step 3, thereby ensuring they won't be completely glued together when you are ready to use them. Check the cubes again every 3–6 hours. Once they are dry, cut them apart and continue with step 5.

5. Now, you will need to count out 25 cubes for the base of the pyramid, 16 cubes for the second level, 9 cubes for the third level, four cubes for the next level, and one cube for the peak.

6. On the piece of cardboard, spread glue in the center, to form a square roughly 4 inches by 4 inches. Set the first 25 blocks on this square, in a grid of 5x5.

7. Spread glue on top of the base layer. Set 16 cubes in a 4x4-block square in the center of the bottom layer.

8. Spread glue on top of the second layer. Set 9 cubes in a 3x3-block square in the center of the second layer.

9. Spread glue on top of the third layer. Set 4 cubes in a 2x2-block square in the center of the third layer.

10. Spread glue on the final cube and place in the center of the fourth layer. Let the glue dry.

CHAPTER FIVE
The First Sumerian Dictator

Encyclopedia Cross-References

Usborne Book of World History: 8–9, 30

Usborne Internet-Linked Encyclopedia: 113

Kingfisher Illustrated History of the World: 24–25

Kingfisher History Encyclopedia: 9

Review Questions — The First Sumerian Dictator

Do you remember what *Mesopotamia* means? You may need to prompt the child for the answer: *Between the rivers.*

What two rivers is Mesopotamia between? *The Tigris and the Euphrates*

Were the cities in Sumer friends with each other? *No, they fought each other.*

What did Sargon do? *He conquered all the city-states and made them into one country.*

What was his country called? *Akkadia* or *the Akkadian Empire*

How did he keep control of it? *He made harsh laws and put his soldiers in the conquered cities to make them obey.*

What do we call it when a ruler uses an army to make sure that people obey without questions? *A military dictatorship.* It's fine to prompt the child for this answer—this is a new concept! We'll be returning to it again.

Narration Exercise — The First Sumerian Dictator

If the child uses the words "military dictatorship" in the narration, make sure he understands what this means! It isn't necessary to use this phrase in the narration since this is only the first introduction to this concept.

"The cities in Sumer all fought with each other. Sargon conquered them all. He made one empire out of them."

OR

"Sargon used soldiers to make people obey. The soldiers went to cities in Sumer. They made the cities follow Sargon."

Additional History Reading

Ancient Egyptians and Their Neighbors: An Activity Guide, by Marian Broida (Chicago Review Press, 1999). There are very few elementary-level books about Sargon and the Akkadian Empire, but this book has appropriate age-level readings and activities centered on the Akkadian people. (Also recommended for Chapters Seven and Eight).

Ancient Agriculture: From Foraging to Farming, by Michael Woods (Runestone Press, 2000). Chapters are divided into sections, each appropriate for reading aloud, covering the food-raising and food-gathering techniques of several different eras. The second chapter covers Sumerian farming and herding in the age of Sargon. (RA 1–3, IR 4–6)

Corresponding Literature Suggestions

An Illustrated Treasury of Read-Aloud Classics for Young People, edited by Becky Koh (Black Dog & Leventhal, 2003). Tales written for reading aloud, from a variety of sources—from *Cinderella* to a chapter of *A Wrinkle in Time*. Includes a tale from the Arabian Nights, retold in classic style by Andrew Lang, which takes place in the same area that Sargon conquered. (RA 1–4, IR 5–up)

The Golden Sandal (A Middle Eastern Cinderella Story), by Rebecca Hickox (Holiday House, 1999). A retelling of the Cinderella story in a Mesopotamian context. (RA)

The Three Princes: A Tale From the Middle East, by Eric Kimmel, illus. Leonard Everett Fisher (Holiday House, 2000). A princess sets her three suitors a task to find out which is most worthy. (RA)

Map Work

Chapter 5: The First Sumerian Dictator (Student Page 13)

1. The area Sumerians lived was called Sumer. Sumer was not one country, like Egypt, but was made of many city-states. Find **Sumer** on your map and underline it.

2. One story tells us that when Sargon was a baby, he floated down the Euphrates River in a basket. Find and trace the **Tigris** and **Euphrates Rivers** in blue.

3. Sargon was found at the edge of a river in the city-state called Kish. Sargon was raised in Kish, and became a servant of the king. Find **Kish** on your map and underline it.

4. Sargon conquered all of Mesopotamia and called his new empire Akkadia. Draw a line through the word "**Mesopotamia**," and write "**Akkadia**" to show Sargon's new empire.

Coloring Page

Sargon, King of Mesopotamia (Student Page 14)

Projects

Art Project: Make a Sumerian Seal

In the old days, very few people knew how to write their names. Instead, they made special seals that they pressed into wet clay. Each person's seal was different, so that people did not get confused.

Materials:
- air-drying clay
- a rolling pin, sculpting tool or sharp pencil
- white glue and water

Directions:

1. Roll out a piece of air-drying clay to the desired size, and about ½-inch thick.

2. With the sculpting tool, carve a pattern into the clay. Be sure to make it deep enough so that it can make a nice impression in the wet clay. Leave it to dry.

3. Roll out another piece of clay that is a bit larger than the seal and about ½-inch thick. When this is done, gently press the dried seal into the wet clay leaving a clear impression.

4. To make your impression into a pendant, use a toothpick to make a hole at the top for the string. Let this piece dry completely. If you want to, you can paint your pendant after that.

5. To give the pendant a nice shine, paint it with a mixture of 2 parts white glue to 1 part water. Brush over the entire piece and let dry. After the pendant has dried, cut a piece of soft cord to the desired length and thread it through the hole in the pendant and tie a knot at the end.

6. You could also use a colored stamp pad with your seal to make cards or decorative stationary.

Word Search Puzzle: Sumerian Inventions

Follow the instructions on Student Page 15.

CHAPTER SIX
The Jewish People

Encyclopedia Cross-References

Usborne Book of World History: N/A

Usborne Internet-Linked Encyclopedia: 142–143

Kingfisher Illustrated History of the World: 50–51

Kingfisher History Encyclopedia: 24–25

Review Questions — God Speaks to Abraham

In our story, why did Terah want to leave Ur? *He was afraid a war would start.*

What was Terah's son named? *Abram* ["*Abraham*" is also acceptable]

Terah and his family went to another city in Mesopotamia—Haran. Why did Abram decide to leave Haran and go to Canaan? *God told him to.*

What did God promise Abraham? *That Abraham would have a son*

Do you remember the name of Abraham's wife? It means "princess." *Sarah*

In the story, how old was Sarah when she had her baby, Isaac? *One hundred years old!*

Narration Exercise — God Speaks to Abraham

Ask the child to summarize the history lesson in two to four sentences. You can prompt him with the questions above. The narration should include the information that Abraham went to Canaan because God told him to. The child can use the name "Abraham" throughout his narration. Acceptable narrations might include:

"Abraham lived in Ur with his father. God told him to go to Canaan. Then he had a baby when his wife was 100." OR

"Abraham and Sarah went to Canaan. God told them to obey him and they would have a baby. Abraham laughed because he was so old, but they had a baby."

Review Questions — Joseph Goes to Egypt

What did Jacob give Joseph to show that he loved him? *A coat of many colors*

What did Joseph's brothers think about this? *They were jealous; they didn't like it.*

What country did Joseph's brothers send him to? *Egypt*

Joseph was the son of Jacob, and Jacob was the son of Isaac. Who was Isaac's father? *Abraham*

What did the Pharaoh dream about? *Seven fat cows and seven skinny cows*

What did his dream mean? *Seven good years would come, then seven years of famine*

After Joseph told him the answers to his dream, what did Pharaoh do? *Made him second-in-command in Egypt*

At the end of the story, where did the Israelites live? *In Egypt*

Narration Exercise — Joseph Goes to Egypt

"Joseph's brothers sold him to Egypt. He was thrown in jail. Then Joseph told the Pharaoh what his dream meant. Pharaoh made him second in command. Joseph's brothers came to get food. Then Joseph told them to all come to Egypt." OR

"Joseph's father loved him best and gave him a colored coat. Joseph's brothers were jealous. They sold him as a slave. Joseph told Pharaoh there would be a famine. He helped Pharaoh get grain and keep it. Joseph's brothers were hungry too. Joseph gave them food and they came to live in Egypt."

Additional History Reading

The Jewish Children's Bible: Genesis, by Sheryl Prenzlau (Pitspopany Press, 1996). Read the story of Joseph from Genesis itself. (RA)

Dance, Sing, Remember: A Celebration of Jewish Holidays (HarperCollins Juvenile Books, 2000). A page or two of text explains the significance and traditions of each of 11 holidays included in the book—a crash course in basic Jewish history! Most include a story, song, activity or recipe. (RA)

Old Testament Days: An Activity Guide, by Nancy I. Sanders (Chicago Review Press, 1999). Basic information and easy activity about life in Old Testament times. (RA)

Corresponding Literature Suggestions

Plays for Learning: Ancient Israel: Legends from the Bible and Jewish Folklore for Grades K–3, by L.E. McCullough (Smith and Kraus, 2001). Twelve brief plays, written for young children to read or perform, based on stories from the Old Testament and the Apocrypha. Some of the plays include stories from the midrash as well (e.g., Falsehood and Wickedness hitch a ride on Noah's ark). Clear explanations of the origins of each story. Not appropriate for parents who prefer to avoid Biblical paraphrase. (RA 1–3, IR 3–5)

The Coat of Many Colors, by Jenny Koralek, illus. Pauline Baynes (Eerdmans Books for Young Readers, 2004). A well-written picture book version of the story of Joseph, with pictures by the original illustrator of the *Chronicles of Narnia*. (RA 1, IR 1–3)

God's People: Stories from the Old Testament, by Geraldine McCaughrean, illus. Anna C. Leplar (Margaret K. McElderry, 1997). Well-told tales ranging from Creation to Esther. **Out of print**, but worth checking your library for. (RA 1–3, IR 3–5)

Corresponding Audiobook Suggestions

Tales from the Old Testament, read by Jim Weiss (Greathall Productions). An exciting introduction to the Bible. Features nondenominational portraits of biblical characters as caring, understandable humans facing extraordinary situations. Available at www.greathall.com.

Map Work

Chapter 6: The Jewish People (Student Page 16)

1. Find **Babylon** on your map. Circle the name in red, since the threat of war between Babylon and Ur was the reason Terah and his family left their home along the river.

2. Terah decided to move from Ur up to the city of Haran. Draw a line in blue from **Ur** up to **Haran**.

3. After Terah died, God told Abram to move to Canaan. Continue your blue line from Haran over to **Canaan.**

4. Abraham and Sarah had a child, Isaac. Isaac had a son named Jacob. Jacob had twelve sons. Joseph was Jacob's favorite son, and one of his youngest. He was sold as a slave by his older brothers and later became a governor of Egypt. Then all of his relatives moved from Canaan down to Egypt. Continue the blue line from Canaan down to **Egypt**, to show the path that the Israelites took.

Projects

Art Project: Make Joseph's Coat
Materials:
- construction paper
- glue, fabric scraps (optional)
- large sheet of butcher paper (or smaller sheets taped together)
- markers, crayons or colored pencils

Directions:
1. Have an adult or older sibling trace your body, wearing a robe, onto the large piece of butcher paper.
2. Decorate the coat with fabric scraps or with colored pencils, markers or crayons.
3. Draw a face for Joseph. Hang on the wall, or on a door.

Alternate Craft Project: Make Joseph's (More Realistic) Coat of Many Colors
Materials:
- button down shirt (If oversized, it will drape down the body more. Buy one inexpensively at a thrift store if needed.)
- paint (fabric paint that is painted on would be best, but tempera paint can be used—it will be more rigid, though)
- scissors

Directions:
1. Cut the collar off the shirt.
2. Paint the shirt in many colors. Let it dry completely.
3. Put it on, and pretend to be Joseph.

Alternatively, you could:
1. Cut a large paper grocery bag into a vest, instead of using a shirt.
2. Use fabric scraps instead of paint. Sew or glue them in place.

Activity Puzzle: The Jewish People Word Search

Follow the instructions on Student Page 17.

Activity Project: Color Your Own Comic Book!

Color in the comic book "Joseph: Lost and Found," on Student Pages 19–22.

CHAPTER SEVEN
Hammurabi and the Babylonians

Encyclopedia Cross-References

Usborne Book of World History: 9, 30–31

Usborne Internet-Linked Encyclopedia: 132–133

Kingfisher Illustrated History of the World: 47

Kingfisher History Encyclopedia: 21

Review Questions — Hammurabi and the Babylonians

Why did Hammurabi want to be king? *So that people would be treated fairly*

What city did Hammurabi rule? *Babylon*

What did Hammurabi write down on a stone monument? *Laws*

What were these laws called? *The Code of Hammurabi*

Who had to obey these laws? *Everyone in Babylonia*

Can you tell me about one of these laws? Allow the child to summarize any of the laws in the chapter.

Narration Exercise — Hammurabi and the Babylonians

Ask the child to summarize the history lesson in two to four sentences. You can prompt him with the questions above. The narration should include the information that Hammurabi was a king of Babylon who wrote laws. Appropriate narrations might be:

"Hammurabi lived in Babylon. He built an empire like Sargon. But he wanted to be fair."

OR

"Babylon was a city in Mesopotamia. The king was Hammurabi. He made the Code of Hammurabi. These were laws for everyone to obey."

Additional History Reading

Ancient Egyptians and Their Neighbors: An Activity Guide, by Marian Broida (Chicago Review Press, 1999). There are no easy-to-locate books about Hammurabi written on an elementary level, but this book (also recommended for Chapters Five and Eight) contains age-appropriate information and activities centered on the early Babylonian civilization.

Ten Kings: And the Worlds They Ruled, by Milton Metzger (Orchard, 2002). Brief and interesting biographical sketches of ten rulers, from Hammurabi through Peter the Great of Russia. The tone is aimed towards upper elementary-school students. **Out of print; check your local library.** (RA 3–4, IR 4–6)

Corresponding Literature Suggestions

Abu Ali: Three Tales of the Middle East, by Dorothy Van Woerkom (Crown, 1976). Three tales about Abu Ali, who counts his donkeys, fools his friends, and finally fools himself. **Out of print; check your local library.** (IR)

The Winged Cat: And Other Tales of Ancient Civilizations, by Deborah Nourse Lattimore (HarperTrophy, 2002). Three short tales, one of which is set in ancient Babylon. Written and illustrated by Lattimore. (RA 2–3, IR 4)

Map Work

Chapter 7: Hammurabi and the Babylonians (Student Page 23)

1. Find Hammurabi's city of **Babylon**, and circle it in red.

2. Hammurabi began by ruling over the city of Babylon, but he soon conquered the southern part of Mesopotamia and named it Babylonia. Find and lightly shade **Babylonia** in red.

Coloring Page

The Ziggurat of Ur (Student Page 24)

Using your crayons, color the picture of the Ziggurat of Ur. This temple was originally built by the Sumerians as a place to worship their moon god.

Projects

Art Project: Make Your Own Law Code Stele

A stele is a carved stone. Hammurabi had many of these markers carved to display his Law Code around his empire. This way his people would know what the laws were and would obey them. So, how about making one for yourself that shows the rules you follow at your house? You can even draw a picture at the top showing your mother, seated in a chair handing them to you—just like Hammurabi received them from the god of justice, Shamash. A children's book called *The Rules*, by Marty Kelley (Zino Press, 2000), might be fun to read before doing this project.

Materials:
- a large sheet of paper (10"x18")
- scissors
- a saucer
- a ruler
- colored pencils or crayons

Directions:

1. Using a saucer, or other round object, draw a curved line on the corners at the top of the paper. Use scissors to trim the pointed parts.

2. Measure down 9" from the top of the page and draw a straight line across the page with your ruler. The top curved portion of the page will be where you draw your picture and the bottom portion will be where you write your rules. Drawing extra lines with your ruler on the bottom portion of the page will make it easier to keep your writing straight.

3. When you're finished, hang your stele in your room so that you don't forget the rules!

Craft Project: Make a Ziggurat Temple

Materials:
- 4–5 different sized light cardboard boxes (e.g., cereal boxes)
- glue
- scissors
- poster paints or spray paint

Directions:

1. Place the largest box on the bottom and glue the next largest box on top of it. Take your third and fourth boxes and continue to glue them down to make your ziggurat.

2. Once the glue has dried, take your ziggurat outside and paint it with a reddish-brown color to simulate the look of dried mud bricks. You can either use the poster or spray paint, whichever you prefer.

3. Take another cardboard box and cut out 2-inch strips that can be used for the steps. The steps should run from the ground to the top floor of the ziggurat.

4. If you don't have a lot of empty boxes sitting around the house, use your LEGO or wooden building blocks instead. You can still use the strips of cardboard for your stairs on your project.

Activity Crossword Puzzle: Name That Place

Follow the instructions on Student Page 25. Answers: Akkadia, Ur, Jericho, Babylon, Tigris, Kish

CHAPTER EIGHT
The Assyrians

Encyclopedia Cross-References

Review Questions — Shamshi-Adad, King of the Whole World

What Assyrian king did we read about? *Shamshi-Adad*

What city did he live in? *Assur*

What was the name of his empire? *The Assyrian Empire*

How did he build his empire? *Through conquering other cities, through cruelty, through fear*

How was the Assyrian king, Shamshi-Adad, different from the Babylonian king, Hammurabi? Discuss the answer with the child: *Shamshi-Adad was a dictator who ruled by fear and cruelty. Hammurabi ruled by a code of laws.* Which kind of king is better?

Narration Exercise — Shamshi-Adad, King of the Whole World

Ask the child to tell the history lesson back to you in two to four sentences. The narration should include the information that Assyria was a cruel empire, and that it was eventually conquered by the Babylonians. It isn't necessary to remember the name of Shamshi-Adad! Acceptable narrations might be:

"The king of Assyria was a dictator. He made people obey him. Assyria became part of Babylon."

OR

"Shamshi-Adad wanted to be king of the whole world. He conquered cities and was very cruel. Then Hammurabi took his kingdom."

Review Questions — The Story of Gilgamesh

Was Gilgamesh a good king, or a bad king? *He was a bad king (although he was very strong).*

When Gilgamesh's people asked Anu the sky-god for help, what did he send? *The monster Enkidu*

Enkidu was half man and half what? *Animal*

What did the trapper's son do when he met Enkidu? *Took him home, taught him how to talk, eat, wear clothes*

When Enkidu and Gilgamesh fought, who won? *Gilgamesh, but he was too tired to keep fighting!*

What did Enkidu do to make the gods angry? *He killed the bull of the gods.*

Why did Gilgamesh decide to go see Utnapishtim, the only immortal man on earth? *He wanted to find the secret of eternal life* OR *He wanted to beat death.*

What is the first thing Utnapishtim told Gilgamesh to do, so that he would live forever? *Stay awake for six days and seven nights* OR *Stay awake for a very long time*

Did Gilgamesh stay awake? *No*

What did Utnapishtim tell Gilgamesh to do then? *Pick a magic plant from the bottom of the sea*

Who ate the magic plant after Gilgamesh picked it? *A snake*

Narration Exercise — The Story of Gilgamesh

This is a long and complex story for a young child to remember! Ask your child to tell you about Gilgamesh and Enkidu, or about Gilgamesh and Utnapishtim, but don't require her to do both. Remind her what the characters are named, since these names are strange and unfamiliar.

"Gilgamesh was a strong king, but he was very bad. The sky god sent a monster down to punish him. The monster was Enkidu. He learned how to talk. He almost beat Gilgamesh at a fight. They got to be friends. Enkidu got sick because he killed the bull of heaven."
OR

"Gilgamesh was sad because his friend was dead. He went to see a man who had lived forever. The man (Utnapishtim) told him to stay awake for a week. He couldn't. So the man told him to pick a magic plant. He did, but a snake ate it, so he got old and died like everyone else."

Additional History Reading

Ancient Egyptians and Their Neighbors: An Activity Guide, by Marian Broida (Chicago Review Press, 1999). Early Assyria, like early Babylonia and Akkadia, isn't popular with the publishers of children's books, but this activity book (also recommended for Chapters Five and Seven) contains good basic information about the earliest Assyrian people.

The Ancient Near East, by Rebecca Steforff (Benchmark, 2005). The three chapters in the book cover the history of ancient Mesopotamia, Anatolia, and Egypt. A fairly advanced book, but the sections on Assyria in the first chapter may be suitable as read-aloud supplemental material. (RA 3, IR 4–6)

Ancient Egyptians and Their Neighbors: An Activity Guide, by Marian Broida (Chicago Review Press, 1999). This book contains a few activities related to ancient Assyria—very little is available for elementary children on this subject. This book is also listed for Chapter Sixteen. (RA)

Corresponding Literature Suggestions

Gilgamesh the King, by Ludmila Zeman (Tundra, 1998). The cruel tyrant, Gilgamesh, learns the true meaning of friendship from Enkidu. (RA)

The Revenge of Ishtar, by Ludmila Zeman (Tundra, 1998). When Gilgamesh and Enkidu slay monsters that threaten the city of Uruk, the goddess Ishtar becomes angry. (RA)

The Last Quest of Gilgamesh, by Ludmila Zeman (Tundra, 1998). Gilgamesh sets out on a quest to conquer death. (RA)

Map Work

Chapter 8: The Assyrians (Student Page 26)

1. Shamshi-Adad lived in a city called Assur, in the north part of Mesopotamia beside the Tigris River. Find Assur and circle it in red.

2. Find the area that Shamshi-Adad conquered. Shade the area in red.

3. Assyria was in the north part of Mesopotamia. But Shamshi-Adad and the Assyrians never tried to conquer Babylon, in the south of Mesopotamia. Find the city of Babylon and circle it in green.

Coloring Page

Gilgamesh and the Lion (Student Page 27)

This picture is based on a carving sixteen feet high, found in Assyria at the entrance of a doorway.

Projects

Art Project: Draw a Picture of Enkidu

Because the story of Gilgamesh is a fairy tale, there's no one way to represent Enkidu. Although the *Story of the World* features one artist's picture of Enkidu, you can draw your own version of what you think he looked like. Remember, Enkidu was supposed to be a wildman—half man and half animal. What do you think he looked like? Did he have fur? Did he have claws? Use your imagination, and draw a picture of Enkidu.

Writing Project: Compose Your Own Fairy Tale

Use your imagination and write a fairy tale of your very own. Your story could be another adventure for Gilgamesh and Enkidu to embark on. Or, you could start from scratch and make up completely new characters and adventures. When you have decided what your tale will be about, tell a parent and they will write it down for you. To make your fairy tale complete, draw a picture to go with it. When you are done, be sure to place your finished story in your notebook to keep it safe.

CHAPTER NINE
The First Cities of India

Encyclopedia Cross-References

Usborne Book of World History: 28–29
Usborne Internet-Linked Encyclopedia: 118–119

Kingfisher Illustrated History of the World: 32–33
Kingfisher History Encyclopedia: 14–15

Review Questions — The River-Road

Why did ancient people use the river as a road? Acceptable answers: *It was easier than traveling on sand or rocks; it was faster than walking or using carts pulled by cows.*

Why did people in ancient Mesopotamia and India build cities near rivers? Acceptable answers: *There was plenty of water for drinking and for crops; it was easier to send food and other things down the water; the rivers were good roads for trade; the rivers were good for fishing.*

Narration Exercise — The River-Road

"People lived near rivers. They used the rivers to travel on. One of these rivers was the Indus River in India."

OR

"People built cities in the Indus Valley. It is in India. They used the river to get around. Sailing on the river was easier than going over the mountains."

Review Questions — The Mystery of Mohenjo-Daro

What is a citadel? *A stronghold at the center of a city*

Tell me some of the things that the people of the Indus Valley built. *Citadels, drains, houses from mud bricks, toilets, public baths*

What happened to the citadel cities? *No one knows for sure, but they were deserted.*

What did the quail decide to do, so that they could escape the hunter? *Stay all together*

Did it work? *Yes!*

Did the quail keep on cooperating with each other? *No, they started to argue and scattered.*

What did the hunter do then? *Caught them for supper*

Narration Exercise — The Mystery of Mohenjo-Daro

Ask your child to tell you about Mohenjo-Daro OR to tell you the story of the hunter and the quail—not both! Acceptable narrations might include:

"People in the Indus Valley built big cities. They had wells, baths, and citadels. One of the cities was Mohenjo-Daro. Then all the cities disappeared, but we don't know why."

OR

"The quail wanted to escape from a hunter and his net. They decided to stay together in one bunch. When the hunter threw his net on them, they all flew up together and got away. But then they started to fight with each other and the hunter caught them one at a time."

Additional History Reading

Exploration into India, by Anita Ganeri (Chelsea House, 2000). Plenty of photographs of Indian cities, countryside, and the Indus river in this elementary survey of India. (RA)

The Ancient World, by Jonathan M. Kenoyer and Kimberly Heuston (Oxford University Press, 2005). For grades five and up, a good introduction to the history and culture of ancient India. Of the twenty-three chapters, five deal with the Harappan civilization. (IR 5–up)

Corresponding Literature Suggestions

One Grain of Rice, by Demi (Scholastic, 1997). A reward of one grain of rice doubles day by day into millions of grains of rice when a selfish raja is outwitted by a clever village girl. (RA)

The Little Brown Jay: A Tale from India, by Elizabeth Claire (Mondo, 1994). A story of generosity. (RA)

Once a Mouse, by Marcia Brown (Aladdin, 1989). As it changes from mouse, to cat, to dog, to tiger, the pet of an Indian hermit becomes increasingly vain. (IR for strong readers)

Map Work

Chapter 9: The First Cities of India (Student Page 28)

1. On your map, find the **Indus River** and trace its path in blue.

2. Find the town of **Mohenjo-Daro**. Circle it in red.

3. The area around the Indus River became known as the **Indus River Valley**. You've already traced the Indus River in blue. Now color the area to either side of the river green.

Coloring Pages

A Ceremonial Mask (Student Page 29)

The people in the Indus River Valley used masks (like this tiger mask) in plays and religious ceremonies.

A Statue from Mohenjo-Daro (Student Page 30)

This picture of the Indus King is based on a sculpture found at Mohenjo-Daro.

Projects

Science Project: What Does It Take to Make a Brick?

This experiment is to find the combination of materials that are needed to make a brick from mud. Have the child mix up different ratios of dirt, sand and straw to find what makes the "best" mud. Remember that too much clay in the dirt will cause the brick to crack when it dries. Because it is coarse, sand keeps the brick from shrinking when it dries—but too much sand makes a brittle brick. See what works best with the type of soils you have in your area. All soils need different combinations.

Materials:
- dirt and sand
- straw, grass or thin twigs
- water
- a bucket
- a small box or milk carton to use as a mold

Directions:

1. Place the dirt, sand and clay material in a large bucket for mixing. Add pieces of straw, grass or thin twigs to the dirt. These will act as a bonding agent. Use your hands to mix the ingredients before adding the water.

2. Add the water slowly and continue mixing the dirt mixture until you get a thick, sturdy mud. You will probably have to experiment to find the best combination of ingredients.

3. Place the mud in any rectangular-shaped container. A small shoebox will work well, as will a milk container cut in half. Place the brick in a very warm place for about 2 weeks. When it appears to be thoroughly dry, remove the brick from the containers.

Craft Project: Make a Mohenjo-Daro Dwelling

Materials:

- a large amount of air-drying clay
- a rolling pin
- a sculpting tool or blunt knife
- white glue
- a ruler
- a paint brush
- thin cardboard
- reddish-brown paint

Directions:

1. Roll the clay out to a ½-inch thickness and start cutting out bricks. You might find that using a ruler as a straight edge and cutting the clay into ½-inch strips first will help. Then, cut 1-inch bricks from the strips.

2. Place the cut bricks on wax paper and let air-dry. When this is done, start building. The houses in Mohenjo-Daro were small rectangular buildings, with flat roofs. Many of them had no windows at all. White glue can be used as cement to hold your building together. Use a piece of thin cardboard for the roof. For a more realistic mud-brick look, paint your building with a brownish colored paint.

Writing Project: What Happened at Mohenjo-Daro?

"It was a dark and windy night as the town of Mohenjo-Daro slept. Little did anyone know that this was their last night…"

No one knows what happened to the people of Mohenjo-Daro. Why did they leave their beautiful city and never return? Was it a flood? Was it an earthquake? Or was it an invading army? Only you know the answer.

Use your imagination and decide what happened to the people of Mohenjo-Daro. When you've decided what your story will be about, tell a parent and they will write it down for you. Make your tale complete by drawing a picture to go with it.

CHAPTER TEN
The Far East: Ancient China

Encyclopedia Cross-References

Usborne Book of World History: 62

Usborne Internet-Linked Encyclopedia: 164–165

Kingfisher Illustrated History of the World: 42–43

Kingfisher History Encyclopedia: 18–19

Review Questions — Lei Zu and the Silkworm

Why is China called "the Far East"? *Because it is all the way to the east on the map, if you live in the Fertile Crescent*

The Chinese people lived between two rivers. Do you remember the name of one of them? The child can answer either "*The Yellow River*" or "*The Yangtze River*"; be sure to tell the child the name of the river she doesn't guess.

What was their valley called? *The Yellow River Valley*

The Chinese first settled in many small villages. Do you remember the name of the emperor who united them into one empire? *Huang Di* (be sure to supply the answer if the child can't remember)

What did Huang Di's wife, Lei Zu, discover? *She discovered the silkworm and learned how to make silk.*

Narration Exercise — Lei Zu and the Silkworm

Ask the child to tell you in her own words how the Empress discovered silk. An acceptable narration might be, "The Empress was eating in the garden. A worm fell into her tea. It was covered with threads! Then the Chinese people learned how to make silk from the threads."

Review Questions — The Pictograms of Ancient China

What Chinese dynasty did we read about today? *The Shang dynasty*

What is a dynasty? *A family that rules one country for years and years*

How long did the Shang dynasty rule? *Around 500 years*

During the Shang dynasty, the Chinese people began to use a special kind of writing. Do you remember what their picture-words are called? *Pictograms*

In pictograms, what do words look like? *Pictures!*

Do you remember any of the pictograms we looked at? *Sun, water, house, bow-and-arrow, soldier*

Narration Exercise — The Pictograms of Ancient China

Rather than asking the child to do a regular Narration Exercise, have him practice drawing one or two of the pictograms from the lesson above.

Review Questions — Farming in Ancient China

What valley did Chin live in? *The Yellow River Valley*

What two rivers ran on either side of the Yellow River Valley? *The Yellow River and the Yangtze River*

What crop did the ancient farmers of China grow? *Rice*

Why did Chin get up so early in the morning? *He was going to help his father in the fields for the first time.*

What kind of ground did the rice grow in? *Wet ground*

What was Chin supposed to do for his father, first thing in the morning? *Find out whether his father was well, and whether he needed food or water*

What story did Chin's grandfather tell? *About a time when the Yellow River flooded*

Narration Exercise — Farming in Ancient China

An acceptable narration for the last part of the chapter might be, "Chin lived in ancient China. He helped his father grow rice. The rice grew where the river flooded."

Additional History Reading

D is for Doufu: An Alphabet of Chinese Culture, by Maywan Shen Krach (Shen's Books, 2000). An introduction to elements of modern and ancient Chinese culture. (RA)

Ancient China, by Dale Anderson (Raintree, 2005). One of the "History in Art" series, this book discusses how historians can use art as a source, and then briefly covers the histories of four dynasties (Shang, Zhou, Qin, and Han) through examining artifacts from each era. (RA 1–3, IR 3–6)

Ancient China, by Neil D. Bramwell (MyReportLinks.com Books, 2004). For students mature enough to do additional research on the internet, this history of ancient China from the earliest civilizations through the Shang dynasty also provides links to reputable web sites which can provide much more information (e.g., National Geographic, several museums in China, the Library of Congress). (IR 4–up)

Ancient Agriculture: From Foraging to Farming, by Michael Woods (Runestone Press, 2000). Chapters are divided into sections, each appropriate for reading aloud, covering the food-raising and food-gathering techniques of several different eras. The fourth chapter covers food production in ancient China. (RA 1–3, IR 4–6)

Corresponding Literature Suggestions

The Story About Ping, by Marjorie Flack (Penguin Young Readers, 2000). A classic children's story; Ping is an adventurous duck who lives on the Yangtze River. (RA, possible IR for some advanced readers)

The Master Swordsman—The Magic Doorway: Two Legends, by Alice Provensen (Simon & Schuster Books for Young Readers, 2001). A very entertaining picture book about the wiles of a master teacher and a master artist. **Out of print; check your local library.** (RA 1–2, IR 1–3)

Cloud Weavers: Ancient Chinese Legends, by Rena Krasno (Pacific View Press, 2003). Brief (2–3 page) stories from ancient China, ranging from legends ("The Moon Goddess and the Rabbit") to stories with historical bases ("Confucius Talks With Children"). (RA 1–2, IR 3–6)

Map Work

Chapter 10: The Far East: Ancient China (Student Page 31)

1. Find the **Yellow River** and the **Yangtze River**. Use a blue crayon to trace the course of the rivers.

2. Lightly shade the **South China Sea** in blue.

3. Color the area between the two rivers in green. This was called the **Yellow River Valley**, and it is where the first Chinese settled down and started to farm.

Coloring Page

Chin and His Father (Student Page 32)

Using your crayons, color in the picture of Chin and his father going off to tend their rice fields.

Projects

Art Project: Make a Ming Bowl
Materials:
- a large piece of air-drying clay
- plastic wrap
- a small round plastic bowl
- a rolling pin
- a sculpting tool or blunt knife
- blue paint
- white glue
- a paint brush

Directions:

1. Roll the clay out into a large square that is about a ¼-inch thick. The square should be large enough to completely cover the plastic bowl and extend about ½-inch around it.

2. Wrap the bowl in plastic wrap and place it upside down on a piece of scrap cardboard or foil. Lay the clay over the upturned bowl and press the clay to the bowl. Use the sculpting tool to trim away the excess clay. Or, you can leave it there so that your bowl has a rim around it. You will need to use your sculpting tool to cut away the straight edges and make a smooth curve. Allow the piece to air-dry over night.

3. The clay bowl can now be removed from the form and painted. Chinese pottery was usually decorated with pictures of birds, flowers, and outdoor scenes. Use the blue paint to create any design that you like. When you have finished, set the bowl to one side to dry completely.

4. To give your bowl a shiny finish, use 2 parts white glue to 1 part water to make the glaze. Paint the glaze over the entire bowl. This can be done in two steps. First paint the outside, and after it has dried, glaze the inside of the bowl.

Writing Project: Make Your Own Pictograms
Materials:
- black poster paint
- a thin paintbrush
- white cardboard or construction paper

Directions:

Ancient Chinese pictograms looked like the things they stood for. What would the pictogram for "table" look like? How about pictograms for "brother," "sister," or "dog"? Make up your own pictograms and paint them in black paint on the white paper. Can your parents figure out what the pictograms stand for?

CHAPTER ELEVEN
Ancient Africa

Encyclopedia Cross-References

Usborne Book of World History: 82

Usborne Internet-Linked Encyclopedia: 172–173

Kingfisher Illustrated History of the World: 58–59

Kingfisher History Encyclopedia: 30–31

Review Questions — Ancient Peoples of West Africa

Do you remember what a continent is? *A large piece of land with many countries on it*

What continent is the Nile River in? *Africa*

Do you remember the name of the large desert in West Africa? *The Sahara Desert*

Was the Sahara Desert always hot and sandy? *No, once it had water and grass and animals in it.*

What did archaeologists find when they dug down into the hard, dry dirt of the Sahara? *Pollen, seeds, bones of animals, turtle shells*

Why did the people of ancient Africa go south? *Because the Sahara began to dry up*

Narration Exercise — Ancient Peoples of West Africa

Ask the child to tell you three things that he has learned about ancient West Africa. These might include (among others):

"The Nile River is in Africa."

"The Sahara Desert is in Africa."

"The Sahara Desert used to be grassy and have water in it."

"People in Africa had to go south when their land dried up."

"Archaeologists found seeds and animal bones in the desert."

"People in Africa made cave paintings."

Review Questions — Anansi and Turtle

What are yams like? *Sweet potatoes*

Why didn't Anansi want to share with Turtle? *He was too hungry!*

What did Anansi tell Turtle to do before he ate? *Wash his hands*

Where did Turtle set his supper table when Anansi came to visit him? *Under the water*

How did Anansi get down to the bottom of the water? *He put rocks in the pockets of his coat.*

What did Turtle tell him to do? *Take his jacket off before he ate*

What happened when Anansi took his coat off? *He popped back up to the surface of the water!*

Narration Exercise — Anansi and Turtle

Ask the child to retell the story in his own words. An acceptable narration might be:

"Anansi the Spider didn't want to share his supper with Turtle. He told Turtle to keep washing his hands until the supper was all gone. Then Anansi went to see Turtle. Turtle didn't want to share either! He put his supper at the bottom of the river. Anansi couldn't get down to the bottom to eat it!"

Review Questions — Anansi and the Make-Believe Food

Do you remember the three kinds of food that Anansi found in the villages? If necessary, prompt the child for the answers: *Cassava, plantains, and rice.*

What do cassava look like? *Potatoes*

What do plantains look like? *Bananas*

Why did Anansi keep on leaving the villages to go to the next one? *Because he thought he would find something better*

Did he get a wonderful meal at the end of the story? *No, he didn't get anything!*

What was the moral of this tale? *Don't be greedy—eat what you're given.*

Narration Exercise — Anansi and the Make-Believe Food

Instead of asking the child to tell you the story again, have her draw a picture of Anansi the Spider with a banana, a potato, and several grains of rice. Should the food have faces?

Additional History Reading

Great African Kingdoms, by Sean Sheehan (Raintree Steck-Vaughn, 1998). This book gives a great overview of the first kingdoms of Africa; a timeline and glossary are also included. (RA)

Look Who Lives In: The Desert, by Alan Baker (Peter Bedrick Books, 1999). Large illustrations and easy text makes it fun to learn about some of the animals that live in the desert. (RA)

Ancient West African Kingdoms, by Jane Shuter (Heinemann, 2002). An easy-to-read guide to the history and culture of Ghana, Mali, and Songhai, with a brief section on modern West Africa. (RA 1–2, IR 2–4)

Corresponding Literature Suggestions

Anansi the Spider: A Tale from the Ashanti, by Gerald McDermott (Henry Holt, 1982). This tale, which tells how mischievous Anansi and his six brave sons helped place the moon in the sky, won a Caldecott Honor Award. (IR for most readers, RA for beginners)

Zomo the Rabbit: A Trickster from West Africa, by Gerald McDermott (Voyager, 1996). Zomo the rabbit, an African trickster, sets out to gain wisdom. This tale originated in Nigeria. The pictures are colorful and enticing, adding to the excitement of the story. (RA)

Rhinos for Lunch and Elephants for Supper! A Maasai Tale, by Tololwa Mollel (Clarion Books, 2000). A tale from East Africa; the animals are frightened by the horrible-sounding monster who has taken over the hare's cave, until a clever frog solves the problem. (RA)

The Pot of Wisdom: Ananse Stories, by Adwoa Badoe (Groundwood, 2001). More tales about the trickster spider, written to be read out loud. (RA 1–3, IR 3–5)

Anansi and the Magic Stick, retold by Eric Kimmel (Holiday House, 2002). A brightly-illustrated picture-book tale of Anansi. (RA 1–2, IR 2–4)

Monkey Business, by Shirley Climo, illus. Erik Brooks (Henry Holt, 2005). Read-aloud tales, including five from ancient Africa (West Africa, the Congo, the Cape Verde Islands, Liberia, and Madagascar). (RA 1–3, IR 3–5)

Corresponding Audiobook Suggestions

Tales From Cultures Far and Near, read by Jim Weiss (Greathall Productions). Classics of many lands— wisdom from China and Japan, an African romance, wildly funny Native American, Arabian and Spanish tales—show that the human beings who tell them all are related. Chapter titles include: A Guest Who Ran (Native American), Two Monks (Japan), The Three Friends of Manuel (Spain), Courting the Wind (West Africa, The Secret Weapon (China), and Djuha: Two Stories (Arabic). Available at www.greathall.com.

Map Work

Chapter 11: Ancient Africa (Student Page 33)

1. On your map, put your finger between the **Tigris** and **Euphrates Rivers**. Put a B in the area of **Babylonia**. You can find Babylonia on the map from Chapter 7 if you need a reminder.

2. Put your finger back on the map, on Babylonia, and move it to the right—that's *east* on you map. Stop when you reach India. Find the **Indus River**, and color the **Indus Valley** green. Remember—the first cities of India were built there.

3. Draw an arrow pointing right off the map. Write "**China**" above the arrow (your mother or father can help). This note tells you that China is further in that direction.

4. Now go back to the Tigris and Euphrates Rivers. The area between the rivers is called "**Mesopotamia**." Color this area green. Nomads first settled here.

5. Now put your finger on Mesopotamia and go left—that's *west* on your map. You'll run into a big sea. What is this sea called?

6. Follow the shore of the Mediterranean Sea down to the Nile River. Circle the label on the map which identifies **Egypt**. Draw a little **pyramid** next to the name "Egypt."

Coloring Page

Anansi and Turtle (Student Page 34)

Color the picture of Anansi being tricked by Turtle.

Projects

Craft Project: Paper Bead Necklace

Materials:

- colored paper (magazine pages, construction paper, wallpaper samples)
- a glue stick
- a pencil
- scissors
- string

Directions:

1. Cut several triangles out of the colored paper. The width of the base should be between 1 and 2 inches, and the height should be around 4 to 6 inches. The wider the base, the easier it is to work with.

2. Starting with the base of the triangle, roll the paper around the pencil. Put some glue on the point of the triangle and press down firmly.

3. Remove the bead from the pencil and continue making beads until there are enough to thread onto the necklace.

4. Cut a length of string (long enough to easily fit over child's head when completed). Tie a large knot at one end of the string. Thread the beads onto the necklace. Tie the ends together when the necklace is complete.

Craft Project: Make Anansi the Spider

Materials:
- 1 1" styrofoam ball
- 1 2" styrofoam ball
- glue
- scissors
- googly eyes
- paint
- pipe cleaners
- a toothpick

Directions:
1. Paint (with brush or spray paint) both styrofoam balls. Let them dry.

2. Attach the smaller ball (head) to the larger ball (body) using part of a toothpick and/or glue.

3. Cut the pipe cleaners into eight appropriate lengths. Attach four per side to the body of the spider and shape them to look like legs.

4. Glue on the eyes and draw or paint a mouth.

Art Project: Painted Hands

Many African peoples painted their hands, feet and other body parts, usually with geometric designs, on special occasions.

Materials:
- construction paper
- paint and brush

Directions:
1. Have an adult or older sibling trace your hands and feet onto the paper. For more fun, ask if you can trace their hands, too.

2. Paint a geometric pattern (squares, triangles, rectangles, diamonds) onto the hands and feet. Let them dry.

3. Decorate your walls, door or dresser with these hands (ask an adult first!). Or hang them in a mobile by taping colored yarn onto the backs of the hands and feet and tying them to a clothes hanger.

Cooking Project: African Feast

Choose which recipes you would like to include in your feast. Follow the directions to prepare the food. An adult should be present to supervise and assist when necessary, for safety reasons. For a festive touch, decorate your hands (see Painted Hands, above) and make some musical instruments to celebrate with. Instructions for a variety of instruments are included below. Have fun!

Chicken With Figs

Ingredients:
- 3–4 pounds chicken legs
- 1 lemon
- ¼ cup brown sugar
- ¼ cup vinegar

- ¼ cup water
- 1–2 tablespoons lemon juice
- 8–16 ounces dried figs
- salt to taste
- parsley

Directions:

1. Preheat oven to 400°.

2. Peel and slice the lemon. Place lemon slices and figs in the bottom of a 9"x13" baking pan. Add the chicken legs.

3. In mixing bowl, combine the brown sugar, vinegar, water, and lemon juice.

4. Pour mixture over the chicken. Sprinkle chicken with salt and parsley.

5. Bake, covered with foil, for about 40 minutes. Remove foil and bake for approximately 20–30 minutes longer or until chicken begins to brown. Baste frequently during the last 20–30 minutes. Remove chicken, figs, and lemon slices and place on a serving tray.

6. Skim off any fat and use the remaining juices as a sauce for the chicken.

Papaya Stir-Fried Rice

Ingredients:
- 1 can chopped papaya, reserve the juice
- 1 red bell pepper, chopped
- ½ red onion, chopped
- 2 tablespoons dried parsley
- 1 tablespoon olive oil (can substitute water)
- salt to taste
- instant rice (4–6 servings)

Directions:

1. Prepare the rice as directed on the package, substituting the papaya juice for an equal amount of water.

2. While the rice is being prepared, combine the papaya, red pepper, onion, parsley and salt in a medium sized bowl.

3. In a large skillet, heat the oil over medium heat. Add the papaya mixture and stir fry until onions are tender.

4. Add the cooked rice to the papaya mixture, and stir fry an additional 2 minutes. Serve immediately.

Fried Plantains

Ingredients:
- ¼ cup cooking oil
- 1 plantain

Directions:

1. Preheat the oil in a large skillet over medium high heat.

2. Peel and cut the plantain into rounds, a bit thicker than ¼".

3. Very carefully, fry the pieces till the edges are very lightly golden brown. Flip them over, and fry the other side. As a guideline, one minute per side should be sufficient. Don't let them get too dark.

4. Remove excess oil with a paper towel. Serve immediately. Add salt and/or garlic to taste.

Date and Banana Bars
Ingredients:
- ¼ cup margarine
- ¾ cup sugar
- 1 egg
- 1 teaspoon vanilla
- 2 medium bananas
- 1 cup flour
- ¼ teaspoon baking soda
- ½ teaspoon baking powder
- ¼ teaspoon salt
- ½ cup chopped dates
- Optional: ¼ cup almonds

Icing:
- 2 tablespoons margarine
- 1 tablespoon lemon juice
- ½ teaspoon vanilla
- ¾ cup powdered sugar

Directions:
1. Cream together the margarine and sugar.
2. Add the egg and vanilla.
3. Stir in the bananas and dry ingredients.
4. Add the dates and almonds.
5. Bake in an 8" x 8" pan at 350° for about 30 minutes or until edges are turning brown.

Date Chewies
Ingredients:
- 1 cup chopped dates
- 2 eggs
- 1 cup sugar
- ¾ cup flour
- 1 teaspoon baking powder
- 1 cup pecans, ground
- ¼ cup powdered sugar

Directions:
1. In a blender, blend eggs and dates together. Set aside.
2. In mixing bowl, combine sugar, flour, baking powder, and pecans. Add in egg mixture.
3. Pour into ungreased cookie sheets. Press the mixture down so it will be as thin as possible.
4. Bake at 350° for 15–20 minutes. Remove from oven and cut into bars while hot.
5. Roll into balls and then roll in the powdered sugar as soon as the chewies are cool enough to handle.

Music Project: Make Instruments for an African Concert

Plate Shakers
Materials:

- 2 paper plates or bowls of the same size
- beans, rice, lentils, pebbles, or small pasta pieces
- tape and/or stapler

Directions:
1. Fill one plate or bowl with beans, rice, lentils, pebbles, or small pasta pieces. (Each will make a slightly different sound, so if you make more than one, fill each with something different).

2. Place the second plate or bowl on top of the first (the bottom of it should be facing you), rims touching. Staple and/or tape the plates together.

3. Decorate. Then, make music.

Cup Shakers
Materials:
- aluminum foil, cling wrap, paper, or balloon
- beans, lentils, rice, pebbles, or small pasta pieces
- rubber band
- plastic cup

Directions:
1. Fill the cup half full with beans, lentils, rice, pebbles, or small pasta pieces. If using pasta, make sure there are no sharp edges or points (in other words, don't use broken spaghetti noodles). Each will make a slightly different sound against the plastic cup. This shaker will sound different from the plate shaker, as well.

2. To cover the cup, you have some options, each of which will alter the sound slightly. You can cover it with a double layer of foil or cling wrap, a single layer of paper (writing paper, or from a magazine), or you can stretch a balloon across the top. Whichever you use, secure it to the cup with a rubber band.

Rustler Shaker Bells
Materials:
- a nail
- several metal bottle caps
- string

Directions:
1. With the nail, have an adult punch a hole into each metal bottle cap.

2. Tie a short piece of string to each lid, through the hole.

3. Bunch all the strings together and tie with a knot.

4. Make some music by shaking these rustling bells.

One-Stringed Plucker
Materials:
- facial tissue box
- rubber band

Directions:
1. Wrap the rubber band around the tissue box, so it goes over the opening in the top.

2. Decorate. Pluck your one-stringed plucker. For variety, add more rubber bands of different widths.

CHAPTER TWELVE
The Middle Kingdom of Egypt

Encyclopedia Cross-References

Usborne Book of World History: 16–23
Usborne Internet-Linked Encyclopedia: 114–117

Kingfisher Illustrated History of the World: 26–27
Kingfisher History Encyclopedia: 10–11

Review Questions — Egypt Invades Nubia

What happened to the Old Kingdom of Egypt? *It became weak and powerless.*

When Amenemhet became pharaoh, what country did he decide to conquer? *Nubia*

Why was Nubia valuable to the Egyptians? *It had gold.*

What new name did the Egyptians give to Nubia? *Kush*

What do we call this time in Egyptian history? *The Middle Kingdom of Egypt*

Narration Exercise — Egypt Invades Nubia

"Egypt was weak. Then it became strong again. This was called the Middle Kingdom. The Egyptians conquered Nubia."

OR

"The Egyptians invaded part of Africa. It was called Nubia. It had iron and gold in it. This was during the Middle Kingdom of Egypt."

OR

"The Egyptians took over part of Africa. They called it Kush. Then the people of Kush became Egyptian. Some even became pharaohs!"

Review Questions — The Hyksos Invade Egypt

What happened to the Middle Kingdom of Egypt? *It became weak because of bad pharaohs.*

Who invaded Egypt and took over the Egyptian throne? *Wandering nomads* [It is nice (but not essential) if the child can remember the name "Hyksos."]

Where were they from? *Canaan*

Did the Egyptians like having the Hyksos for kings? *No! They thought the Hyksos were unclean shepherds.*

How did the Egyptians get rid of the Hyksos? *Egyptian princes got together and used the Hyksos' own weapons to drive them out*

Narration Exercise — The Hyksos Invade Egypt

"Egypt became weak again. Nomads came from Canaan and took over. They had good weapons and fought with chariots. Then the Egyptians chased them out."

OR

"The Middle Kingdom ended because nomads invaded. They ruled Egypt. Then Egyptians used bows and arrows and chariots to drive them out."

Additional History Reading

The Pharaohs of Ancient Egypt, by Elizabeth Payne (Sagebrush, 1999). This read-aloud book has a brief chapter about the life of each important pharaoh of Egypt. (RA)

Life in Ancient Egypt: A Coloring Book, by John Green (Dover, 1989). Detailed and interesting pictures of life in ancient Egypt, along with brief descriptions. (RA and activity)

Ancient Egypt (Ms. Frizzle's Adventures), by Joanna Cole (Scholastic, 2003). Ms. Frizzle takes a vacation from the Magic School Bus—and ends up in ancient Egypt. (RA)

Corresponding Literature Suggestions

Rimonah of the Flashing Sword: A North African Tale, by Eric Kimmel (Holiday House, 1995). This story of princesses and heroes mixes African and Egyptian elements. (RA)

Temple Cat, by Andrew Clements (Clarion, 2001). A temple cat in ancient Egypt runs away from his temple and catches fish like a normal cat. (RA)

Egyptian Gods and Goddesses, by Henry Barker (Grossett & Dunlap, 1999). An All Aboard Reading Level 2 book with stories about the most important gods and goddesses of Egypt's Middle Kingdom. (RA, but probably an IR for advanced readers)

Map Work

Chapter 12: The Middle Kingdom of Egypt (Student Page 35)

1. On your map, circle the area around the Nile (**Egypt**) with a red crayon.

2. Nubia is south of Egypt, in Africa. Label **Nubia** at the bottom of your map, just to the left of the **Nile River**.

3. Find **Canaan**. Draw an H for Hyksos in Canaan. Then draw a line from Canaan down into Egypt. The Hyksos came down from Canaan when they conquered Egypt.

Coloring Page

Hyksos Jewelry (Student Page 36)

These brooches were worn by Hyksos women. You can wear them as jewelry or as giant belt buckles!

Projects

Craft Project: Make a Monkey Doll
Materials:
- clean, old sock
- dried beans, peas or seeds
- fabric paint or permanent markers
- felt or fabric scraps (brown, if you want a monkey with brown arms, legs and tail)
- glue (hot glue works best)
- ribbon

Directions:
1. Fill the sock with beans, peas or seeds. Tie the end tightly with the ribbon.

2. Cut out four strips from the felt (for arms and legs), plus one longer strip (for the tail). Glue these parts to the filled sock to make arms, legs, and a tail.

3. Cut out two ear shapes from the felt, and glue to the head of your monkey.

4. Paint or draw a face onto your monkey.

5. Now you can deliver your gift to the Egyptians, or pretend you are the Egyptian and thank the Nubians for such a wonderful gift.

Craft Project: Make a Golden Bracelet

Materials:
- gold paint and brushes
- scissors
- toilet paper tube

Directions:
1. Cut the toilet paper tube in half, making two shorter tubes.
2. Cut each of the smaller tubes lengthwise (end to end).
3. Paint the outside of the tubes gold. Let them dry completely.
4. To wear your gold bracelets, gently open the tube, where it has been split, and wrap around your upper arm. It will fit tightly enough that it shouldn't fall off. If it is too tight, take it off, and gently open the tube wider, bending the cardboard a bit. Try it on again. Wear one bracelet on each arm. What a nice gift from the Nubians!

Activity Project: Burn Incense

Materials:
- Incense (can be purchased at some grocery and drug stores, and at many gift stores)
- matches
- adult supervision (Do NOT do this activity without an adult supervising)
- flat, wide candle stick (to hold incense cone) or incense holder (any fire- and heat-proof surface would be suitable)

Directions:
1. Tomb pictures show Nubians carrying incense, among other things, to the Egyptians to give as gifts. Have an adult light the incense with the matches, as directed on the package. After burning, be sure to put out the ember completely. If the package doesn't direct you as to the best way to do this, douse it in water.
2. With the assistance of an adult, try a few different scents of incense. Which do you like best?

Activity Project: Make an Egyptian Chariot and Horse

Materials:
- 3 dowels (1 dowel cut into 3 pieces)
- hot glue
- plastic horse
- small gift box (without the lid) OR pint milk carton (one side removed)
- wooden wheels (from a craft store)

Directions:
1. Poke one of the dowel pieces through the box or milk carton. Hot glue a wooden wheel to each end of the dowel. Be sure you don't glue the dowel to the box side.
2. Take the two remaining dowel pieces, glue one dowel rod on opposite sides of the box above the wheels, letting them extend forward.
3. Back the horse in, between the dowel rods. Then, tape the rods to the horse's sides.
4. Put a plastic person in the chariot and join the Egyptian princes who rebelled against the Hyksos.

CHAPTER THIRTEEN
The New Kingdom of Egypt

Encyclopedia Cross-References

Usborne Book of World History: 33–39   *Kingfisher Illustrated History of the World*: 54–55
Usborne Internet-Linked Encyclopedia: 135–137   *Kingfisher History Encyclopedia*: 26–27

Review Questions — The General and the Woman Pharaoh

We've already learned about the Old Kingdom and the Middle Kingdom of Egypt. What is this time in Egypt's history called? *The New Kingdom*

We read about two pharaohs today. Do you remember their names? Prompt the child if necessary: *Thutmose* and *Hatshepsut*

What did Thutmose do? *He made Egypt bigger.*

What did Hatshepsut do? *She became pharaoh even though she was a woman.*

What did Hatshepsut wear? *Men's clothes and a false beard!*

Narration Exercise — The General and the Woman Pharaoh

Ask the child to retell the story of EITHER Thutmose OR Hatshepsut. Acceptable narrations might include:

"Thutmose wanted to make Egypt bigger. He fought the Nubians and he even fought the Hyksos. He made Egypt twice as big!"

OR

"Hatshepsut wanted to be pharaoh. The Egyptians didn't think a woman could be pharaoh. So Hatshepsut pretended to be a man. She put on a false beard and fought with her army."

Review Questions — Amenhotep and King Tut

What is polytheism? *The worship of many different gods*

What is monotheism? *The worship of just one god*

Did the Egyptians worship just one god, or many gods? *Many gods.* That means that they were polytheists.

Did Amenhotep worship just one god, or many gods? *Just one god*

Did the Egyptians like this? *No! They wanted all their gods back.*

Where was King Tut buried? *In the Valley of the Kings*

Who discovered his tomb? *A man named Howard Carter.*

Did robbers steal Tut's treasure? *No.* Why not? *They couldn't find his tomb.*

Why did people think there was a curse on the tomb? *Because some people who opened it died, and Howard Carter's canary was swallowed by a cobra*

Narration Exercise — Amenhotep and King Tut

Ask the child to retell the story of Amenhotep.

"The Egyptians worshipped many different gods. One pharaoh wanted them to worship just one god. But they didn't want to."

OR

"Polytheism means having lots of gods. The Egyptians had lots of gods. A pharaoh tried to make them be monotheists. That means having just one god."

OR

Ask the child to draw a picture of King Tut's mummy or of Howard Carter discovering the tomb full of treasure. Ask him to describe the picture to you. Write the description on the bottom of the picture.

Additional History Reading

The Pharaohs of Ancient Egypt, by Elizabeth Payne (Sagebrush, 1999). This read-aloud book has a brief chapter about the life of each important pharaoh of Egypt. (RA)

Tut's Mummy—Lost...and Found, by Judy Donnelly (Random House, 1988). A simple account of the mummy's discovery. (IR for many readers, RA for beginners)

Pharaohs and Pyramids (Time Traveler Series), by Tony Allan and Philippa Wingate (EDC Publications, 2003). An Usborne book about the days of the pharaohs; simple text and good pictures.

Look What Came From Egypt (Machines at Work), by Miles Harvey (Franklin Watts, 1999). Oriented towards the science of ancient Egypt. (RA)

Corresponding Literature Suggestions

His Majesty, Queen Hatshepsut, by Dorothy Sharp Carter (HarperCollins, 1987). The story of the thirteen-year-old Hatshepsut. (RA)

Tutankhamen's Gift, by Robert Sabuda (Aladdin, 1997). The story of King Tut's childhood—especially good for the youngest children in the family who may feel left out at times. (RA)

Tut, Tut (The Time Warp Trio), by Jon Scieszka (Puffin, 2004). A silly but entertaining trip through time. For advanced readers to tackle alone. (IR for advanced readers)

Mara, Daughter of the Nile, by Eloise McGraw (Puffin, 1985). Mara is a young slave girl who escapes from her cruel master and finds herself in the hands of two new enemies. Too long to read in one day, but this might make a good family reading project, especially if an older child can take on the project of reading to the younger ones. (RA)

Tales of Ancient Egypt, selected and retold by Roger Lancelyn Green (Puffin, 1996). Green's stories are classics in their own right. This collection of tales includes a story about Hatshepsut, as well as fables about the Egyptian gods. (RA 1–3, IR 3–6)

Corresponding Audiobook Suggestions

The Cat of Bubastes, by G.A. Henty, read by Jim Weiss (Greathall Productions). Mr. Henty gives his readers a fascinating picture of the ancient Egyptians at the height of their civilization. A story of heroism and loyalty, it is filled with action (battles with a crocodile and with desert bandits) and interesting details of life in Egypt. Available at www.greathall.com.

Map Work

Chapter 13: The New Kingdom of Egypt (Student Page 37)

1. On your map, circle the area that is known as the **Valley of the Kings**.

2. Review the locations of **Canaan**, the **Mediterranean Sea**, and the **Red Sea**.

Coloring Page

The Mask of King Tut (Student Page 38)

Projects

Craft Project: Make Hatshepsut's False Beard
Materials:
- colored tissue paper
- fabric elastic, ¼" to ½" width (the sort used in clothing)
- white glue
- a paint brush (for glue)
- scrap paper
- a toilet paper tube

Directions:
1. The toilet paper tube will be the "base" for your false beard. Cover it with thin strips of tissue paper, glued to the tube at one end and hanging free at the other. To avoid getting your hands sticky, you can use a paint brush to paint glue onto the tissue paper, and to apply the tissue to the tube. Let the beard dry by setting one end of the tube on a piece of cling wrap or scrap paper.

2. Once the beard is dry, punch two holes opposite each other at one end of the tube. Thread the fabric elastic through one hole, and tie a knot on the inside of the tube.

3. Put the beard up to your chin, and measure how long the elastic needs to be to reach around your head to the other side of the tube. An older sibling or adult could help you with this task. Cut the elastic at the appropriate length (this will keep the beard on your face, so you don't want it to be too loose or too tight).

4. Thread the free end of the elastic into the open hole in the tube. Tie a knot on the inside of the tube. Try the beard on. If it is too loose, pull the knot tighter. You may need to undo the original knot first, or perhaps just tie a second knot to take up the slack.

5. Wear your beard and pretend to be Hatshepsut, the first woman Pharaoh.

Craft Project: Make One of Hatshepsut's Monuments

During Queen Hatshepsut's reign, she had many monuments built. Do you know what a monument is? A monument is usually built to serve as a memorial to a person or group of people who have died. An ancient monument could be a statue of a person, a statue of a god, a large building, a pillar with a story written on it, or a large stone with words carved on it. In ancient times, monuments were often statues of people; sometimes they were also large buildings, or pillars with words written on them.

Imagine that you are a king or queen in ancient times. What important things have happened in your country? (Look back over the chapters you've already read, if you can't remember.) What event or person would you like to make a monument to?

Optional Idea: Think of something that is important to you. This could be someone special, a favorite toy, or a favorite activity. Make a monument (model) of it.

Materials:
- glue (optional: paint)
- white bread
- mixing bowl

Directions:
1. Mix together bread and glue, using one tablespoon of glue for every two slices of white bread. Mix together until the consistency of clay is reached. It will eventually pull away from the sides of the bowl and will not be sticky.

2. Shape mixture into a monument. Mix more dough if you want to make a larger monument.

3. Most ancient monuments are made of plain stone—but some of them may have been painted, in colors that have now worn away. If you want to, paint your monument in bright colors.

Craft Project: Make an Egyptian Death Mask

Kings, queens, and other people of nobility and high class in ancient Egypt were mummified and buried in highly decorated coffins. Each mummy wore a "death mask" which was made in the likeness of the person being buried. The Egyptians believed that every person had a spirit called "ka" which separated from the body at death. To live in the afterlife, the ka would need to find the body it belonged to. The death masks (and the coffins, which were also crafted to look like the person within) helped the ka to recognize the body it belonged with.

Materials:
- circular balloon
- cling wrap-covered bowl
- newspaper
- paste (made of glue and water, or salt, flour, and water)
- scissors
- paint, gold glitter, etc. (optional)

Directions:
1. Make the paste. You can use a glue and water mixture (1–2 parts glue to 1 part water) or a flour paste mixture (1 part water with two parts flour and a little salt OR 1 part flour to 5 parts water—for both mixtures, boil three minutes and then cool before using).

2. Blow up balloon. Place it on cling wrap-covered bowl.

3. Cut strips of newspaper. Cover entire front surface of balloon by dipping strips into paste and then carefully putting on balloon. Let dry completely.

4. Add facial features (with string, crumpled paper, foil, buttons, etc.). Use masking tape to hold in place.

5. Add 2–3 more layers of papier maché over the features. Allow each layer to dry before adding the next.

6. Pop balloon. You can now paint the mask with bright colors and gold glitter, so that it resembles the death mask of a pharaoh (optional).

Craft Project: Be an Archaeologist

Archaeologist Howard Carter discovered King Tut's tombs and its treasures after years of searching. Pretend to be an archaeologist discovering a tomb! You'll need a parent or older sibling to help you out.

Directions:
1. PARENT OR OLDER SIBLING: Choose a small, out-of-the-way, secret place in the house (or outdoors, if the weather is nice) to be "King Tut's Tomb." Select a number of small treasures from around the house

(toys from the child's room, stuffed animals, small pieces of candy or other approved treats—a new toy is nice but not essential). Don't choose too many treasures, since the child will need to draw pictures of the treasures as soon as he finds them. Arrange these treasures in the "tomb." Make a simple map for the child to follow, and tell him to go find the tomb!

2. CHILD: Before an archaeologist can move anything in a tomb, he has to draw a picture of its original place. When you discover your "tomb," don't touch any of the treasures! Instead, get a piece of paper and a crayon or pencil. Draw each item in the tomb, just as you see it. (Ask your parent or sibling for help.) After you've drawn your "tomb picture," you can play with the treasures!

CHAPTER FOURTEEN
The Israelites Leave Egypt

Encyclopedia Cross-References

Usborne Book of World History: N/A

Usborne Internet-Linked Encyclopedia: 142

Kingfisher Illustrated History of the World: 50–51

Kingfisher History Encyclopedia: 24

Review Questions — The Baby Moses

Who were the Israelites descended from? *Abraham*. [Take a moment to talk about what a "descendant" is, if necessary.]

Did the Israelites worship one god or many gods? *One god*

Were they monotheists or polytheists? *Monotheists*

Why did they go to Egypt? *Because of a famine in Canaan*

What happened to them in Egypt? *They became slaves.*

Who led them back out of Egypt? *Moses*

What terrible command did the pharaoh give? *To kill all the baby boys of the Israelites*

What did Moses's mother do to save his life? *Put him in the Nile River in a basket*

Who took him out? *The princess of Egypt*

Narration Exercise — The Baby Moses

The narration should EITHER say that the Israelites went to Egypt, and were made into slaves by the pharaoh, OR should retell the story of Moses. (If the child wants to include both parts of the lesson in the narration, that's fine, but don't require this.)

"The Israelites went to Egypt because of a famine. There were many of them and the Egyptians were afraid of them. The Egyptians made them into slaves."

OR

"Moses' mother wanted to keep him safe. She hid him. Then she put him in a basket on the river. The daughter of the pharaoh found him. Then his mother got to take care of him again."

Review Questions — The Exodus from Egypt

How many plagues did God send on Egypt? *Ten*

Did the pharaoh finally let the Israelites go? *Yes*

What happened when they got to the Red Sea? *The water parted* OR *God parted the water* OR *Moses parted the water.*

What was this great escape from Egypt called? *The Exodus*

Where did the Israelites go next? *Back to Canaan!*

Narration Exercise — The Exodus from Egypt

Ask the child to tell you about the Israelite flight from Egypt. Prompt her to use the word "Exodus." Acceptable narrations might include:

"The Israelites were in Egypt. The pharaoh didn't want to let them go, so God made them have plagues. Then they left Egypt. This was called the Exodus."

OR

"Israel was in Egypt. They were slaves. Moses led them out of Egypt to Canaan. They went across the Red Sea. This was the Exodus."

Additional History Reading

Exodus from Egypt, by Mary Auld (Franklin Watts, 2000). A simple and straightforward retelling of the exodus story, told on a level that most children can read independently. (IR, but RA for children who are not yet reading independently)

Exodus, by Brian Wildsmith (Eerdmans, 1998). Another simple retelling; the sentences are more difficult than those in the Auld book, but the illustrations are spectacular. (RA)

Israel (Countries of the World), by Frederick Fisher (Gareth Stevens, 2000). A simple guide to the Israel of today, with a brief glance back at Israel's history as a nation. (RA; you'll want to skip some of the text altogether because of complexity)

Eyewitness: Bible Lands, by Jonathan N. Tubb (DK Publishing, 2000). A guide to the geography, customs, and history of Israel. Much of the text is too difficult for elementary children, but the pictures are beautiful. (RA)

Miriam and Her Brother Moses, by Jean Marzollo (Little, Brown, 2004). Designed to be read aloud, this well-illustrated retelling comes from Miriam's point of view. For young readers. (RA 1–2, IR 3–4)

Corresponding Literature Suggestions

The Moses Basket, by Jenny Koralek, illus. Pauline Baynes (Eerdmans, 2003). A picture-book retelling of the Biblical story of Moses' birth and adoption, with pictures by the original illustrator of the *Chronicles of Narnia*. (RA 1, IR 2–3)

Moses: The Long Road to Freedom, by Ann Keay Beneduce, illus. Gennady Spirin (Orchard, 2004). A more advanced picture book, with small print but detailed, Renaissance-style paintings. (RA 1–3, IR 3–5)

Angels Sweep the Desert Floor: Bible Legends About Moses in the Wilderness, by Miriam Chaikin, illus. Alexander Koshkin (Clarion, 2002). Fictional account of 18 stories set during the 40 years of Moses' wanderings in the desert. Not appropriate for parents who want to avoid biblical paraphrase. (RA 2–3, IR 4–6)

Map Work

Chapter 14: The Israelites Leave Egypt (Student Page 39)

1. On your map, draw a line from **Egypt** up to **Canaan**. The Israelites fled from Egypt up to Canaan, the land God promised to Abraham.

2. Find the **Red Sea** on your map and shade it in blue. Remember that when Moses led the Israelites away from Egypt, he led them through the Red Sea.

Coloring Page

Moses Parting the Red Sea (Student Page 40)

Craft Project: Make Baby Moses' Basket

Materials:
- newspaper
- scissors
- glue or glue stick, tape or stapler
- paints and brushes

Directions:

1. Take 8 sheets of 13½" x 22" newspaper and roll each sheet into a tight tube. Start at the long edge. Glue the open edge to the rest of the tube and flatten the roll. These will be the reeds for your basket.

2. Lay four of the reeds side by side on the table. Weave the remaining four through the first four. Manipulate the strips until they fit tightly together and form a bottom for the basket. Fold the leftover ends of the reeds up to form the sides or spokes of your basket.

3. Cut newspaper sheets into four 11" x 27" rectangles. Roll these into tight tubes starting with the long end first. Tape or staple the end of a reed to the bottom of a spoke reed. Weave the reed in and out of the spokes working your way around the basket.

4. Tuck the end behind a spoke and fasten with glue or stapler. Weave in the other reeds, working your way up and around the basket. Fold the leftover tops of the spokes into the basket and tuck them behind a reed.

5. Now paint your basket inside and out. A coat or two of polyurethane will preserve your basket.

Craft Project: Make a Red Sea Diorama

Materials:
- large shoebox
- construction paper and tissue paper
- crayons and markers
- glue and tape
- string and scissors
- small rocks and clipart
- small plastic figures (plastic soldiers will do in a pinch!)

Directions:

1. Decorate the inside of your shoebox to look like the Red Sea—glue blue construction paper onto the walls of your box, or color them blue with markers (or paint).

2. Add brown paper on the shoebox bottom, for the sea floor.

3. Glue or tape down a few rocks on your sea floor. Draw fish on the walls and floor, if you want to.

4. Glue the feet of the small plastic figures in a line down the middle of the shoebox. These are the Israelites, walking through the sea. (If you use plastic soldiers, you might want to cut or twist their weapons off!)

5. Cut a small square hole in one end of the shoebox, to use for a peephole.

6. Cut a larger square hole in the far end of the shoebox. Glue or tape one layer of tissue paper across it. (This allows light to come in.

7. Put the shoebox lid on. Now hold the shoebox up to a light and peer in. You'll see an underwater scene!

Activity Project: Moses and the Ten Plagues Stickerbook
Materials:
- colored pencils
- scissors
- Bible
- Student Page 41—(you may want to have this laminated)
- contact paper (available at office supply stores)
- a photocopy of the three sticker pages (Student Pages 42–44), copied onto label sheets such as Avery's Removable Laser Labels (8½" x 11" full sheet).

Directions:
1. Color the "Moses and the Ten Plagues" page with colored pencils. Cover it with contact paper when it is finished. (Optional: when it is finished, have it laminated in thick plastic at your local copy store. This is a cheap and simple procedure.)

2. Read through the appropriate sections of the Biblical story (Exodus 2–15; try a modern translation such as the New International Version or a children's version such as the Living Bible). As you read, follow the directions on the sticker pages. Cut out each sticker and place it on the "Moses and the Ten Plagues" page, as directed.

NOTE: The Avery *Removable* Labels work best with this project, although the regular Avery Labels will also do. Make sure you photocopy onto the laser labels and not the ink jet labels, as the ink jet copy will peel off. The tenth plague does not have a sticker. This plague was a very somber one, which the Israelites remembered long after it happened, and you should use your own discretion in explaining this plague to small children. Read Exodus 11–12:35 to hear about the end of the plagues and the beginning of the Hebrew nation.

Activity Project: Famine Experiment

(Please note, this experiment will take a few weeks!) Discuss the famine in Canaan. Ask the child to explain why there was a shortage of food, why animals might have died, etc.
Materials:
- two small disposable containers
- potting soil
- handful of bean seeds

Directions:
1. Cut a few drain holes in the bottom of the containers. Mark one container with a W and one with an F. The one marked W stands for water. The one marked F stands for famine.

2. Fill containers with potting soil.

3. Plant a couple of bean seeds per container.

4. Place both containers on a tray and leave in a warm location.

5. Water the W container frequently. Water the F container no more than once a week, adding only a small amount of water.

6. After a few weeks, discuss the differences in the plants and why there are differences.

CHAPTER FIFTEEN
The Phoenicians

Encyclopedia Cross-References

Usborne Book of World History: 50–51

Usborne Internet-Linked Encyclopedia: 144–145

Kingfisher Illustrated History of the World: 56–57

Kingfisher History Encyclopedia: 28–29

Review Questions — Phoenician Traders

Where did the Phoenicians live? *In Canaan*

What were they good at? *Sailing their boats*

The Phoenicians made glass. Do you remember what two things they made glass from? *Sand and lye*

What special way of shaping glass did the Phoenicians invent? *Glass blowing*

What did they make their purple dye from? *Snails*

Why was purple called "the color of kings"? *Because it was so expensive*

Narration Exercise — Phoenician Traders

Ask the child to list four things that the Phoenicians sold to other countries. Acceptable answers include: cedar trees, logs, beautiful furniture, salt, dried fish, embroidered cloth, tin, metals, glass, purple dye, and purple cloth.

Review Questions — The Founding of Carthage

What is a colony? Prompt child for the answer: *A little settlement of people*

Do you remember the name of the little Phoenician colony that grew into a big city? *Carthage*

What queen helped to start Carthage? *Dido*

Why did Dido have to leave her home? *She was afraid of her brother.*

Why did Dido want to start the city of Carthage near the water? *So that ships would visit her city and trade with her*

Narration Exercise — The Founding of Carthage

Ask the child, "How did Dido use the bull-hide to get the land she wanted?" An acceptable answer might be, "She told the man who owned the land that she only wanted enough to go under a bull hide. Then she cut it up into lots of small pieces and laid it all around a big piece of land."

Additional History Reading

Ancient Israelites and Their Neighbors: An Activity Guide, by Marian Broida (Chicago Review Press, 2003). This book contains a few activities related to ancient Phoenicia—very little is available for elementary children on this subject. (RA)

Eyewitness Anthologies: Ancient Civilizations, by James, Pearson, and Tubb (Dorling Kindersley, 1998). This book contains one section ("The Phoenicians," pp. 18–19) that includes pictures of artifacts from ancient Phoenicia (seals, pots, motifs, glassware, etc.). **Out of print; check your local library.**

The Phoenicians: Mysterious Sea People, by Katherine E. Reece (Rourke, 2005). A good, basic introduction to the Phoenicians. Includes two-page chapters such as "Where Was Phoenicia?" and "What Did the Phoenicians Wear?" (RA 2–3, IR 4–5)

Corresponding Literature Suggestions

In Search of a Homeland: The Story of the Aeneid, by Penelope Lively, illus. Ian Andrews (Frances Lincoln, 2006). Aeneas meets Dido, among other adventures; you may want to read all of the text to a young child, but the illustrations are lovely. (RA)

Roman Myths and Legends, retold by Anthony Masters (Peter Bedrick Books, 2000). Stories from Roman mythology, including Romulus and Remus, Cupid and Psyche, Dido and Aeneas, and Horatius at the bridge. (RA 1–3, IR 3–5)

Roman Myths, by Geraldine McCaughrean, illus. Emma Chichester Clark (Margaret K. McElderry, 2001). May be **out of print**, but worth checking your library for. Colorful, engaging read-aloud tales include two about Aeneas, Romulus and Remus, and the kidnapping of the Sabine women. (RA 1–3, IR 3–6)

Map Work

Chapter 15: The Phoenicians (Student Page 45)

1. On your map, find the Phoenician cities of **Tyre** and **Carthage** and circle their names using a red pencil.

2. With a green pencil, color in the area known as **Phoenicia**. Then, using the same green pencil, color the areas that were controlled by the Phoenicians. These areas are already marked on your map. If you need a reminder, see the map in your book.

3. Color the **Mediterranean Sea** in blue. This is where the Phoenician sailors did most of their trading.

Coloring Page

A Phoenician Ship (Student Page 46)

Projects

Craft Project: Make Pretend Colored Glass
Materials:

- wax paper
- crayon shavings—red, blue, and yellow
- colored threads
- a picture (see below)
- iron, ironing board, and old newspapers

Directions:

1. Choose a picture to encase in your project. This could be a drawing, a picture from a magazine, a Coloring Page, a photocopied illustration from your favorite book, or even a sticker or stamp.

2. Cut out two identical shapes from the wax paper. The shape can be anything of your choosing—a circle, a square, a rectangle, or even a hexagon. Be sure that the shapes of wax paper are larger than the picture.

3. Place one piece of wax paper on the table. Place the picture on the wax paper. Add the crayon shavings and colored threads and then place other piece of wax paper over the top.

4. Set up the ironing board and place a layer or two of newspaper over the ironing board. Place the project on the newspaper and then add more layers of newspaper. Using a low level of heat, iron the "glass" (carefully) until crayon shavings have melted. This step needs to be done by an adult.

5. When the "glass" has cooled, trim up any rough edges. Hang in window or put in history notebook.

Craft Project: Make Purple Dye

The Phoenicians used snails, but you can use fruits and vegetables for a short cut!

Method One:
Materials:
- head of purple cabbage
- alum (at most grocery stores)

Directions:
1. Chop the cabbage into small pieces.

2. In a large saucepan, boil cabbage for about an hour.

3. After the cabbage is partially cooled, drain the colored water from the cabbage. Discard the cabbage. The water will be turquoise in color.

4. Add about a tablespoon of alum to the colored water. You may need more or less depending upon the quantity of water. This will turn the colored water into a nice shade of purple.

5. Use the dye to color any cotton material—a shirt, cotton yarn to use in a project, a handkerchief.

6. Try to set the dye using cold salt water. (This will not always work and color will fade.)

Method Two:
Materials:
- 1 package of frozen blueberries

Directions:
1. In saucepan, boil whole blueberries for about an hour.

2. After partially cooled, drain the colored water from the blueberries. Discard the berries.

3. The colored water is ready for dyeing.

Craft Project: Use Phoenician Dye to Make a Colored Pasta Necklace
Materials:
- dye water from cabbage or blueberries
- string or yarn
- elbow macaroni or pasta shapes (such as hearts or Christmas trees—which are available during the holiday seasons)

Directions:
1. In bowl, pour a cup or two of the dye and add a handful of pasta. Keep the pasta in the dye until it has changed its color. This will take a few minutes.

2. Remove the pasta from dye and set it to dry in a safe place.

3. Add more pasta to the dye and continue process until there is enough colored pasta to make a necklace.

4. After the pasta is completely dried, string onto a length of yarn that is long enough to fit easily over your head.

5. Securely tie the ends together.

Cooking Project: Make Phoenician Bread (Pita Bread)
Ingredients:
- 6 cups flour
- 2 teaspoons salt

- 1 tablespoon yeast
- 2 cups warm water
- 1 tablespoon honey
- some butter and extra flour for preparation

Directions:

1. Let the yeast dissolve in the warm water. Stir the honey in the water and yeast mixture. Then add the salt and flour, slowly. Stir until it becomes tough to mix.

2. Put the dough on a surface lightly covered with flour.

3. Knead for about 10 minutes. Then place the dough in a buttered bowl (make sure all sides are buttered). Cover the bowl with plastic wrap or a damp dishtowel.

4. Let dough rise for about 2 hours. It should double in size.

5. After punching down the dough, shape it into 10 balls.

6. Set them aside for about 15 minutes, then shape into approx. 6 or 7" round shapes (like mini pizza crusts).

7. Preheat oven to 450 degrees. Place dough on a cookie sheet. Bake for 10 to 12 minutes on the lowest rack in the oven. Makes about 10 Pita Bread rounds.

CHAPTER SIXTEEN
The Return of Assyria

Encyclopedia Cross-References

Usborne Book of World History: 50–51

Usborne Internet-Linked Encyclopedia: 144–145

Kingfisher Illustrated History of the World: 56–57

Kingfisher History Encyclopedia: 28–29

Review Questions — Ashurbanipal's Attack

Can you tell me two countries that Assyria conquered? *Egypt, Canaan* [the answers Mesopotamia, Babylon, and Asia Minor are also acceptable].

What did Ashurbanipal like to do for fun? *Hunt lions with bows and arrows*

What kind of shields did the Assyrians use? *Basket shields tied together with leather*

How did the Assyrian soldiers break through city walls? *They built ramps out of dirt and pushed wooden towers on wheels up the ramps.*

Did the people in the Assyrian empire like their king? *No, they hated him for his cruelty.*

Narration Exercise — Ashurbanipal's Attack

"The Assyrians wanted to make their empire big again. They conquered everyone around them. Their king knew how to break into cities with walls. The Assyrians were very cruel to the cities they beat."

Review Questions — The Library of Nineveh

What city did Ashurbanipal live in? *Nineveh*

Can you tell me two things that Ashurbanipal did to make Nineveh beautiful? *He built a beautiful palace, decorated the gates of the city, planted gardens, and made sculptures.*

Why did Ashurbanipal decide to collect a library? *So that people would remember him*

Were the library books made out of paper? *No, they were made out of clay.*

Some of the clay tablets had the history of Assyria written on them. Can you tell me two other kinds of writing from Ashurbanipal's library? *Stories, prayers, facts about the sun, moon and sky, medicine, law, and science*

Can we still read Ashurbanipal's library today? *Yes, some of the clay tablets can still be read today.*

Narration Exercise — The Library of Nineveh

"Ashurbanipal lived in Nineveh. It was a beautiful city with gardens in it. He wanted to be remembered. He made a library out of clay tablets."

OR

"The first library was in Nineveh. The king collected stories and other writings. He kept them in big rooms so that people could read them a long time afterwards."

Additional History Reading

Ancient Egyptians and Their Neighbors: An Activity Guide, by Marian Broida (Chicago Review Press, 1999). This book contains a few activities related to ancient Assyria—very little is available for elementary children on this subject. (RA)

Corresponding Literature Suggestions

The Story of Jonah, by Mary Auld (Franklin Watts, 2000). Jonah was sent to Assyria's capital city, Nineveh, but he didn't want to go! (IR)

Illustrated Jewish Bible for Children, by Selina Hastings (DK Publishing, 1997). A beautifully illustrated version of Jonah's journey to Nineveh. (RA)

The Seven Voyages of Sinbad the Sailor, by John Yeoman, illus. Quentin Blake (Chrysalis Books, 2003). Sinbad's mythical voyages took place around the time of Nineveh's height. (RA)

Map Work

Chapter 16: The Return of Assyria (Student Page 47)

1. On your map, find Ashurbanipal's city, **Nineveh**, and circle the name in red.

2. Use a green crayon or pencil to underline **Assyria**—the area that Ashurbanipal ruled.

3. Use a blue crayon to color in all of the seas. See if you can read all of their names.

Coloring Page

A Bas Relief From Ancient Assyria (Student Page 48)

Projects

Craft Project: Make an Assyrian Siege Tower

The Assyrians are ready to lay siege to another town and are in need of a tower. Now is your time to bring out the LEGO bricks and try your hand at building one. The Assyrian army used these moveable towers to protect themselves as they used their battering rams to smash the city walls of their enemies.

1. First, make a wheeled base by attaching your LEGO wheels to a flat LEGO base.

2. Next, build a three-sided tower on top of the base. The siege tower was built on a wheeled base and had a three-sided tower built on the front portion of the vehicle. The archers stood inside the tower and shot arrows as the tower was pushed closer and closer to the city walls.

3. Add a battering ram—a long LEGO brick, sticking out from the front of your tower, as the battering ram.

Writing Project: Make a Book for Ashurbanipal's Library

Ashurbanipal was the first king to start collecting stories and putting then in one place, his library at Nineveh. You can make a book too and add it to his collection.

Materials:
- 2 sheets blank paper (8½" x 11")
- 1 sheet of colored paper
- markers, crayons, stickers, and glitter
- a length of ribbon or cord

Directions:

1. Place the colored paper and the blank paper in a stack. Fold them in half (into a 5½" x 8½" booklet) with the colored paper on the outside.

2. Punch two holes along the folded edge, spacing them about 3 inches apart. Get a piece of ribbon, thread it through the holes and tie a bow. This will help keep your book together. If you prefer, you can place three staples along the folded edge instead.

3. On the outside cover of your book, write a title. For example it could be titled "My Favorite Things."

4. Ancient people often told stories through pictures. Use markers, crayons, stickers and glitter to tell a story!

CHAPTER SEVENTEEN
Babylon Takes Over Again!

Encyclopedia Cross-References

Usborne Book of World History: 58–59
Usborne Internet-Linked Encyclopedia: 150–151

Kingfisher Illustrated History of the World: 70–71
Kingfisher History Encyclopedia: 36–37

Review Questions — Nebuchadnezzar's Madness

What did the Assyrians do to Babylon when they conquered it? *They flooded it (destroyed it).*

What did the Babylonians do to Nineveh when they conquered Assyria? *They destroyed it and smashed some of Ashurbanipal's clay tablets.*

Was the Babylonian empire as big as the Assyrian empire? *No*

Do you remember the name of Babylon's most famous king? He built the Ishtar Gate in Babylon. *Nebuchadnezzar*

What happened to Nebuchadnezzar after he thought he was a god? *He went mad (thought he was an animal).*

Did he get better? *Yes*

Narration Exercise — Nebuchadnezzar's Madness

"Assyria was destroyed by Babylon. The king of Babylon thought he was a god. Then he went mad and ate grass like a cow. Finally he got better again."

OR

"Nebuchadnezzar was the king of Babylon. He was a great king, but he thought he was greater than God. So he lost his mind. He thought he was an animal. When he said that he was only a man, he got better."

Review Questions — The Hanging Gardens of Babylon

Why was Nebuchadnezzar afraid of Persia? *He thought Persia would attack him.*

Why was Persia afraid of Nebuchadnezzar? *The Persians thought Nebuchadnezzar would attack them.*

Why was Amytis homesick? *Because she missed the mountains*

What did Nebuchadnezzar build to make Amytis happy? *The Hanging Gardens of Babylon*

We've studied three of the Seven Wonders of the Ancient World. What three have we learned about? *The Great Pyramid, the Sphinx, and the Hanging Gardens of Babylon*

Narration Exercise — The Hanging Gardens of Babylon

"Nebuchadnezzar married a princess who missed her home. He built her a big garden on a hill to make her happy. It was called the Hanging Gardens of Babylon."

OR

Ask your child to draw a picture of the Hanging Gardens of Babylon and to describe the picture to you. Write the description on the bottom of the picture.

Additional History Reading

Great Wonders of the World, by Russell Ash (DK Publishing, 2000). The ancient wonders, including the Hanging Gardens of Babylon, beautifully illustrated and explained; also includes modern and natural wonders of the world. (RA 1–3, IR 4–7)

The Seven Wonders of the Ancient World, by Reg Cox and Neil Morris, illus. James Field (Chelsea House, 2000). Links the Seven Wonders to broader cultural developments, including those in Babylon. (RA)

Seven Wonders of the Ancient World, by Mary Hoffman, illus. M.P. Robertson (Frances Lincoln, 2004). The tale of a fictional slave who travels to see the real Wonders of the World. Includes a map, good illustrations, and historical details. (RA 1–3, IR 3–6)

Seven Wonders of the Ancient World, by Lynn Curlee (Atheneum, 2002). Factual information about each of the seven wonders. Includes non-explicit side view illustration of naked Greek athletes running. (RA 1–3, IR 4–5)

Wonders of the World (Fast Forward Series), by Mark Bergin (Franklin Watts, 1999). "Split-level" pages give dual views of the wonders during and after construction. (RA 1–3, IR 3–5)

Corresponding Literature Suggestions

1001 Arabian Nights (Oxford Story Collections), by Geraldine McCaughrean, illus. Rosamund Fowler (Oxford University Press Children's Books, 2000). A long and fascinating collection of stories from the ancient Near East. (RA)

The Legend of the Persian Carpet, by Tomie dePaola (Putnam, 1993). A traditional folk-tale from Nebuchadnezzar's part of the world, retold in picture-book form. (RA 1–2, IR 2–4)

Forty Fortunes: A Tale of Iran, by Aaron Shepard (Clarion Books, 1999). A well-intentioned fortune-telling peasant unwittingly tricks a band of local thieves into returning the king's stolen treasure; set in the area of ancient Babylonia. **Out of print; check your local library.** (RA)

King Nimrod's Tower, by Leon Garfield (Lothrop, Lee & Shepard, 1982). Against a background of the building of the Tower of Babel, a boy tries to train a stray dog—and God watches over all. **Out of print; check your local library.** (RA)

The King in the Garden, by Leon Garfield (Lothrop, Lee & Shepard, 1984). A little girl named Abigail finds mad King Nebuchadnezzar eating the flowers in her garden and helps him return to his palace and to God. **Out of print; check your local library.** (RA)

Map Work

Chapter 17: Babylon Takes Over Again (Student Page 49)

1. On your map, find Nebuchadnezzar's city of **Babylon** and circle it in red.

2. Find the city of **Nineveh** on your map. Put a red X across the name Nineveh to show that Nebuchadnezzar destroyed it.

3. Find the city of **Jerusalem**, also destroyed by Nebuchadnezzar. Just like you did with Nineveh, put a red X across the name Jerusalem.

Coloring Page

Marduk and Tiamat (Student Page 50) — PARENTS, PLEASE PREVIEW

Marduk, the most important Babylonian god. Here he's fighting another god, named Tiamat, who's in the form of a dragon.

Art Project: Draw the Hanging Gardens of Babylon

You have just finished reading the story of why Nebuchadnezzar built the Hanging Gardens in Babylon. But no one knows what the gardens actually looked like. We only know of their existence because we have copies of ancient Greek and Rome texts that describe them. Many people believe that the gardens were made up of terraces stacked one on top of another. It probably resembled a ziggurat with plants! Trees, shrubs and flowers were brought in from all around the vast empire and planted in the garden. The finished result was a magnificent green emerald in the desert landscape.

Use your crayons and your imagination to draw a picture of how you think the Hanging Gardens of Babylon looked. Your drawing just might be the one that best depicts how the gardens really looked so long ago.

Science Project: Build a Babylonian Mountain Garden

Materials:

- dirt, water and large bucket
- large square of cardboard
- grass seeds
- wild flower seeds (optional)

Directions:

1. Fill a large bucket with dirt. Add water and mix with your hands until you form a wet, but not mushy, clay-dirt mixture. Let the mixture sit in the bucket for a day.

2. Place a stiff piece of cardboard (about three times larger than the mouth of the bucket) on top of the bucket. Place one hand on top of the cardboard and the other hand under the bucket. Then turn your hands over quickly so that the dirt will slide out of the bucket onto the cardboard. Put the cardboard and bucket on the ground. Slowly lift the bucket off of your mountain. Use your hands to pat down any dirt that didn't stay formed to your mountain.

3. Sprinkle grass seeds all over the mountain (follow the seed pack instructions). Use your hands to gently press the seeds to the sides of your mountain, so that they will adhere. If you want, you can sprinkle wild flower seeds on the top.

4. Be sure to gently water your mountain daily and keep it outside in a sunny place. Behold, a Babylonian Mountain Garden!

CHAPTER EIGHTEEN
Life in Early Crete

Encyclopedia Cross-References

Review Questions — Bull-Jumpers and Sailors

Why did the Minoans hold bull-jumping festivals? *To honor the gods of Crete*

Were the bull-jumpers treated well? *Yes; they were given food, beautiful clothes, jewelry, and gold.*

Was bull-jumping dangerous? *Yes; bull-jumpers were often killed.*

What did pirates do in the Mediterranean Sea? *They attacked and robbed people who tried to sail on the sea.*

What did the Minoans build to get rid of the pirates? *Ships*

What is a navy? *An army that fights on water*

Narration Exercise — Bull-Jumpers and Sailors

"The Minoans lived on Crete. They jumped over bulls to worship their gods. The king of the Minoans wanted a navy. He built ships to drive pirates away."

Review Questions — King Minos and the Minotaur

What kind of monster was the Minotaur? *Half man and half bull*

Why did King Minos tell Athens to send him seven girls and boys every year? *To feed them to the Minotaur*

Where did the Minotaur live? *Under the palace, in a maze*

How did Theseus get out of the maze? *With a ball of wool that Ariadne gave him*

What color sail was Theseus supposed to put on his ship? *A white sail*

What happened when he forgot to put on the white sail? *His father jumped off a cliff.*

The father of Theseus was called King Aegeus. What sea was named after him? *The Aegean Sea*

Narration Exercise — King Minos and the Minotaur

Ask the child to retell the story of Theseus and the Minotaur to you. Aim for a narration of four to six sentences; if the child wants to include every detail, suggest a more condensed version of the story. (For example, if the child says, "Theseus went down to the seaside. He found out that people were being sent to Athens for the Minotaur to eat. He said he wanted to go. His father didn't want him to go," suggest, "We could just say, 'Theseus wanted to go to Athens, even though his father told him not to.'")

OR

Ask the child to draw a scene from the story and to describe the picture to you. Write this description at the bottom of the page.

Review Questions — The Mysterious End of the Minoans

Why did the Minoans leave Crete? *Because a volcano erupted nearby*

What island did the volcano erupt on? *Thera*

What happened to Thera? *It sank beneath the sea.*

What did the volcano do to the air and land of Crete? *A tidal wave hit Crete; ash, dust, and rock covered the fields and towns, so that people couldn't breathe and crops couldn't grow.*

Narration Exercise — The Mysterious End of the Minoans

Ask the child to tell you why the Minoans had to leave Crete. Acceptable narrations might include, "A volcano erupted near Crete. All the people on Crete had to leave."

OR

"A volcano blew up the island of Thera. The ash and the dust fell all over Crete, and the people couldn't grow crops any more. So they had to leave."

Additional History Reading

Where Was Atlantis? by Brian Innes (Raintree Steck-Vaughn, 1999). The legend of Atlantis may have been based on the destruction of the island of Thera; this book (along with others that may be at your library) discusses this factual foundation. (RA)

Atlantis: The Lost City (DK Eyewitness Readers: Level 4), by Andrew Donkin (Sagebrush, 2001). This 2–3rd grade reader begins with Plato telling the story of Atlantis, and then discusses the possible evidence. (RA 1–2, IR 2–4)

The Mystery of Atlantis, by Holly Wallace (Heinemann, 2001). Slightly more difficult than the Eyewitness Reader listed above, this text focuses on various theories about the disappearance of Atlantis and the evidence for each. (RA 1–3, IR 3–5)

Ancient Aegean [videorecording], produced and directed by JWM Productions (Schlessinger Media, 1998). Join archaeologist Arizona Smith and a young detective-in-training as they explore the mysteries of the ancient Minoan civilization. You can buy this video from Amazon.com, but check your local library first.

Corresponding Literature Suggestions

Monster in the Maze: The Story of the Minotaur (All Aboard Reading, Level 2), by Stephanie Spinner (Penguin, 2000). This version can be read independently by advanced readers, and even beginners should be able to read a page or two alone. (IR/RA)

Atlantis: The Legend of a Lost City, by Christina Balit (Henry Holt, 2000). A retelling of the ancient Greek legend about the creation of Atlantis by Zeus, and its sinking to the bottom of the sea. (RA)

The Hero and the Minotaur: The Fantastic Adventures of Theseus, by Robert Byrd (Dutton, 2005). This retelling includes the story of Icarus; illustrations are very un-scary. (RA 1–3, IR 3–4)

Corresponding Audiobook Suggestions

Heroes in Mythology, read by Jim Weiss (Greathall Productions). Three of the world's greatest adventures—Theseus and the Minotaur, Prometheus, Bearer of Fire, and Odin and the Norse Men—each featuring a quest for wisdom. Available at www.greathall.com.

Map Work

Chapter 18: Life in Early Crete (Student Page 51)

1. On your map, find the **Aegean Sea**. Shade it lightly in blue.

2. Find the island of **Crete** and color it yellow.

3. Find **Athens** and circle it in green. Then draw a line from Athens to Crete. This is the path that Theseus took.

4. Can you find the island of **Thera**? Circle it in red to remind you that a volcano erupted there!

Coloring Page

Bull Jumper (Student Page 52)

Projects

Activity Project: The Minotaur's Maze

Help Theseus slay the Minotaur—color the maze and help Theseus find his way through the labyrinth to the Minotaur at the center. (Student Page 53)

Craft Project: Build Your Own Labyrinth
Materials:
- cardboard sheet
- clay (variation: LEGOs or building blocks)

Directions:

1. Roll the clay into long, skinny (snake-like) pieces.

2. Place the clay on the cardboard to make your own Labyrinth.

3. Tape a piece of string at the start and wind it through your Labyrinth so you can find your way out.

Variation: Use your LEGOs or blocks instead of clay.

Craft Project: Build a Minoan Ship

Note: Archaeologists disagree over whether most Minoan boats had sails.
Suggested Materials (many different things will work for this project):
- styrofoam or plastic container (takeout, or from grocery store meat counter)
- styrofoam floral arranger
- styrofoam plate
- small wooden dowel
- hot glue
- paints (optional)

Directions:

1. Wash the container well. This is the hull of your boat. If you plan to paint it, do that now.

2. Glue a 1½-inch thick piece of styrofoam floral arranger to the inside floor of the hull. This will hold the mast up.

3. Push the dowel rod into the styrofoam floral arranger and glue. This is the mast for your boat.

4. Cut a rectangular sail from the styrofoam plate.

5. Poke a small hole in the top and bottom of the sail. Gently push the dowel rod through the bottom hole then through the top hole.

Take this project a step further and make some oars for your ship.

Materials:
- thin dowel rod or 3 bamboo skewers
- 1 package of "Woodsies," small, medium and large circles, teardrops and ovals (available at craft stores)
- wood glue

Directions:
1. Cut the dowel rod or skewers into 6-inch lengths. These are the oars.
2. Glue a large oval Woodsie on the end of each oar to make the paddle end.
3. Carefully poke three evenly spaced holes on each side of the hull.
4. Poke the ends of the oars through the holes so the paddles are outside the hull.
5. Glue a small oval Woodsie on the end of each oar for a handle.

Craft Project: Make an Erupting Volcano

(This project is a little messy, but is a lot of fun!)

Materials:
- plaster of Paris or self-hardening clay
- an 8 oz. drink bottle
- pie tin or plastic plant saucer
- water proof paint
- baking soda and vinegar
- red and yellow food coloring
- liquid dish soap
- funnel
- water

Directions
1. Spread newspapers and wax paper over work area.
2. Mix plaster of Paris with just enough water to make thick clay.
3. Working quickly, shape the plaster of Paris or clay around the bottle to resemble a mountain. Use small amounts of water to smooth the surface. Let volcano dry completely.
4. Paint your volcano, let it dry, and then put it in the pie plate or plant saucer.
5. Use the funnel to pour ¼ cup of water and 1 or 2 tablespoons of baking soda into the bottle. Add about three drops of yellow food coloring.
6. Mix red food coloring and liquid soap with ½ cup of vinegar.
7. Quickly pour vinegar mixture into the bottle and stand back!

What's happening here? The baking soda reacts with the vinegar and carbon dioxide gas is produced. As the gas bubbles build up in the bottle the liquid or "lava" is forced out. Experiment with different mixtures of the ingredients to create different effects.

Take this one step further and make an ancient city out of clay to place at the foot of your volcano.

CHAPTER NINETEEN
The Early Greeks

Encyclopedia Cross-References

Usborne Book of World History: 42–45

Usborne Internet-Linked Encyclopedia: 128–131

Kingfisher Illustrated History of the World: 40–41

Kingfisher History Encyclopedia: 17

Review Questions — The Mycenaeans

What were the people who came from Greece to conquer Crete called? *The Mycenaeans.*

What were the Mycenaeans good at? *Fighting*

Where did the Mycenaeans build colonies? *Around the Aegean Sea*

Can you tell me a little bit about how the Mycenaean Greeks lived? Prompt the child if necessary for the following answers: *They lived in houses, had jobs, and went to school.*

Narration Exercise — The Mycenaeans

"After the volcano erupted near Crete, other people took over. They were called Mycenaeans. They used helmets and shields and chariots to fight."

Review Questions — The Greek Dark Ages

How did the barbarians live? Prompt the child if necessary for the following answers: *They wandered around, couldn't read or write, and spent their time fighting other people.*

What did the Mycenaean Greeks have that made them such strong fighters? *Bronze weapons and chariots*

What kind of weapons did the barbarians have? *Iron weapons that were stronger than bronze weapons*

When the Greeks and the barbarians fought, who won? *The barbarians*

Do you remember why we call this time the Dark Ages? *Because the barbarians didn't leave us any written history or records about the time that they lived in Greece*

Narration Exercise — The Greek Dark Ages

If necessary, prompt the child to use the phrase "Dark Ages."

"The Greeks thought they were strong. But barbarians were stronger. They took over Greece. This was the 'Dark Ages,' when they didn't write anything."

OR

"Greeks lived like regular people. Barbarians wandered around fighting. The barbarians conquered the Greeks, but they didn't keep histories. This was the 'Dark Ages.'"

Additional History Reading

Footsteps in Time: The Greeks, by Sally Hewitt (Frankling Watts, 2001). Introduces young children to ancient Greece using crafts and activities. (RA)

How Would You Survive as an Ancient Greek? by Fiona MacDonald (Franklin Watts, 1996). Presents an account of everyday life in Ancient Greece. (RA)

You Wouldn't Want to Be a Slave in Ancient Greece: A Life You'd Rather Not Have, by Fiona MacDonald (Franklin Watts, 2000). Entertaining guide to the life of an ancient Greek slave, with cartoon-like illustrations. Good historical information. (RA 1–2, IR 3–5)

Ancient Greece (Nature Company Discover Libraries), by Louise Schofield (Barnes and Noble, 2003). Spectacular pictures and information about the earliest Greeks. (RA)

The Best Book of Ancient Greece, by Belinda Weber (Kingfisher, 2005). Colorful and easy-to-read sections on the Minoans, Mycenaeans, Trojans, Spartans, Athenians, and various aspects of daily life. Excellent for young students (some parents may wish to preview the picture of the Minotaur on p. 28).

Corresponding Literature Suggestions

Usborne Greek Myths for Young Children, by Heather Amery (Usborne, 2000). Simplified retelling of Greek myths. (RA, possible IR for advanced readers)

D'Aulaire's Book of Greek Myths, by Edgar Parin d'Aulaire (Delacorte, 1992). A classic in its own right, this introduction to the gods and goddesses of Ancient Greece has beautiful illustrations by Caldecott Award winners.

The Trojan Horse, by Emily Little (Random House, 1988). The Greek assault on Troy took place during the Mycenaean period; this retelling can be read independently by strong readers. (IR, RA for beginners)

The Trojan Horse, by Warwick Hutton (Margaret K. McElderry, 1987). This picture-book retelling is **out of print**, but still remains a classic and is stocked at most libraries. (RA)

Map Work

Chapter 19: The Early Greeks (Student Page 54)

1. On your map, find the cities of **Mycenae**, **Thebes**, and **Athens**.

2. Choose your favorite color, and color **Greece**.

3. Draw an arrow from the **Mediterranean Sea** up into Greece. This shows that the Sea People invaded Greece.

4. On your map, find the land above and to the left (that is, north and west) of Thebes. Draw an arrow from this land down into Greece. This shows that **Dorians** came from the north to invade Greece.

Coloring Page

Greek War Chariot (Student Page 55)

This picture of a warrior in his chariot is based on a fresco found in Pylos.

Projects

Craft Project: Make an Easy Mycenaean Helmet
Materials:
- cardboard box the size of your head
- scissors
- paints

Directions:

1. Cut eyeholes so you can see out of your helmet when it's on your head.

2. Paint the box bronze.

3. Get ready for battle!

Craft Project: Make a Realistic Mycenaean Helmet

Some Mycenaean helmets were made of bronze. Bronze is a metal made by mixing tin and copper.

Materials:

- old cap with bill cut off
- heavy cardboard
- papier maché clay (Celluclay, available at craft stores)
- masking tape, scissors
- sealer paint (optional)
- bronze paint
- polyurethane (optional)

Note: Make this helmet a little too large all the way around to allow for shrinkage.

Directions:

1. Put the cap on and attach cardboard to the bottom of the cap from the back of your head to your ears. Attach another section of cardboard around your face. Use wedges of cardboard to attach the back section to the front. Make sure the bottom of the helmet is a little bigger around than the top.

2. With a pin, mark places for eyeholes and mouth. After you cut out the mouth and eyeholes, it should look like this.

3. Cover the outside of the cap with strips of masking tape.

4. Stuff the cap with tightly wadded up newspaper or plastic bags and prop up your helmet so it is not touching the table.

5. Mix the papier maché clay according to directions and spread over the outside of helmet. Use water on your hands to help smooth the clay. The surface will have a rough hammered appearance. Let this dry completely.

6. When the outside of the helmet is completely dry, turn it over and apply papier maché clay to the inside. Do not cover the cap on the inside of the helmet. Let this dry completely.

7. Apply sealer paint (optional), then bronze paint, then polyurethane (optional) letting each coat dry completely before applying the next one.

8. Take it a step further and line your helmet like the Mycenaeans did. Glue cloth or fake fur inside. Paint gold trim around the edges. Your finished helmet will look something like the helmet at the top of the page (you can add the crest if you like!).

Craft Project: Make a Mycenaean Shield

Materials:

- cardboard
- scissors
- glue
- paint

Directions:

1. Draw a circle or oval shape on a heavy piece of cardboard and cut it out.

2. You need two handles on the back of your shield, one for your hand to hold on to and another to put your forearm through. Lay your arm across the back of the shield and measure where the handles should go.

3. Glue or tape the handles onto the shield

4. Paint and decorate your shield. (Some Mycenaean warriors painted scary faces or animals on their shields and some warriors had bronze shields.)

Craft Project: Make a Simple Greek Vase

Much of what we know about the Ancient Greeks comes from the pictures they painted on their beautiful pottery.

Materials:
- copy of vase outline (Student Page 56)
- colors and or paints
- construction paper

Directions:

1. Draw a design onto the vase outline.

2. Cut out and decorate your vase using colors, paints or construction paper.

Craft Project: Make a Realistic Greek Vase

Materials:
- 7" balloon
- newspaper torn into 2" by 4" strips
- glue (white school glue or wallpaper paste)
- small plastic cup
- jar lid
- foam brushes
- paints
- polyurethane

Directions:

1. Blow up the balloon and tape the jar lid on the bottom so it stands upright.

2. Spread glue on the balloon with a foam brush.

3. Put strips of newspaper on the balloon and brush glue on top. Cover the entire balloon and jar lid. Continue layering newspapers and glue until you have about 6 layers of newspaper on balloon.

4. Tie a string around the knot in the balloon and hang up to dry.

5. When the vase is completely dry cut a hole in the top of the balloon and let the air out. The balloon should come right out.

6. Carefully cut a hole in the top of the vase and fit the plastic cup into the hole.

7. Cover the plastic cup with several layers of newspaper and glue. Set aside to dry.

8. Paint and decorate your vase. Spray a coat of polyurethane on your vase for durability.

CHAPTER TWENTY
Greece Gets Civilized Again

Encyclopedia Cross-References

Usborne Book of World History: 64

Kingfisher Illustrated History of the World: 72

Usborne Internet-Linked Encyclopedia: 141, 154, 156–157

Kingfisher History Encyclopedia: 38

Review Questions — Greece Gets an Alphabet

What happened to the barbarians who lived in Greece? *They became civilized—built houses, learned how to read, etc.* (any details the child wants to repeat from the lesson are fine).

Did they kill their neighbors for fun? *No.* What did they do instead? *Wrestled, raced, danced*

Did the women go out and find food? *No, they stayed indoors.*

The barbarians were now called Greeks. They learned to read and write. Can you tell me about the letters that they used? Ask the child to point back to some of the Greek letters and tell you what they represent.

Narration Exercise — Greece Gets an Alphabet

Instead of a Narration Exercise today, help the child to write her first name (middle and last name is optional) in Greek letters. (Greek Alphabet—Student Page 59)

Review Questions — The Stories of Homer

What hero is the Odyssey named after? *Odysseus*

Why did Poseidon get angry at Odysseus and his men? *Because they forgot to thank him for their victory over Troy*

What was the one-eyed monster called? *Cyclops*

How did the Greeks know the stories of Odysseus and Troy, in the days when they couldn't read and write? *They told them to their children and grandchildren*

Who first wrote down these stories? *The poet Homer*

How did Odysseus get revenge on the Cyclops? *He blinded him/put his eye out.*

How did the men get out of the cave? *They held on to the Cyclops' sheep when he let them out in the morning.*

Why did Odysseus tell the Cyclops that his name was Noman? *So that anyone who came to rescue the Cyclops would think that no man was hurting him*

After Odysseus made fun of the Cyclops, what did the Cyclops do? *Asked Poseidon to keep him from reaching home*

Why do you think Odysseus decided to make fun of the Cyclops? Why didn't he just sail quietly away? Discuss this with the child. Possible answers: *Pride, foolishness, he wanted to boast* Would it have been better if he'd just left without making any more noise? *Yes*

Narration Exercise — The Stories of Homer

"Odysseus and his men were headed home. They landed on an island where a monster lived. The monster ate two of the men. Odysseus tricked the monster into going to sleep and put his eye out. Then he and his men sneaked out of the cave. The Cyclops cursed Odysseus before he left."

OR

"Odysseus landed on an island. A monster who lived there ate two of his men. Odysseus was trapped in the monster's cave and couldn't get out. Odysseus told the monster that his name was Noman, and then put out his eye. The monster told everyone that Noman was killing him. Then Odysseus and his men held onto the sheep to get out of the cave."

Review Questions — The First Olympic Games

What god was honored by the first Olympic games? *Zeus, the king of the gods*

What mountain was the Olympics named after? *Mount Olympus, where the gods were supposed to live*

What is a virtue? *Something good about a person*

What virtues did the Olympic Games reward? *Strength and courage*

Who was allowed to compete in the Olympic games? *Men from Greece*

Narration Exercise — The First Olympic Games

Ask the child to draw a picture of an Olympic competition. She should describe the picture to you; write the description on the bottom of the picture, and put it into the History Notebook.

OR

Ask the child to tell you three things about the Olympic games. Write them down and put them into the History Notebook. Sample narrations might include:

"The Olympics started in ancient Greece. They were held to worship Zeus. Only men could go."

OR

"The Olympics started because two cities made peace. They were held every four years. The winners got olive branches for medals."

Additional History Reading

I Wonder Why the Greeks Built Temples and Other Questions About Ancient Greece, by Fiona MacDonald (Kingfisher, 1997). Presents information in a question-and-answer format using double-page spreads and large, full-color illustration. (RA)

Count Your Way Through Greece, by Jim Haskins and Kathleen Benson (Chrorhoda Books, 1996). The authors use the numbers one through ten to explain Greek history and culture. (RA)

Footsteps in Time: The Greeks, by Sally Hewitt (Children's Press, 1998). Introduces young children to ancient Greece using crafts and activities. (RA and activity)

A Coloring Book of the Trojan War: The Iliad, Vol. 2, by John K. Anderson, illus. Harry Knill, (Bellerophon Books, 1995). Detailed pictures based on original Greek sources (vase paintings from ancient Greece); also contains some Greek text. (RA and activity)

Corresponding Literature Suggestions

The Librarian Who Measured the Earth, by Kathryn Lasky (Little Brown, 1994). Describes the life and work of Eratosthenes, the Greek geographer and astronomer who accurately measured the circumference of the Earth. (RA)

How the Greeks Won the War: Step Into Reading, by Emily Little (Sagebrush, 1999). A retelling of the Trojan War with simple sentences and vocabulary (on a second or third grade reading level). (RA, IR for advanced readers)

Black Ships Before Troy: The Story of the Iliad, by Rosemary Sutcliff (Laurel Leaf, 2005). A simple and beautifully illustrated (but lengthy) retelling of the Trojan War; good for a read-aloud project that extends over a couple of weeks. (RA)

The Wanderings of Odysseus: The Story of the Odyssey, by Rosemary Sutcliff (Frances Lincoln, 2005). Fascinating and beautifully illustrated, but not long. Some scary pictures. (RA)

Run With Me, Nike! by Cassandra Case (Soundprints, 1999). This simple picture book tells the story of a young Olympic competitor in ancient times. (RA)

Hour of the Olympics (Magic Tree House #16), by Mary Pope Osborne (Random House, 1998). Jack and Annie go to ancient Greece, where they race against time to witness the very first Olympic Games! (RA)

Archimedes Takes a Bath, by Joan M. Lexau (Crowell, 1969). Young Xanthius has the job of seeing that absent-minded Archimedes eats and bathes occasionally. His success has much to do with the formulation of Archimedes' principle. **Out of print; check your local library.** (RA)

Corresponding Audiobook Suggestions

She and He Adventures in Mythology, by Jim Weiss (Greathall Productions, 1999). Upbeat and exciting yet deeply moving, this unique collection of myths addresses respect between men and women and the value of love and honor. Available at www.greathall.com.

Galileo and the Stargazers, including: Archimedes and the Golden Crown, by Jim Weiss (Greathall Productions, 1999). Adventure, laughter, mystery … amid scientific fact. Available at www.greathall.com.

Greek Myths, by Jim Weiss (Greathall Productions, 1997). Make Hercules, King Midas, and Perseus and Medusa understandable to children, with strong emphasis on character over violence. Available at www.greathall.com.

Map Work

Chapter 20: Greece Gets Civilized Again (Student Page 57)

1. On your map, find the country of **Greece** and color it green.

2. Find **Mount Olympus** and circle it in red.

3. Find **Troy** and circle it in blue. What sea did the Greeks cross to find the Trojans?

4. Optional: Color all the islands of Greece in your favorite color. How many islands are there?

Coloring Page

The Cyclops (Student Page 58) — PARENTS, PLEASE PREVIEW

Projects

Activity Project: Write Your Name with Greek Letters

Using Student Page 59, write your name—and the names of your friends and family—in Greek.

Activity Project: Make Greek Instruments

The Greeks loved music and dancing. There are very few records of the songs the Greeks played but we do know about the instruments that they used because they painted pictures of them on pottery.

Make a Timpanon

A timpanon is a tambourine that the Greeks used to provide rhythm. It was made from animal skin stretched tightly over a frame.

Materials:

- 2 Styrofoam plates or pie tins
- glue
- hole punch
- ribbon
- paints

Directions:

1. Glue the two plates together at the rim, so that they form a hollow "shell."

2. Paint or decorate as desired.

3. Punch evenly spaced holes around edges of plates.

4. Lace ribbon through the holes and tie ends together leaving streamers. Tap your timpanon for rhythm!

Make a Greek Flute:

Materials:

- cardboard roll from toilet paper
- wax paper
- rubber band
- pencil or ice pick

Directions:

1. Punch three holes on one side of the cardboard roll using a pencil or ice pick (adult help required!).

2. Stretch wax paper over one end and fasten with a rubber band.

3. Hum in your flute. Using your fingers, cover the holes one at a time to make different sounds.

Make Finger Cymbals:

Materials:

- 2 small metal jar lids
- 2 pieces of pipe cleaner
- ice pick

Directions:

1. Punch two holes in each jar lid (make sure that a grown-up helps!).

2. Put a piece of pipe cleaner through holes and fasten the jar lids to your thumb and longest finger. Now put on your favorite music and pretend you are in Ancient Greece. Make up a dance and play your instruments while dancing.

Craft Project: Make a Greek Loom

The Ancient Greeks had to make all their own clothes. They even had to weave their own cloth!

Materials:

- sturdy piece of cardboard or Styrofoam tray
- string
- knife
- all kinds of paper, yarn, ribbon, pipe cleaners—you can even use dried grasses and flowers!

Directions:
1. For an adult: Cut slots or Vs all the way down both ends of the cardboard, leaving a space about ½-inch between each slit.
2. Student: Attach string at top left corner of cardboard and wind it around the Vs of the cardboard. Do this from top to bottom. Parallel lines will be formed. Securely attach string at bottom of cardboard.
3. Weave your chosen materials in and out, going over one string then under the next.
4. When finished weaving, carefully cut the strings and tie the ends together. You can attach your woven piece to a dowel rod or a twig and hang it on the wall.

Craft Project: Make an Olympic Wreath

The winners at the ancient Olympic received olive branch wreaths as a prize.

Materials:
- small (green) branches or twigs from trees or bushes or artificial greenery
- floral wire
- hot glue gun
- construction paper leaves, real leaves or artificial leaves

Directions:
1. Bend a tree branch or two, using light pressure, to form a circle. If green enough, they won't snap.
2. Secure the ends by using floral wire.
3. Continue wrapping the rest of the branches around the form until it resembles a wreath. Use floral wire and, if necessary, a hot glue gun (make sure an adult helps out!) to hold all of the branches in place.
4. Glue leaves onto your "olive" branch wreath.

Activity Project: Have an Olympic Games / Greek Feast Party

Invite several friends over to participate in some fun games. Award the winners an olive branch wreath or provide the materials and let each participant make their own wreath. Then enjoy some Greek food and dancing. You can also look in your area for Greek Festivals hosted by Greek Orthodox churches.

Suggested Games:
- crab walk or bear walk to a finish line
- wheel barrow race—hold your partner's ankles like the handles of a wheelbarrow while he uses his hands to race to the finish line.
- skip, hop or jump backward or somersault or cartwheel to the finish line.
- frisbee discus throwing—see who can throw a Frisbee the farthest!
- long jump or high jump
- hula hoop competition—who can keep it going the longest?
- obstacle course race—create an obstacle course and see who can finish it first. The obstacles can be physical (jump a barrier, crawl through a tire) or they can be tasks (stop at each corner and do jumping jacks, pushups, somersaults, etc.).

Greek Food Suggestions:

Hummus

Ingredients:
- 2 15 oz. cans of chick peas rinsed and drained
- 6 tablespoons tahini (sesame seed butter)
- 2 to 3 garlic cloves pressed
- ¼ cup olive oil
- lemon juice

- salt
- pepper

Directions:
1. Mix all of the ingredients together in your food processor or mash with a potato masher. Serve with warmed pita bread

Greek Pilaf
Ingredients:
- 1½ cups raw brown rice
- 2¼ cups water or chicken broth
- 1½ tablespoons olive oil
- 1½ cups minced onion
- ½ cup minced celery
- ½ cup toasted pine nuts
- 4 or 5 garlic cloves pressed
- 2 teaspoons lemon juice
- salt and pepper

Directions:
1. Place rice and water in a saucepan. Boil, cover and simmer for about 40 minutes or until tender.
2. Sauté onion, celery and garlic in olive oil until vegetables are tender. Add salt, pepper and pine nuts and sauté for five minutes.
3. Mix rice with sautéed mixture and add lemon juice.

Stuffed Grape Leaves
Ingredients:
- About 24 grape leaves 3 to 4 inches wide (Grape leaves can be found in larger grocery stores or specialty food stores. You can pick your own in the spring when they are tender.)
- Greek pilaf
- spaghetti sauce

Directions:
1. Preheat oven to 350 degrees and lightly grease a baking dish.
2. Place a heaping spoonful of Greek Pilaf on each leaf and roll it up, tucking in the ends.
3. Place the stuffed leaves in the baking dish and bake for 20 minutes.
4. Serve with spaghetti sauce or squeeze lemon juice on top.

Ekmek

Ingredients:

Syrup:
- 2 teaspoons honey
- ⅔ cup inexpensive brandy
- 1 cup sugar
- 1 cup water

Cake:
- 1 package square melba toast (or Jacobsen's Snack Toast)
- ground cinnamon
- pudding/custard (such as vanilla instant pudding)

Top Layer:
- real whipped cream (NOT Cool Whip)
- ground cinnamon
- slivered almonds or pistachios

Directions:

1. Assemble syrup ingredients in a pan and boil for about 15 minutes (while you're making the pudding). Mix the instant pudding. When the pudding is done, remove syrup from heat and let cool. Line a glass dish with melba toast (cake is actually the toast that has soaked up the syrup). Pour cooled syrup over toast (syrup should cover toast slices completely). Sprinkle lightly with cinnamon. Pour instant pudding over toast. Pour whipped cream over pudding. Sprinkle with slivered almonds & cinnamon.

CHAPTER TWENTY-ONE
The Medes and the Persians

Encyclopedia Cross-References

Usborne Book of World History: 66

Usborne Internet-Linked Encyclopedia: 152–153

Kingfisher Illustrated History of the World: 74–74

Kingfisher History Encyclopedia: 40–41

Review Questions — A New Empire

What was the name of the shepherd tribe at the edge of Media? *Persia, or the Persians*

What country did the Persians obey? *The Medes, or Media*

Why did the Persian king, Astyges, want to get rid of his grandson? *He dreamed that the baby would grow up and take his throne away.*

What was the baby's name? *Cyrus*

After Cyrus became king of the Persians, what did he do? *He conquered Media too.*

Narration Exercise — A New Empire

The child should know the name Cyrus, but she doesn't need to know the other proper names of characters in the story. Acceptable narrations might include:

"The king of Persia was afraid of his grandson. The baby was named Cyrus. When he grew up, he took over the throne. Then he conquered the Medes."

OR

"Cyrus grew up and became king of the Persians. Then he also took over Media. He became a great ruler."

Review Questions — Cyrus the Great

Was Cyrus a good king? *Yes, he was very fair.*

Can you tell me one of the fair things Cyrus did? *He let the Medes have some power in his empire.* OR *He let the Jews go back to Palestine.*

What was King Croesus known for? *His gold—he was richer than anyone else.*

Why did the Babylonians let Cyrus into their city? *Because they did not like their own king*

Narration Exercise — Cyrus the Great

Now ask the child to tell back to you the story of Cyrus's conquests in two to four sentences. Use the above questions to prompt the child if necessary. The narration should include the information that Cyrus conquered Babylon. Acceptable narrations might include:

"Cyrus conquered lots of other nations. One was ruled by a rich king named Croesus. He had lots of gold. He also conquered Babylon."

OR

"Cyrus was a good king. His people liked him. Babylon let him in because he was better than their king. Cyrus ruled a large empire."

Additional History Reading

The Persian Empire, by Karen Zeinert (Benchmark, 1996). This descriptive book highlights the history of the Persian Empire and its contributions to modern life. Intended for slightly older children; you'll want to read selected sections. (RA)

Ancient Persia, by Neil Bramwell (MyReportLinks.com Books, 2004). For students mature enough to do additional research on the internet, this history of ancient Persia during the rule of Cyrus also provides links to reputable web sites which can provide much more information (e.g., the University of Chicago, the Library of Congress). (IR 4–up)

Corresponding Literature Suggestions

King Midas and the Golden Touch, by Charlotte Craft (HarperTrophy, 2003). The legend of King Midas may be based on Croesus, the rich king of Asia Minor. For a longer project, listen to the unabridged audio of Lynn Reid Banks's *The Adventures of King Midas* (try your local library). (RA)

Esther's Story, by Diane Wolkstein (HarperCollins, 1995). The story of Esther took place during the expansion of the Persian Empire, among the Jews who were in exile in the Persian capital city. (RA)

The Legend of the Persian Carpet, by Tomie dePaola (Putnam, 1993). This simple read-aloud has detailed and accurate pictures of Persian architecture. (RA 1–2, IR 2–4)

The Persian Cinderella, by Shirley Climo and Robert Florczak (HarperCollins, 2001). This retelling sets the story in ancient Persia, with beautiful detailed paintings for illustrations. (RA)

Ali and the Magic Stew, by Shulamith Levey Oppenheim, illus. Winslow Pels (Boyds Mill Press, 2002). An easy picture-book tale of a young Persian boy (during Muslim times, so the setting is later). (RA 1, IR 2–4)

Map Work

Chapter 21: The Medes and the Persians (Student Page 60)

1. On your map, trace the dotted line that goes all the way around the **Persian Empire**. Remember that the Persian Empire swallowed up the empires of Media and Babylonia.

2. Find the **Persian Gulf** and color it blue. Why do you think it is call the *Persian* Gulf?

3. The ancient Persian Empire had four rivers in it. Trace each one in blue. What are the names of the **four rivers**?

4. Two countries we have already studied—**Egypt** and **Canaan**—fall within the boundaries of the Persian Empire. Find those two countries and circle their names in red.

5. Persia was becoming the most powerful country in the east. Soon, they would meet the Greeks in battle. Find **Greece** on your map and color it in green.

Coloring Page

Cyrus the Great (Student Page 61)

This picture of Cyrus the Great is based on a bas-relief found in Pasargade, the capital city of Persia founded by Cyrus.

Craft Project: Make the Persian Ruler's Silver Plate

The Persian Kingdom was full of silver. To us, silver is valuable. (Do you have anything silver in your home? How about a picture frame, jewelry, or special dinnerware?) Silver was valuable to the Persians as well. Workers of this precious metal made beautiful silver plates and bowls, decorating them with pictures of their favorite warriors or heroes—some of whom were famous hunters. They also made beautiful silver crowns. Some were so heavy that the kings couldn't even wear them!

Materials:
- cardboard
- dinner plate
- foil (Reynolds Wrap works best)
- pencil
- craft knife
- scratch paper

Directions:

1. Put the dinner plate face down on a large piece of cardboard and trace the plate.

2. Using a craft knife, cut out the plate shape from the cardboard.

3. Wrap the cardboard plate with foil. Tack down the foil on the back of your cardboard plate with glue or tape. Cut away any extra foil, making sure that it lies down flat.

4. Using your scratch paper, draw some pictures of heroes: a king on a throne, a hunter, or a warrior on a horse. Stick figures are just fine!

5. When you have a drawing that you like, place the paper on the silver plate, right where you want your picture to be. Trace over the lines of your drawing with your pencil, pushing medium-hard so that your pencil tip dents the foil beneath.

6. Take the scratch paper off. See your picture on your Ruler's Plate!

Craft Project: Make Persian Puppets

Materials:
- several brown paper lunch bags (one for each puppet)
- crayons, markers, colored pencils, or pastels
- construction paper, fabric scraps
- buttons, felt, glitter, or sequins
- yarn
- glue
- scissors

Directions:

1. Read over the story of Cyrus and how he became king of the Persians. Decide which characters in the story would make good puppets.

2. Use the paper bags as puppet bases. Put your hand into each one and open and close the fold for a mouth. Draw lips around each "mouth" and use buttons, sequins, or construction paper circles to make eyes.

3. Glue strands of yarn on the top crease of the puppet for hair.

4. Use your other art materials to decorate the puppets.

5. Get behind your sofa, put your hand into the puppet, and push the puppet up above the back of the sofa. Now you have a stage! Act out part of the story of Cyrus for your parents or grandparents.

Activity Project: Play the Conquer Mesopotamia Game

Materials:

- 1 die (2 dice for faster play)
- the "Conquer Mesopotamia" gameboard (Student Page 62)

The board works best if it is enlarged (to 11"x14") and photocopied onto cardstock. You can also color it as an additional art project.

Directions:

1. Object of the game: Be the first one to the FINISH line!
2. Keep your *Story of the World* nearby for quick answer checks.
3. Players should select different objects to represent them on the board (button, bean, coin, LEGO, small plastic animal, etc.) All playing pieces should be placed on START.
4. Roll the die (or dice). The highest number goes first.
5. Going clockwise, each player should throw the dice and move the prescribed number of spaces. When a player lands on a square that contains a symbol, she should check the corresponding symbol and follow the instructions.

CHAPTER TWENTY-TWO
Sparta and Athens

Encyclopedia Cross-References

Usborne Book of World History: 67–69

Usborne Internet-Linked Encyclopedia: 154–159

Kingfisher Illustrated History of the World: 82–89

Kingfisher History Encyclopedia: 52–55

Review Questions — Life in Sparta

Did the Greek cities all obey the same king? *No, each city had its own king.*

What did all Spartan boys grow up to be? *Soldiers*

What did they learn in school? Acceptable answers: *How to fight; how to be tough; how to be strong*

If you were a Spartan boy and you hurt yourself, what would you do? *Be brave and silent! You wouldn't cry. You would pretend that you were fine.*

What were Spartan girls supposed to do? *Have children who would be good fighters.*

Narration Exercise — Life in Sparta

Ask the child to tell you two important things about Sparta. Prompt him if necessary! Any two of the following are acceptable:

Boys were supposed to be soldiers.

Spartan boys went away to camp to learn how to fight.

Men were supposed to be tough (or brave, or strong, or silent).

Spartans weren't supposed to complain.

The Spartans didn't obey the same king as other Greeks.

Review Questions — Life in Athens

What is a democracy? [Prompt the child for the answer:] *A country where people vote on the laws and on who becomes the leaders.*

Did Athens think fighting was the most important thing for boys to learn? *No*

What kinds of things did Athenian boys learn in school? *Mathematics, reading, writing, poetry, music*

What did Athenian girls learn how to do? *Keep house*

What happens to ignorant people who don't know the laws? *Other people can make them do things.*

Why is it important to be educated? [Discuss the answer with your child:] *So that you know what the laws are; so that you know how to vote on laws and leaders; so that tyrants can't tell you what to do*

Narration Exercise — Life in Athens

Ask the child to tell you two important things about Athens. Prompt him if necessary! Any two of the following are acceptable:

Athens was a democracy.

In Athens, people voted on the laws and on the leaders.

People in Athens were educated.

Boys learned how to read and write (or do math, or play music, or memorize poetry).

Girls learned how to keep house.

Plato was a famous man in Athens.

They didn't want tyrants to be in charge.

Additional History Reading

Time Traveler: Children Through Time (DK Eyewitness Reader), by Angela Bull (Dorling Kindersley, 1999). A colorful, interesting book that draws children into the ancient cultures, including the Greeks! Part of a series that focuses on encouraging young readers. (RA for beginning readers, IR for advanced)

Ancient Greece: DK Eyewitness, by Ann Pearson (Dorling Kindersley, 2004). This book is packed with information bites that make it a good reference. Descriptive of many aspects of ancient Greece, using pictures, drawings, actors dressed up, and more. Fantastic pictures of artifacts! (RA)

How Would You Survive As An Ancient Greek? by Fiona MacDonald (Franklin Watts, 1996). A creative look at life as a Greek, complete with questions leading you on a journey to find the answer. Illustrations are enticing. Read the main text quickly, or spend more time studying the details. (RA)

Inside Ancient Athens, by Fiona MacDonald (Enchanted Lion, 2005). Simple explanations of Greek life as lived in Athens, with attention to Athenian government, theater, and wars. (RA 1–3, IR 3–6)

A Coloring Book of Ancient Greece (Bellerophon Books, 2000) is available at www.bellerophonbooks.com. Real Greek art, simplified for young artists to color, along with interesting explanatory text. (RA and activity)

Spend the Day in Ancient Greece! Projects and Activities that Bring the Past to Life, by Linda Honan (Jossey Bass, 1998). Weave on a loom, paint an amphora, build a racing chariot. These are a few of the fun projects taught in this book. Each section centers around a child in ancient Greece and tasks he or she has to do. (RA and activity)

Ancient Greece! 40 Hands-On Activities to Experience This Wondrous Age, by Avery Hart and Paul Mantell (Williamson Publishing, 1999). This collection of activities and information that can be used with older children if you are multi-leveling. (RA and activity)

Top Secret: A Handbook of Codes, Ciphers, and Secret Writing, by Paul B. Janeczko, illus. Jenna Lareau (Candlewick Press, 2004). Pages 48–54 cover two ciphers developed by the ancient Greeks: the Greek square, invented by Polybius, and the Greek skytale, a cipher which comes from ancient Sparta. (RA 1–3, IR 3–6)

Corresponding Literature Suggestions

D'Aulaire's Book of Greek Myths, by Edgar Parin d'Aulaire (Bantam Doubleday Dell, 1962). This introduction to the gods and goddesses of Ancient Greece has beautiful illustrations by Caldecott Award winners. (RA)

Mr. Semolina-Semolinus: A Greek Folktale, by Anthony Manna and Christodoula Mitakidou (Aladdin, 2003). Take a break from myths and read another old Greek story—a folktale about a princess who makes the perfect man out of cookie dough (since she can't find one in real life). (RA)

Bright-Eyed Athena: Stories from Ancient Greece, by Richard Woff (Getty Museum Publications, 1999). A group of weaving women in Athens tell stories about the city's protector. (RA)

Map Work

Chapter 22: Sparta and Athens (Student Page 63)

1. On your map, find the city of **Athens**. Circle it in red.

2. Now find **Sparta**, and circle it in yellow.

3. The Athenians and Spartans could reach each other in two ways—by land and by sea. Draw a blue line to show the sea route between the two. If the Athenians wanted to sail over to Sparta, they would use this path.

4. Now draw a green line to show the land route between the two. If the Spartans wanted to march an army over to Athens, they would use this path.

Coloring Page

A Spartan Warrior (Student Page 64)

Projects

Craft Project: Make a Greek Bowl
Materials:
- terra-cotta clay (available at craft stores) or Sculpey clay
- small round bowl that can be baked in the oven
- foil
- baking sheet
- red and black acrylic paint

Directions:

1. Place the bowl on the baking sheet and spread a piece of foil over it.

2. Break the clay up in small chunks about half the size of a child's hand. Flatten these pieces, but not too thin. Place each piece on the inside of the bowl, smoothing the edges together with water. When the bowl is completely covered, smooth off the top edge.

3. Bake following terra-cotta or Sculpey clay instructions.

4. After your clay pot has cooled, take it out of the small round bowl.

5. Paint a design on the sides using black and red paint!

Activity Project: Write on an Athenian Wax Tablet
Materials:
- a small brick of lard or shortening
- plastic lid from a yogurt or margarine tub
- table knife
- toothpicks

Directions:

1. An hour before you plan to use your wax tablet, spread the lard the inside of the plastic lid so that the edges provide a frame for your tablet. Place in the refrigerator and let it solidify.

2. When you're ready, take out and write a message, or draw a picture on the lard with a toothpick.

3. When you're finished, smooth it over with the knife and write something new. This is similar to how the sturdy wax tablets were used. The Greek boys used them at school and the Greek girls used them in their housework.

Craft Project: Make "No-Sew" Greek Clothes

How do we know how the Greeks dressed in ancient days? Archeologists get a pretty good picture from the artwork that has been left to us. Bowls, beautifully carved statues, and letters found give us peeks into their daily lives. Spartan soldiers were depicted in their uniforms. Their long red cloak was their most prized possession. If you want to be a Spartan, make sure you use an old red T-shirt!

Materials:

- old white pillowcase
- Dad or Mom's old colorful T-shirt
- scissors
- jute rope or twine

Directions:

1. Place a white pillowcase flat on a table. Cut out a hole in the middle of the folded edge on the short side. This will be the neck hole.

2. On the longer, folded sides, cut out arm holes at the top corner edge on the side close to the neck hole. Slip it over your head. Voila! Your chiton.

3. Use the rope as a belt for the chiton.

4. Do your hair like a Greek! Girls often wore their hair in ponytails or buns. Sometimes they would wrap a ribbon in a criss-cross fashion around their heads. Boys wore a band of material around their heads.

5. To make your cloak, use the old T-shirt and make a cut down the middle front, from the neck to the bottom seam. Slip it on over your chiton. Add sandals and you're ready to visit ancient Greece!

Craft Project: Make Greek Stickers (Student Page 65)

Using the stencils provided, pick one of the following options. Put your stickers on your bike helmet, in your scrapbook, or anywhere else you're allowed to stick them!

Homemade Greek Stickers:

Materials:

- 2 envelopes unflavored gelatin
- 1 cup water
- ½ teaspoon peppermint extract
- small saucepan
- photocopy of the Greek stickers (Student Page 65)

Directions:

1. Mix the gelatin and the water together in a pan. Heat the mix over medium heat until the gelatin is dissolved. Add the peppermint extract and let cool.

2. Color the Greek stickers with colored pencils, markers or crayons. Once done, cut them out. Paint a thin layer of the homemade sticky-gum on the back of your pictures and let dry. Now your Greek stickers are ready to be licked and stuck! (Ask mom for suggestions on where to stick them!)

Regular Greek Stickers:

Materials:

- Avery sticky-back paper and Student Page 65

Directions:

1. Photocopy Greek stencils on a sheet of Avery 8½ x 11 full sheet of sticky-back paper.

2. Color and cut them out. Peel off the backs whenever you're ready to stick your stickers.

Craft Project: Greek Charm Bracelet

Materials:

- photocopy of the stencils on Student Page 65
- hole punch, colored pencils
- sandpaper
- elastic gold cording (in the bead section of your craft store)
- plastic deli containers, #6 recyclable, flat sides cut out for use

Directions:

1. Cut up a deli plastic container, freeing the usable top and bottom. Sand one side of the plastic until it is cloudy and you can feel the roughness on every part of it. This is so that the color will stick.

2. Lay the plastic on top of the stencil pattern. Trace it on to the plastic, making sure you are working on the scratched side. Then fill in the stencil with the colored pencils. You can use markers as well, but the pencils seem to work best.

3. Decide where you want to punch your hole for the "charm" to hang from your bracelet, and use the hole punch to create the hole.

4. Use your elastic cording and measure around your wrist or around your neck. Leave enough string to knot each charm to your cording. (You may need to re-punch some of the holes.) String the charm and make a knot so it will stay put. Finish by tying the elastic cord ends together.

Activity Project: Make Greek Tattoos

Materials:

- pure henna (from health food stores) or henna hair coloring that is 100% henna
- stencils photocopied on to cardstock and cut out (use the cardstock with the empty spaces)
- small paint brush, non-toxic body crayons (optional)

Directions:

1. Mix the henna with boiling hot water until it is like wet sand and let cool.

2. Put cut-out stencil outline over skin. Brush the henna in the stenciled area. Let sit for a few minutes. This washes off after a few washings. Add details with non-toxic body crayons, if available.

Note: Most people are not allergic to henna. Though it is natural, we recommend that new users put a very small amount on their skin first as a test. If skin gets red or irritated, do not use.

Activity Project: Make Spartan and Greek Paper Dolls

Materials:

- colored pencils, scissors
- Scotch Removable Double Stick Tape
- photocopy of the paper dolls (Student Pages 66–68) on card stock, and clothes on regular white paper

Directions:

1. Color the Greek figures and their clothes and then cut them all out. The Spartan soldier's pride was his flaming red wool cloak and the helmets of the Greek soldiers were passed down from generation to generation.

2. Use the Scotch Removable Double Stick Tape to keep the outfits on your dolls.

3. Options: Laminate your dolls and their clothes (stick-on laminate sheets are available at most office supply stores). Or attach dolls to thin balsam wood and cut out using a craft knife. Photocopy the dolls and clothes twice or more for a family or army.

CHAPTER TWENTY-THREE
The Greek Gods

Encyclopedia Cross-References

Usborne Book of World History: N/A
Usborne Internet-Linked Encyclopedia: N/A

Kingfisher Illustrated History of the World: N/A
Kingfisher History Encyclopedia: 48 (one illustration)

Review Questions — The Greek Gods

Were the Greeks monotheists? *No*

Were they polytheists? *Yes*

Does a polytheist believe in one god or many gods? *Many gods*

Why did Zeus start a war on earth? *Because there were too many people on earth*

Can you name any of the other gods from the story? *Hera, Aphrodite, Athena, Eris, Poseidon*

Narration Exercise — The Greek Gods

Ask the child to retell the story. An acceptable narration might read, "Zeus wanted to get rid of some of the people on earth. So he started a war on earth. All the gods took sides."

OR

"Paris had to say which goddess was the most beautiful. He picked Aphrodite. The other goddesses got mad. A war started."

Additional History Reading

An Ancient Greek Temple: The Story of the Building of the Temples of Ancient Greece, by John Malam, illus. Mark Bergin (Peter Bedrick Books, 2001). A beautifully illustrated look at the building of a Greek temple from the quarry to the finished product. (RA)

Trojan Horse: The World's Greatest Adventure, a DK Eyewitness Reader, by David Clement-Davies (Dorling Kindersley, 1999). Wonderfully crafted paperback with detailed information on side bars of each page. Pictures of gold coins and the pipes are some of the features which make this book a terrific read! (RA)

Corresponding Literature Suggestions

Greek Gods and Goddesses, by Geraldine McCaughrean (Margaret K. McElderry, 1997). McCaughrean's paraphrases are always interesting and sometimes surprising. (RA)

The Gods and Goddesses of Olympus, by Aliki (HarperTrophy, 1997). Colorful pictures and lively, short tales of the central Greek gods. (RA) Note: This book is the basis for one of the Activity Projects in this chapter.

The Illustrated Book of Myths: Tales and Legends of the World, by Neil Philip (Dorling Kindersley, 1995). This book has several examples of myths from several cultures, divided into subjects. Philip weaves in several enjoyable Greek myths. Short chapters are well-illustrated. (RA)

Corresponding Audiobook Suggestions

Greek Myths, read by Jim Weiss (Greathall Productions). Makes Hercules, King Midas, and Perseus and Medusa understandable to children, with strong emphasis on character over violence. Available at www.greathall.com.

She and He: Adventures in Mythology, read by Jim Weiss (Greathall Productions). Upbeat and exciting yet deeply moving, this unique collection of myths addresses the equality of the sexes and the value of love and honor. Available at www.greathall.com.

Map Work

Chapter 23: The Greek Gods (Student Page 69)

This map is the same map of Greece you've seen in recent chapters—19, 20, and 22. But on this map, the names are missing. Can you find them? Try to find:

1. The country of **Greece**
2. The island of **Crete**
3. The **Aegean Sea**
4. The city of **Athens**
5. The city of **Sparta**
6. The city of **Troy**
7. **Mount Olympus**

(PARENT: You can offer a small reward—a chocolate chip, for example—for each name the child can identify. Offer the student a chance to look back at the map of Greece before trying to identify places on the new map.)

Coloring Page

Aphrodite and Zeus (Student Page 70)

Projects

Activity Project: Make an Olympus Family Tree

Once you have read through *The Gods and Goddesses of Olympus* by Aliki, consider making a family tree of the Greek and Roman gods and goddesses—a little bit like you did for your family in the beginning of this book! The Greeks thought their gods were like a big, very unhappy family.

Materials:
- large twig with several branches
- small clay pot or empty container (a coffee can works), filled with rocks, sand or clay
- green construction paper
- string, ribbon, or hot glue
- double stick tape or glue

Directions:

1. Stabilize your tree branch in a pot using rocks, sand or clay.

2. Go outside and find your favorite leaf shape. Trace one leaf shape onto your green construction paper for each Greek god and goddess you will include.

3. Write the name of the god or goddess on the leaf. You can also draw a picture of the character on the other side of the leaf. Or you may write the Greek name on one side and the Roman name for the god or goddess on the other (use chart on Student Page 71).

4. Using string, ribbon or hot glue, attach the leaf for the god who is in charge, Zeus, at the top of your "tree." Place the other leaves in order, from the most important gods near the treetop down to the least important near the bottom.

Art Project: Draw a Home for the Greek Gods
Materials:
- long sheet of newspaper print (Check with your local newspaper printers for the end roll. Inexpensive and very versatile!) OR a piece of white construction paper, 11" x 14"
- colored pencils or thin markers
- an ink pad and your thumb

Directions:
1. Imagine what it might be like to live on the top of a mountain. Illustrators for books about the Greek gods and goddesses had to imagine this. Take your piece of paper and think through how you want to set up your home for the Greek gods. You may want to draw it in pencil first. What would you include in your home for the Greek gods? Maybe their thrones, or the fire that Hestia might be stoking, a valley for Pan's sheep, a bed for Hypnos or a long road for Nike to race on? If you need ideas, go through Aliki's book or another of the recommended readings on the Greek gods and goddesses.

2. After you've set up their home, use your thumb-print to make your gods and goddesses. Put your thumb on the ink pad, and then on the paper where you want the head of your character to be.

3. Now add eyes, nose, and mouth with your markers. Add a body to each head with another thumb-print, or draw a body with your markers. Add arms and legs with your markers.

4. Decorate each character so that you remember who they are. Zeus might have a golden crown and a beard; Cupid could have a heart in his hand, while Helios might have sun-rays coming out of his head!

Craft Project: Make a Golden Apple
Materials:
- small strips of newspaper
- a wad of newspaper squished to the size of an adult fist
- toothpick, snapped in half
- masking tape
- wallpaper paste (NOTE: you can also use a mixture of one part flour to two parts water)
- gold and brown paint, permanent black marker

Directions:
1. Make sure your wad of newspaper is tightly packed into a round, apple shape.

2. Secure a toothpick into the newspaper ball, on the top of your apple.

3. Use masking tape to secure the loose ends of newspaper into place. Put another piece of masking tape over the toothpick so that the toothpick pushes through the tape; this will keep the toothpick in place.

4. Mix wallpaper paste (if you bought it dry) and dip the newspaper strips into it until they are completely wet with the glue, but not dripping heavily. Place the strips over the newspaper ball until it is covered with one layer. Repeat this step until the ball and stem are covered in four layers. Let the apple dry.

5. After the apple is dry, paint your apple gold and print the message Zeus put on his mischievous golden apple: "For the Most Beautiful," with your black permanent marker. Paint the stem brown.

Activity Project: Greek Gods and Goddesses Wordsearch
Follow the instructions on Student Page 72. Answers are to the right:

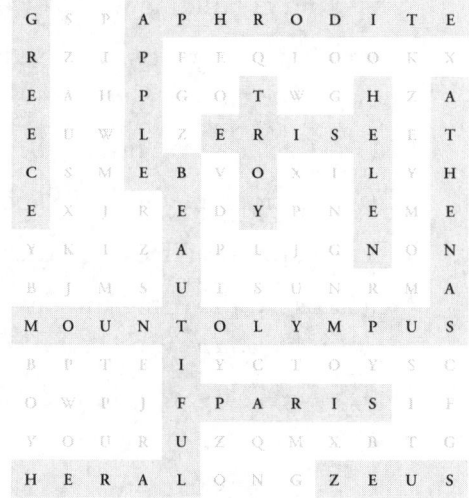

CHAPTER TWENTY-FOUR
The Wars of the Greeks

Encyclopedia Cross-References

Usborne Book of World History: 67

Usborne Internet-Linked Encyclopedia: 154–155

Kingfisher Illustrated History of the World: 80–83

Kingfisher History Encyclopedia: 52–53

Review Questions — Greece's War with Persia

Why did Athens and Sparta decide to be friends and allies? *Because they were afraid of the Persians*

What did the Athenians and Spartans do to the messenger sent by the Persian king? *They threw him down a well.*

What did Persia do then? *Attacked!*

What two armies fought the Battle of Marathon? *Persia and Athens*

Who won? *Athens*

Why didn't the Spartans come help the Athenians? *They were having a religious festival.*

What happened to the runner who took the good news to Athens? *He died of exhaustion.*

Was the Battle of Marathon the end of Greece's war with Persia? *No*

The last battle in the war with Persia was the Battle of Salamis. Who won—the Greeks or the Persians? *The Greeks, and the Greek cities stayed independent!*

Narration Exercise — Greece's War with Persia

The narration should include the information that Athens and Sparta united to fight the Persians, and that the Persians eventually lost the war. Acceptable narrations might include:

"Athens and Sparta weren't friends. But they fought the Persians together. They won a famous battle at Marathon. Persia lost the war."

OR

"Persia attacked Greece. The Greek cities fought back all together. Persia was defeated. One of the battles was at Marathon."

Review Questions — The Greeks Fight Each Other

What kind of building was the Parthenon? *A temple*

In one of the wall *friezes*, or carved pictures, inside the Parthenon, Greek soldiers are fighting strange creatures. What were they? *Centaurs—half man, half horse.*

Did the Greeks go on making beautiful art in peace? *No, they fought with each other.*

What two cities fought the Peloponnesian War? *Sparta and Athens*

When Sparta was attacking Athens, what happened inside the city of Athens that made it weaker? *The plague*

Alcibiades led the Athenians out of the city to attack the Spartans. But what did he do when the Athenians lost? *He joined the Spartans. He led the Spartans into Athens.*

Which Greek city won the fight? *Sparta finally conquered Athens.*

Narration Exercise — The Greeks Fight Each Other

The narration should include the information that the Greeks made lifelike art, and that Sparta and Athens fought until both cities were weak. Acceptable narrations might include:

"The Greeks knew how to make statues that looked like real people. They built beautiful buildings. But they kept on fighting with each other."

OR

"Athens and Sparta were at peace for a little while. They did beautiful art. Then they started fighting with each other again. They got weak from fighting."

Additional History Reading

The Greeks (Footsteps in Time), by Sally Hewitt (Franklin Watts, 2001). Covers Greek culture and lifestyles with pretty illustrations and simple text on a first to second grade level. (RA)

I Wonder Why the Greeks Built Temples? And Other Questions and Ancient Greece, by Fiona MacDonald (Kingfisher, 1997). Questions and answers about Greek accomplishments, with full-page color illustrations. (RA)

The Parthenon (Great Buildings), by Peter Chrisp (Raintree, 1997). Using lively drawings and pictures of carvings and ancient objects, this book covers the building of the Parthenon; it even introduces young students to the war between the Greeks and Persians, the reason for the Parthenon's destruction. (RA)

Corresponding Literature Suggestions

The Aesop for Children, by Milo Winter (Barnes and Noble, 1993). The famous moral stories from Greek times in an illustrated, easy-to-read edition. (RA)

Cupid and Psyche, by M. Charlotte Craft (HarperCollins, 1996). This child-appropriate retelling of the story of Cupid and Psyche has stunning illustrations. (RA)

The Flying Horse: The Story of Pegasus (All Aboard Reading, Level 1), by Jane B. Mason. A Greek story that most beginners can read alone. (IR)

Apollo & Daphne: Masterpieces of Greek Mythology, by Antonia Barber (J. Paul Getty Museum Publications, 1999). Retellings of Greek and Roman myths (intended for slightly older students) are accompanied by great paintings based on these stories. (RA)

Map Work

Chapter 24: The Wars of the Greeks (Student Page 73)

1. On your map, find **Sparta** and **Athens**. Draw a red line connecting them to show that they often fought each other.

2. The Persian Empire wanted to conquer Greece. Athens and Sparta decided to stop fighting against each other, and become friends and allies so that they could defend themselves against the Persians. Color the **Persian Empire** yellow. Then, draw an arrow from the Persian Empire across the **Aegean Sea**, toward **Marathon**.

3. After the Battle of Marathon, a messenger ran from Marathon to Athens to bring the news that the Athenians had driven back the Persian threat. Draw a blue line to show his path.

4. The Persians and Greeks went on fighting until the Greeks finally defeated the Persians, once and for all, in a great sea battle at a place called Salamis. After this battle, the Persians finally gave up attacking Greece. Find **Salamis** on your map.

Coloring Page

The Parthenon (Student Page 74)

The Parthenon was a temple built to honor Athena, the goddess of war.

Projects

Cooking Project: Ice-Cream Greek Ship and Gingerbread Parthenon

Ice Cream Greek Boat

The Greek leader Themosticles went to the Oracle of Delphi and asked her how the Greeks could win the war against the dreaded Persians. Her answer puzzled everyone but this great leader. She said, "The wooden wall will save you." Themosticles knew what she meant—the Greeks needed to build a whole fleet of wooden ships, and then line them up side by side like a great floating wall to keep the Persians away.

Below and to the right is a picture of a fighting ship.

Do you see how the front of the ship is curved? The ships were designed to ram into enemy ships. When the Greeks fought the Persians at Salamis, they rammed into the Persian ships until the Persians were destroyed.

Materials:

- inexpensive box of vanilla ice cream, frozen VERY hard
- table knife and spoon, glass of warm water
- toothpicks
- skewer
- white paper cut in the shape of a sail
- cookie sheet or brownie pan
- heavy whipping cream, whipped up
- blue food coloring
- black, red, and white cans of icing (best choice: Betty Crocker's Easy Flow Decorating Icing)

Directions:

1. Open the box of ice cream and peel the paper away from the ice cream block.

2. Ask an adult to use a large knife to cut the block lengthwise into two long rectangles. Put the rectangles end-to-end on the cookie sheet.

3. Work fast! Dip the table knife and spoon in the warm water. Use the knife for carving and the spoon for scooping. Carve sharp ends into your ice cream, and scoop a hollow out of the middle. Use your hands if you need to! Keep dipping the knife and spoon into the warm water. You should also keep a warm damp towel nearby to warm your hands now and then. If the ice cream begins to melt, slide your cookie sheet back into the freezer and take a break until the ice cream refreezes.

4. Refreeze the ice cream at least 15 minutes before the next step. Then, when you have the boat shaped, slide the toothpicks into the sides for "oars."

5. Mix a few drops of blue food coloring with your whipped cream. Spread the whipped cream over the cookie sheet and around the boat for "water."

6. Use the frosting to decorate your ship. Line the sides and edges; give your ship an eye and mouth, as in the picture above.

7. Slide your paper sail onto the skewer and push the skewer into the middle of the boat.

8. Take a picture (quick!), and then eat!

NOTE TO PARENT: This is an exciting but messy project. A perfectly-shaped boat is impossible, and the frosting tends to slide off, especially if the ice cream is melting.

Gingerbread Parthenon

Once the battle of Marathon was won, the people of Athens wanted to thank their goddess Athena for their victory. So they built her a temple—the Parthenon.

Materials:

- gingerbread dough (recipe below)
- canned or homemade white frosting (1 can for 2 Parthenons)
- rolling pin and greased baking sheet
- photocopy of the Parthenon coloring sheet (Student Page 74), with the Parthenon cut out
- toothpicks and table knife

Gingerbread dough

- ¾ cup shortening
- ¾ cup brown sugar
- ¾ cup dark molasses
- ¼ cup cold water
- 1 teaspoon vanilla
- 4 ½ cups all purpose flour
- 2 teaspoons ground cinnamon
- ½ teaspoon ground ginger
- ½ teaspoon ground nutmeg
- ¾ teaspoon salt

Directions:

1. Beat together shortening, sugar, molasses, and water.

2. In a separate bowl, mix flour, spices, and salt.

3. Add dry ingredients to the shortening mix and blend together.

4. Take out of the bowl and form a ball. If you are making this ahead of time, put a teaspoon of flour into a Ziploc bag and shake. Put the dough in and set in refrigerator up to four days. This is enough dough to make two Parthenons!

5. As if you were making a standard gingerbread house, use the Parthenon templates to make a Gingerbread Parthenon.

Activity Project: Make a "Stone" Sculpture

Stone sculptors were busy people in ancient Greece! They worked hard making beautiful statues and friezes, using tools of different sizes and shapes. They were so good that when Greek towns and cities were conquered, the stone art work was carted off as bounty for the conqueror!

Materials:

- bar of Ivory soap, or another soft soap bar
- table knife
- white paper and pencil

Directions:

1. Place the bar of soap on the white paper and draw around it. Now you can see how much space you have to work with. On the square you traced, draw the design you want to carve.

2. When your design is finished, draw it carefully onto the flat side of the bar of soap.

3. Now use your knife to carefully shave away the soap around the outside lines of your design.

4. Remember: make your designs simple, without too many details! You might want to start with a very simple shape such as a fish. Shave off the edges to make the front rounded. Then carve out triangles on the top side and bottom side to make the back fin. Careful! If you carve too much off, the back fin will fall off. Dig out a place in the front to form the eyes. There's your first statue!

Craft Project: Make Athenian Coins

The Greeks were at war with each other. Money was one cause of this war—Athens tried to force all the other city-states to stop using coins of their own. Instead, they would have to use the special coins Athens made. These coins had the picture of Athena, goddess of war and patron of the city of Athens, on one side, and her symbol, an owl, on the other.

Materials:
- yellow quick-dry clay such as Sculpey (sold by Rainbow Resource Center, www.rainbowresource.com, and at craft stores)
- toothpick
- quarter, dime, and nickel
- encyclopedia picture of an owl
- glass pie plate

Directions:
1. Preheat the oven to 250 degrees.

2. Knead clay until it is easy to mold. Roll it out flat, about ⅛-inch thick.

3. Using the quarter as a guide, cut the clay around it with the point of the toothpick. This will form a round, coin-like shape.

4. Now use the toothpick to draw a picture of a woman's head on one side of the coin. (A round head with eyes, nose, and a mouth is just fine!) You can draw hair or a helmet on her head, and if you have room you can draw a sword beside her. This is Athena, the goddess of war.

5. Turn the clay over and draw the head of an owl on the other side. The owl has big round eyes and triangular ears!

6. Now design a coin of your own. What picture will you draw on the first side? What symbol will you use on the second side? Look at the quarter, dime, and nickel. Whose picture is on each coin? What symbol is on the other side of the coin?

7. Bake your Athenian coins on a glass pie plate for 20 minutes. Allow them to cool.

Activity Project: Play the Peloponnesian War Game

Materials:
- 1 die (2 dice for faster play)
- The "Peloponnesian War" gameboard (Student Page 75)

The board works best if it is enlarged (to 11" x 14") and photocopied onto cardstock. You can also color it as an additional art project.

Directions:
1. Object of the game: Be the first one to the center of the board after going around it once

2. This game is for two players or teams. Players or teams should select different objects to represent them on the board (button, bean, coin, LEGO, small plastic animal, etc.) Each player should have four pieces.

3. One player/team should put all four pieces onto the Athens star; the other player/team should put theirs in the Sparta star (like in the game of *Sorry*).

4. Take turns rolling the dice (or die). You must roll a one to move one of your pieces out of your star. If you are playing with two dice, you can roll a one on either die (ignore the number on the remaining die if you choose to move a piece out of your star).

5. Move your pieces all around the board in the direction of the arrows. If you land directly on an opponent's piece, you can send it back to its star!

5. Go around the board until you reach your port—the port right in front of your star. The first player to get all four pieces into the right port wins!

CHAPTER TWENTY-FIVE
Alexander the Great

Encyclopedia Cross-References

Usborne Book of World History: 70–71

Usborne Internet-Linked Encyclopedia: 160–161

Kingfisher Illustrated History of the World: 90–95

Kingfisher History Encyclopedia: 56

Review Questions — Philip and His Son

Who attacked the Greek cities? *Philip*

What country did he rule? *Macedonia*

What was the name of Philip's son? *Alexander the Great*

What does "Alexander" mean? *Ruler of men*

Do you remember the name of Alexander's horse? *Bucephalus*

How did Alexander tame his horse? *He turned the horse so that it couldn't see its shadow.*

How did Alexander solve the problem of the Gordian Knot? *He cut it in half.*

Narration Exercise — Philip and His Son

Ask the child to retell the story of Bucephalus OR of the Gordian Knot. Three to four sentences is long enough. The child can choose to illustrate the story, if she wants to. Appropriate retellings might include:

"Alexander's father was going to buy a horse. The horse was too wild for him. Alexander told his father that he would tame the horse. He did, and his father bought the horse for him."

OR

"Alexander the Great saw a chariot with a huge knot on it. No one could untie the knot. So he cut it in half with his sword. This meant that he would conquer Asia."

Review Questions — Alexander's Invasions

What three Wonders of the Ancient World have we learned about? *The Hanging Gardens of Babylon, the Great Pyramid, the Pharos*

What was the Pharos? *A giant lighthouse*

What was the name of the city Alexander built in Egypt? *Alexandria*

Why did Alexander stop before he conquered all of India? *His soldiers refused to go any further.*

Narration Exercise — Alexander's Invasions

Ask the child: What three things did we learn about in this lesson? Prompt him if necessary:

1. Alexander didn't finish conquering India because his soldiers rebelled.

2. Alexander built a city in Egypt called Alexandria OR Alexander built many new cities.

3. The Pharos was a huge lighthouse in the harbor of Alexandria.

Review Questions — The Death of Alexander

How did Alexander the Great die? *No one knows why he died. He got weak.*

How many pieces did Alexander's empire get divided into? *Three*

What did Ptolemy do in Egypt? *Finished the city of Alexandria and built a library.*

What is another name for the Seleucids? *The Syrians*

Did the three generals who ruled Alexander's kingdom make friends with each other? *No, they fought.*

Narration Exercise — The Death of Alexander

"Alexander the Great had a huge kingdom. When he died, his generals split it into three parts. Then they all fought with each other."

Additional History Reading

Alexander the Great: The Greatest Ruler of the Ancient World (What's Their Story), by Andrew Langley (Oxford University Press Children's Books, 1998). A simple, nicely-illustrated picture-book biography. (RA, but may be IR for strong readers)

The Greek News, by Anton Powell and Philip Steele (Candlewick Press, 1999). The cover story of this "Greek newspaper" (full of silliness and good information) is about Alexander the Great. (RA)

The World in the Time of Alexander the Great, by Fiona MacDonald (Chelsea House, 2000). Good illustrations and straightforward text; covers what was going on in the rest of the world during Alexander's conquests. Excellent for reinforcing the chronological flow of world history. (RA 1–3 (sections); IR 4–6)

Alexander the Great: Macedonian King and Conqueror, by Bernard Randall (Rosen, 2004). A biography of Alexander, more detailed and a little more difficult than the Pancella biography below. (IR 4–7)

Alexander the Great, by Peggy Pancella (Heinemann, 2004). A very readable and heavily illustrated biography of Alexander the Great, divided into two-page "chapters" that could easily be read aloud. (RA 1–2, IR 3–5)

Corresponding Literature Suggestions

Solomon and the Ant: And Other Jewish Folktales, by Sheldon Oberman (Boyds Mill Press, 2006). Forty-three traditional Jewish tales, written for reading out loud; includes "The Seven Questions of Alexander the Great," a mythical encounter between Alexander and the wise men of Jerusalem. (RA 1–3, IR 3–6)

The Great Alexander the Great, by Joe Lasker (Viking Press, 1983). Alexander's life, from the time of the taming of Bucephalus to the end; illustrated, and very easy to read. **Out of print; check your local library.** (IR)

Ten Kings: And the Worlds They Ruled, by Milton Metzger (Orchard, 2002). Brief and interesting biographical sketches of ten rulers, from Hammurabi through Peter the Great of Russia. Includes Alexander the Great. The tone is aimed towards upper elementary-school students. **Out of print; check your local library.** (RA 3–4, IR 4–6)

Map Work

Chapter 25: Alexander the Great (Student Page 76)

1. On your map, find the city that Alexander named for himself. Circle it in red. What country is it in?

2. Trace the **Nile River** in blue. Don't forget the **Nile Delta**!

3. Trace the borders of Alexander's empire in red. Then shade his empire lightly in red.

4. Find and trace in blue the **Tigris**, **Euphrates**, and **Indus** rivers. How many rivers were inside Alexander's empire?

Coloring Page

Alexander the Great and Bucephalus (Student Page 77)

Projects

Craft Project: Make a Bucephalus Stick Horse

Materials:

- broomstick (available at hardware stores)
- piece of heavy cardboard
- template of horse's head (Student Page 78; enlarge this for best results)
- glue and yarn
- nylon rope, cotton rope, or old belt
- crayons or paint

Directions:

1. Make two copies of the horse template out of cardboard.

2. Cut out a hole in the horse's mouth on both templates (a rope can be tied here to make reins).

3. Paint or color heads and glue yarn (for the mane) along the inside of one of the necks.

4. Attach cardboard heads together by stapling the edges (leave the bottom open).

5. Set assembled head on broomstick. Staple the bottom of the neck on either side of the broomstick (you can also use duct tape for extra security).

6. Thread cotton or soft nylon rope (or an old leather belt) through the mouth hole. Tie ends together in a loop, long enough for the child to hold while astride the broomstick.

Activity Project: Tie a Gordian Knot

Alexander cut the Gordian Knot because it was too complicated for him to untie. If you tie these knots, can you untie them? What if you tie them several different times?

Materials:

- two heavy pieces of string or rope
- Student Page 78

Directions:

1. Begin with the bowline knot—a knot in one piece of rope. First, make a loop in the rope and push the free end up through the loop from the bottom (Step One). Next, pass the free end around the rope above the loop (Step Two). Finally, bring the free end back down through the loop and pull it tight (Step Three).

2. Now try a sheet bend. This knot ties two pieces of rope together. First, make a loop in one rope. Pass the end of the second rope through the end loop and then around the first rope further up (Step One). Next, pull the end of the second rope through the loop in the first rope and tighten (Step Two).

Activity Project: Make the Pharos Lighthouse

Materials:

- 1 11½ oz. mixed nut can (or any can the same size)
- 1 small Pringles can
- lighthouse top template (Student Page 79); make one copy on cardstock
- lighthouse base template (Student Page 80); make two copies on cardstock
- yellow cling wrap
- tape, glue, scissors, and crayons

Directions:

1. Color the pieces of the lighthouse.

2. Cut out both pieces of the base template. The bottom will be slightly larger than the middle and you will need both copies of the bottom to go around the nut can. Turn empty nut can upside down. Wrap the two sections around the nut can and cut end to fit. Tape or glue in place with the railing sticking up over the bottom of the can.

3. Cut out the lighthouse middle template. Turn the Pringles can upside down and wrap it with the middle template. Tape or glue in place.

4. Glue top of Pringles can to bottom of nut can.

5. Cut out the lighthouse top template. Cut out windows. Attach yellow cling wrap to the inside of the template. This will make your lighthouse look like it is lit.

6. Fold the top and glue the large tab to the inside to make a rectangular shape. Fold the bottom tabs and tape to the top of the Pringles can. Set your lighthouse in a window so the sunlight will shine through the top.

Story Project: Being Brave

Discuss the reasons why you think Alexander was a brave person. Make a list of the things that made Alexander brave. Then think about a time when you were brave. Draw a picture or narrate a story about that time in your life.

Activity Project: Play the Alexander the Great Game
Materials:

- 1 die (2 dice for faster play)
- the "Alexander the Great" gameboard (Student Page 81)

The board works best if it is enlarged (to 11"x14") and photocopied onto cardstock. You can also color it as an additional art project.

Directions:

1. Object of the game: Be the first one to the finish line! Keep your copy of *The Story of the World* close by for quick answer checks.

2. Players should select different objects to represent them on the board (button, bean, coin, LEGO, small plastic animal, etc.).

3. All players begin at the START. Roll the dice and the highest number goes first.

4. Roll again and begin the journey through the life of Alexander the Great. When you land on a square that has a symbol, look for the corresponding symbol and follow the instructions.

CHAPTER TWENTY-SIX
The People of the Americas

Encyclopedia Cross-References

Usborne Book of World History: 63, 80, 81   *Kingfisher Illustrated History of the World*: 62, 63, 134, 135
Usborne Internet-Linked Encyclopedia: 176–181   *Kingfisher History Encyclopedia*: 32, 76, 77

Review Questions — The Nazca Drawings

What is a continent? *A big mass of land*

There are three different "Americas." The first is South America; what are the other two? *North America and Central America*

South America has flat land in the middle. What does it have all down one edge? *Mountains*

Do you remember the name of the South American tribe that made drawings on the ground? *The Nazca*

How big were the drawings? *Hundreds of miles across!*

Do you remember what some of the drawings were? *Spiders, pelicans, hummingbirds, flowers, spirals, squares, patterns*

Archaeologists don't know how the Nazca people made their drawings, but they have two guesses. What methods might the Nazca have used to draw these big lines? *They may have used math or the position of the stars.*

Narration Exercise — The Nazca Drawings

"The Nazca lived in South America. They made big drawings on the ground. Some of the drawings were of birds and flowers."
OR
"There are three Americas—North America, Central America, and South America. Tribes lived in South America a long time ago. They hunted and grew things like other people in ancient times. One tribe was called the Nazca."

Review Questions — The Heads of the Olmecs

What does "Meso" mean? *Between*

What does "Mesoamerica" mean? *Between the Americas*

What is the other name that we use for "Mesoamerica?" *Central America*

Do you remember the name of the tribe that lived in Central America? *The Olmecs*

Where did the rich Olmec people live? *In the city, up on a hill*

Where did the poor people live? *Down on the plain below*

What kind of pyramid did the Olmecs build in the middle of their city? *A dirt pyramid*

What kind of sculptures did they make? *Giant heads of their rulers*

Narration Exercise — The Heads of the Olmecs

"Central America is in the middle between North America and South America. The Olmec people lived there. They made huge giant stone heads that didn't have any bodies."

OR

"The Olmecs lived in a place called Central America. They built a dirt pyramid at the center of their city. The rich people lived up in the city, and the poor people lived down on the ground."

Review Questions — Rabbit Shoots the Sun

What two countries are now in North America? *Canada and the United States*

Way up in the northern part of North America, where it is too cold to grow crops, what did ancient people eat? *Seals, polar bears, birds, caribou, mosses, lichens, whales*

How about people in the middle part of North America—what did they eat? *Corn, buffalo, fish*

Did the people of North America live in cities? *No, they were nomads.*

In the story of "Rabbit Shoots the Sun," why did Rabbit decide to shoot the sun? *Because it was so hot and dry*

What happened when Rabbit's arrow hit the sun? *Fire came out and started to burn up the world.*

What color did the bush turn when the fire scorched it? *Yellow*

Was Rabbit still brave and bold at the end of the story? *No, he was timid and shy.*

Did the sun still jump over the edge of the world in a hurry? *No, it crept up a little at a time.*

Narration Exercise — Rabbit Shoots the Sun

Ask the child to tell you two things about the people who lived in the far northern parts of North America, and two things about the people who lived down in the warmer part of North America. Acceptable answers might be:

"People in the cold part of North America hunted seals and gathered moss to eat. People where it was warmer hunted buffalo and grew corn."
OR
"People in North America were nomads. Up where it was cold, they hunted whales and polar bears. Further down they grew corn and wheat, and they went fishing and hunting."
OR
Ask your child to retell the story of "Rabbit Shoots the Sun." An acceptable retelling might be,

"Rabbit was mad at the sun for making it so hot and dry. He shot the sun with an arrow, but fire poured out all over the world and made it brown. Rabbit had to hide. Now Rabbit is very shy and the sun is afraid to jump up over the edge of the world."

Additional History Reading

You Wouldn't Want to Be an Aztec Sacrifice! by Fiona MacDonald (Franklin Watts, 2000). Colorful guide to ancient Aztec civilization. (RA)

Machu Picchu: The Story of the Amazing Incas and Their City in the Clouds, by Elizabeth Mann (Mikaya Press, 2000). With beautiful paintings of Incan times and photographs of Incan artifacts, this book describes Inca life and explores the building of the greatest Inca city. (RA)

Who Were the First North Americans, by Philippa Wingate (EDC Publications, 2003). This Usborne book has bright, cartoon-like illustrations and a good, brief summary of ancient cultures in North America. (RA)

Life in Ancient Mexico Coloring Book, by John Green (Dover, 1991). Detailed scenes of ancient South American culture.

A Coloring Book of Incas, Aztecs, and Mayas (Bellerophon Books, 1985). All Bellerophon coloring books use simplified adaptation of actual images from the culture under study.

The Lost World of the Anasazi: Exploring the Mysteries of the Chaco Canyon, by Peter Lourie (Boyds Mill Press, 2003). The Anasazi were an ancient North American people; this well-photographed volume, a supplement to the stories of South and Central American peoples found in *The Story of the World*, shows the ruins they left behind. (RA 1–3, IR 4–6)

Corresponding Literature Suggestions

Note: Numerous North, Central, and South American tales have been published as picture books; you can use many books other than those listed below for this chapter.

Stories from the Amazon, by Saviour Pirotta (Raintree Steck-Vaughn, 2000). A collection of folk tales from the Central American rain forest region. (RA)

The Two Mountains: An Aztec Legend, by Eric Kimmel (Shen's Books, 2000). The children of the sun and moon fall in love, even though their families are opposed. (RA)

Jabuti the Tortoise, by Gerald McDermott (Voyager, 2005). This very brightly colored picture book version of a South American legend tells how the tortoise's shell was cracked, why the toucan is so bright, and explains a host of other natural phenomena. (RA)

Thirteen Moons on Turtle's Back: A Native American Year of Moons, by Joseph Bruchac (Putnam, 1997). Tales from a wide range of Native American traditions are beautifully illustrated with watercolors; each story explains the importance of a season to a particular tribe. (RA)

Is My Friend at Home? Pueblo Fireside Tales, by John Bierhorst (Farrar, Straus and Giroux, 2001). Seven stories about friendship; each one also explains some aspect of nature. (RA)

Keepers of the Earth: Native American Stories and Environmental Activities for Young Children, by Michael J. Caduto and Joseph Bruchac (Fulcrum Publishing, 1997). Retellings of 25 legends from 20 different cultures combined with scientific information and hands-on activities. Joseph Bruchac has written many other books about Native Americans. (RA)

Map Work

Chapter 26: The People of the Americas (Student Page 82)

1. On your map, find **South America**. Color it with your favorite color.

2. Choose another color and shade in **Central America**.

3. Choose a third color to shade in **North America**.

Coloring Page

Rabbit Shoots the Sun (Student Page 83)

For the Student: Color the "Rabbit Shoots the Sun" comic strip while your parent reads the story aloud. Then cut out each frame, shuffle them and see if you can tell the story while you put the frames back in order.

Projects

Craft Project: Make a Seed Mosaic Map

The foods we eat today come from different places all over the world. Many were first grown in the Americas! Some foods that originated in the Americas are corn, beans, sunflowers, tomatoes, peanuts, peppers, potatoes, pumpkins, squash, and strawberries.

Materials:
- corn, any kind of beans, peanuts, as well as sunflower, tomato, pepper, pumpkin, and squash seeds
- copy of the map of the Americas used with this chapter
- glue

Directions:
1. Brush glue all over your map.

2. Pick out which seeds you want to use on each continent and glue them on. You can use smaller seeds for the flat land and larger seeds for the mountains.

Craft Project: Make a Native American Headband
Materials:
- posterboard or lightweight cardboard
- scissors and tape (stapler or glue)
- crayons, markers, stickers, construction paper, etc.

Directions:
1. Measure around your head with a measuring tape. Now cut a two-inch wide strip of posterboard the same length.

2. Decorate your headband. Fake feathers can be attached or made from construction paper.

3. Tape headband at ends.

Craft Project: Make a Native American Sand Painting
Materials:
- sand
- food coloring or powder paints
- piece of cardboard

Directions:
1. Draw outline of picture on piece of cardboard.

2. Make colored sand by stirring food coloring (3 drops at a time) or powder paints (1 tablespoon at a time) into ½ cup of sand. Use a metal spoon and a metal mixing bowl (sometimes coloring will stain plastic).

3. Working with one color at a time, spread glue over appropriate area. Sprinkle on colored sand. Continue until picture is complete.

Activity Project: Make a Nazca Line Drawing

Do you remember reading about the huge Nazca line drawings that can only be seen from the air? How hard is it to draw a picture if you can't see what you are doing?

Materials:
- white crayon
- white paper
- watercolor paints

Directions:
1. Using the white crayon, draw a picture of your choice on white paper. Notice how difficult it is to draw a picture when you can't see exactly what you are doing. Be sure and press down hard with your crayon.

2. Using watercolor paints, paint over the entire sheet of paper.

3. Let dry. How did your "invisible drawing" turn out?

Cooking Project: Make Tapioca Pudding:

Ingredients:
- ¾ cup sugar
- 1 egg
- 3 tablespoons minute tapioca
- 2¾ cup milk
- 1 teaspoon vanilla

Directions:
1. Mix together above ingredients (except for the vanilla) and let stand for five minutes. Cook and stir until mixture comes to a full boil. Remove and add 1 teaspoon vanilla.

Microwave Directions:
1. Mix together above ingredients and let stand for five minutes. Microwave on high for approximately 10–12 minutes, stirring every two minutes until the mixture boils.

Cooking Project: Make Navajo Fry Bread

This recipe comes from the ancient people of North America!

Ingredients:
- 4 cups white flour
- 1 tablespoon baking powder
- 1 teaspoon salt
- 1 ½ cups warm water
- 1 cup shortening

Directions:
1. Mix together flour, baking powder, and salt. Add water.

2. Knead until dough is soft and elastic and does not stick to bowl. If necessary add more water.

3. Shape dough into balls. Pat the balls back and forth by hand until dough is about ¼-inch thick. Dough should be round. Make a small hole in the center.

4. Melt the shortening in a fry pan. Brown on both sides. Pat dry on paper towel.

5. Eat plain, or use these in place of a tortilla and make tacos.

CHAPTER TWENTY-SEVEN
The Rise of Rome

Encyclopedia Cross-References

Usborne Book of World History: 86

Usborne Internet-Linked Encyclopedia: 184

Kingfisher Illustrated History of the World: 66, 67, 104, 105

Kingfisher History Encyclopedia: 34, 35

Review Questions — Romulus and Remus

Can you tell me the names of three empires that came before Rome? We have studied about all of them. Acceptable answers include: *Assyria, Babylon, Media, Persia, Greece, Macedon* or *Alexander the Great's kingdom*

Who founded the city of Rome in the legend that we read? *Romulus*

Who raised Romulus? *First a wolf, then a shepherd*

What was Romulus's twin brother named? *Remus*

Why did Romulus name his city Rome? *He named it after himself* OR *Rome sounds like Romulus.*

How many hills was Rome built on? *Seven hills*

Narration Exercise — Romulus and Remus

Now ask the child to retell the story of Romulus and Remus in three to five sentences. Make sure the child includes the information that Rome was named after Romulus. An acceptable story might sound like this:

"Romulus and Remus were twins. A wolf raised them. They built a town at Rome. Romulus killed Remus and became king. He named Rome after himself."

OR

Have the child draw a picture of some part of the story of Romulus and Remus. Ask the child to describe the picture to you. Write the child's description on the bottom of the paper. Put the picture in the History Notebook.

Review Questions — The Power of Rome

What important tribe of people lived in Italy? *The Etruscans*

Whose alphabet and gods did they borrow? *The Greeks*

Did the Romans fight with the Etruscans? *Yes*

Did they learn anything from them? *Yes*

Do you remember anything that the Roman kings borrowed from the Etruscans? Any of the following are acceptable: *How to dress, about the Greek gods, painting, music, special robes called togas, fasces (the rods with axe blade)*

In a democracy, who makes the laws and chooses the leaders? *The people*

How do they do this? *They vote.*

What does monarchy mean? *Rule by a king*

What two symbols of power did the Roman kings have? *The fasces (bundle of rods with an axe in the middle) and the purple-bordered robe*

How many kings did Rome have? *Seven*

Who ruled Rome once the Romans got rid of their kings? *Two consuls*

Was Rome a democracy? *No*

Narration Exercise — The Power of Rome

Ask the child to tell you about the history lesson in four or five sentences. He should include the information that Rome was ruled by kings first, and that the kings were followed by consuls. Acceptable narrations might include:

"At first Rome had kings. Rome got rid of the kings and had consuls instead. There were two of them."

OR

"The Etruscans lived in Italy. They taught the Romans about painting and other things. Rome had kings, but then the people wanted to help with government. They had consuls instead of kings."

Additional History Reading

Who Were the Romans? (Usborne Starting Point History), by Phil Roxbee Cox (Usborne, 2002). A very elementary, easy-to-read introduction to Roman culture, put out by Usborne Books. (RA)

The Roman News: The Greatest Newspaper in Civilization, by Andrew Langley (Candlewick Press, 1999). "News stories" about ancient Roman life, with silly headlines and colorful illustrations. A good way to introduce young children to Rome. (RA)

Tools of the Ancient Romans: A Kid's Guide to the History and Science of Life in Ancient Rome, by Rachel Dickinson (Nomad, 2006). Even though it is aimed at older students, the book includes many activities and pictures that will work for younger children as well. (RA and activity)

Corresponding Literature Suggestions

Roman Myths, by Geraldine McCaughrean, illus. Emma Chichester Clark (Margaret K. McElderry, 2001). May be **out of print**, but worth checking your library for. Colorful, engaging read-aloud tales include two about Aeneas, Romulus and Remus, and the kidnapping of the Sabine women. (RA 1–3, IR 3–6)

Roman Myths and Legends, retold by Anthony Masters (Peter Bedrick Books, 2000). Stories from Roman mythology, including Romulus and Remus, Cupid and Psyche, Dido and Aeneas, and Horatius at the bridge. (RA 1–3, IR 3–5)

Romulus and Remus (Ready to Read, Level 2), by Anne Rockwell (Aladdin, 1997). In this young-readers version of the legend of the twin founders of Rome, Romulus does not kill Remus; instead, Remus goes away to hunt with the wolves. Available as a board book. **Out of print; check your local library.** (IR for many children, RA for very early beginners)

Map Work

Chapter 27: The Rise of Rome (Student Page 84)

1. On your map, circle **Rome** with a red crayon. Rome is in Italy.

2. The Etruscans lived and ruled the area north of Rome. Find the borders on your map, and outline them in blue.

Coloring Page

Romulus and Remus (Student Page 85)

Projects

Craft Project: Make a Roman Hairpiece

In ancient Rome, fancy hairstyles became very popular. Sometimes it was difficult to get the right look with natural hair—so many Romans wore wigs or hairpieces.

Materials:

- black, brown or yellow (or any color hair you desire) yarn and construction paper
- glue, stapler, scissors
- bobby pins

Directions:

1. Cut yarn into the length of "hair" desired. Braid the yarn into plaits.

2. Cut a strip of construction paper, long enough to fit around the child's head. Staple the ends together.

3. Glue the braids onto the construction paper. Use bobby pins to keep the hairpiece in place.

Craft Project: Make the Fasces

Materials:

- handful of craft sticks, straws, pencils or twigs
- red yarn or ribbon
- cardboard
- aluminum foil

Directions:

1. Cut out the shape of an axe blade from a piece of cardboard.

2. Cover the axe blade (both sides) with aluminum foil.

3. Form your craft sticks into a bundle.

4. Starting at the bottom, wrap the yarn completely around the bundle, then wind the yarn up and around the bundle of sticks. Wrap the yarn completely around the top and then glue down wherever needed.

5. Glue the axe blade between two of the sticks.

Craft Project: Make a Saturnalia Gift

Saturnalia was a festival to honor Saturn, the god of agriculture. Romans celebrated this festival by exchanging gifts and eating. The most common gifts were small clay figures.

Materials:

- easy-bake clay such as Sculpey
- baking sheet, wax paper
- cookie cutters (small ones, if available—animal shapes work great!)
- rolling pin
- pencil, plastic knife

Directions:

1. Roll out about ¼ block of clay until flat on wax paper. Use cookie cutter to cut out shape. Trim with plastic knife, if needed.

2. Use a pencil to poke eyes or any details. You may also wish to add small pieces of another color clay for features on your shape.

3. Bake 20 minutes at 275 degrees. For Sculpey, see package instructions.

Activity Project: Run a Popinas (Roman take-out restaurant)

Materials:

- "Roman coins" (either make some pretend ones out of aluminum foil, or use pennies)
- poster board and markers
- canned lentil soup
- bread
- olives
- fruit
- grape juice
- bowls, spoons, glasses, serving utensils
- large pot for soup (or crock-pot)

Directions:

1. Paintings outside the popinas advertised what was on the menu. Make posters with pictures of the items you will be selling (bread, soup, fruit, grape juice, olives, etc.)

2. Heat the soup in pan or crock-pot (adult help needed!).

3. Cut up fruit and bread and arrange it on a platter or plate (adult help needed!).

4. Open for business (maybe a family dinner). Be sure to bring lots of coins to pay for the hard work!

5. If you want to, serve the Roman dish below:

Cecina

Ingredients:

- olive oil
- salt
- basil leaves (dried or fresh)
- 2 cans chick peas

Directions:

1. Heat oven to 375 degrees.

2. Drain beans, but save the liquid. Mash beans in a bowl.

3. Add 2 tablespoons olive oil and enough liquid as needed to make a smooth paste.

4. Oil a cookie sheet or pizza pan with olive oil. Spread batter on the pan, shaping into a circle.

5. Drizzle on a tablespoon or two of olive oil. Sprinkle with basil. Bake for 45 minutes.

CHAPTER TWENTY-EIGHT
The Roman Empire

Encyclopedia Cross-References

Usborne Book of World History: 86

Usborne Internet-Linked Encyclopedia: 188–191

Kingfisher Illustrated History of the World: 117, 127

Kingfisher History Encyclopedia: 62, 63

Review Questions — The Roman Gods

Whose gods did the Romans worship? *The Greek gods, with different names*

Can you tell me any of their names? *Jupiter, Ceres, Proserpine, Pluto, Neptune, Mars*

Why did Proserpine have to stay with Pluto for six months of the year? *Because she ate some seeds from a pomegranate*

What season of the year comes when Proserpine is underground with Pluto? *Winter*

Narration Exercise — The Roman Gods

Ask the child to draw a picture of Proserpine and Ceres, Proserpine and Pluto, or Ceres looking for her daughter. Ask the child to describe the picture. Write the description on the bottom of the picture.

Review Questions — The Roman Builders

Can you tell me three things that the Romans built? *Roads, aqueducts, and apartment buildings*

What were the Roman roads made out of? *Sand, gravel, stone, concrete*

Can you still see Roman roads today? *Yes*

What did aqueducts do? *Carried water into the city*

What did the Romans use the water for? *Drinking, cooking, and public baths*

Narration Exercise — The Roman Builders

Ask the child to tell you three things that the Romans built, and to tell you one fact about each of these things. Write these down for the child and put them into the History Notebook. An acceptable answer might be:

"Roads. They were made of sand and gravel."

"Aqueducts. They carried water."

"Apartments. They were made of concrete."

Review Questions — The Roman Gladiators

What did gladiators do? *Fought with each other or with wild animals while an audience watched*

Why did Servius have to be a gladiator? *He didn't have any choice because he was a prisoner.*

Where did Servius learn how to fight? *In the gladiator school*

Did he want to be a fighter? *No*

What happened when he fought in the arena? *He didn't kill his opponent.*

Narration Exercise — The Roman Gladiators

Say to your child, "Can you tell me the story of Servius very briefly—in just a couple of sentences? Begin with 'Servius was captured...' and go from there." Note to parent: This exercise is developing your child's ability to summarize the main points of a story. Talk to the child about the story. Guide her towards a summary that sounds like this: "Servius was captured by Roman soldiers. They took him to Rome and forced him to go to gladiator school."

Review Questions — The Gladiator School

Did Servius feel lucky to be a gladiator? *No, he hated it.*

Do you remember what a *secutor* is? Prompt child if necessary: *a fighter who chases net-fighters*

What did Servius do in his first match when the net-fighter stumbled? *Let him live, let him get away*

Did the Romans like to see gladiators die? *Most of them did. A few, like Seneca, did not.*

Narration Exercise — The Gladiator School

Say to your child, "Can you tell me the end of Servius' story? First, let's read what you told me last time. Read the child the summary of the first part of the story. Now can you finish the story?" Note to parent: Aim for two to three sentences. An acceptable summary might be:

"Servius learned how to fight. But when he went to the arena, he didn't want to kill the other man. So he let him live."

Additional History Reading

Gladiator, by Richard Watkins (Houghton Mifflin, 2000). Dramatic black-and-white pictures of gladiators, and descriptions of each type of gladiator armor. (RA)

The Roman Colosseum (Wonders of the World), by Elizabeth Mann (Mikaya, 1998). This book is to be "explored," not necessarily read word-for-word; look at the pictures, read the captions, and read those pages that the child finds most interesting. (RA)

Rome Antics, by David Macaulay (Houghton Mifflin, 1997). Macaulay takes a pigeon's-eye view and leads young readers through the streets of early Rome. Beautifully done, like all Macaulay's books. (RA)

City: A Story of Roman Planning and Construction, by David Macaulay (Houghton Mifflin, 1983). Follow the development of a Roman town from its earliest days. (RA)

Roman Roads and Aqueducts (Building History Series), by Don Nardo (Lucent, 2000). This well-researched account is packed with detailed information about the technical principles of construction and architectural features. Probably best for advanced readers and children with strong engineering interests. (RA)

You Wouldn't Want to Be a Roman Gladiator, by John Malam (Franklin Watts, 2000). Entertaining guide to the life of a Gallic captive trained to be a gladiator, with cartoon-like illustrations. Good historical information. (RA 1–2, IR 3–5)

Corresponding Literature Suggestions

Classic Myths to Read Aloud, by William F. Russell (Crown, 1992). A collection of Greek and Roman myths, designed to be read aloud to children five and older. (RA)

Asterix the Gladiator, by Rene de Goscinny (Orion, 2004). This comic-strip tale of adventure is as much fun for grown-ups as for children. (RA)

See You Later, Gladiator (Time Warp Trio), by Jon Scieszka (Puffin, 2004). *Gratias tibi ago quia me gladio tuo non fodisti*. That's "thank you for not poking me with your sword," a useful phrase for the hapless time-traveling trio, Sam, Fred, and Joe, when they find themselves flunking out of gladiator school in ancient Rome. (RA)

Aesop's Fables, by Jerry Pinkney (SeaStar Books, 2000). Readable retellings and very attractive illustrations. (RA 1–2, IR 3–6)

Map Work

Chapter 28: The Roman Empire (Student Page 86)

1. Find the island of **Sicily**. Color it yellow.

2. What is Italy shaped like?

3. What does it look like it is doing to the island of Sicily?

Coloring Page

Gladiators in the Arena (Student Page 87) — PARENTS, PLEASE PREVIEW

Projects

Craft Project: Make a Roman Archway and Aqueduct

As the Roman towns grew, the architects put their beautiful archways to use as water-conduits, in structures known as aqueducts. The aqueducts were a series of connected archways built to bring the water from its source to a holding tank in the town which would distribute the water through out in a piping network, like those in use today.

Materials:
- photocopy of arch pattern (Student Page 88)
- sand dough (recipe follows)
- rolling pin
- table knife
- baking sheet
- cardboard inside roll from paper towels
- empty yogurt cup
- plastic straw
- scissors
- full glass of water

Directions:
1. Pre-heat oven to 250 degrees.

2. Cut out the archway pattern.

3. Divide your sand dough into two parts. Wrap up the dough you are not using to prevent drying. Pat or roll out the first ½-inch to 1-inch thickness and place the archway pattern on top. Using a table knife, cut around the pattern. Save the scraps with the rest of the dough not being used.

4. Carefully lift your first arch on to a baking sheet.

5. Repeat with the other slab of dough, only with the second arch, add ¼ inch more dough on the top. This is so that when the archways are hooked together, there is a gradual sloping down to the water tank. (You can make additional archways as long as each is slightly taller than the last.)

6. Bake the archways for 20 minutes. Let them cool for 15 minutes.

7. To make your archways stand, lift them one at a time and stand them on the baking sheet. Brace the bottoms with more sand dough built up on the sides slightly. When all are standing, bring them together and smooth in sand dough between them, hooking them securely.

8. Gather a glob of sand dough the size of two jumbo marbles. Pat it down in the palm of your hand and press it on to the side of a rolling pin. This will create a kind of cradle for the cardboard tube to sit on. Add these cradles to the top of each archway, checking to make sure there is a gradual sloping downward. Bake the aqueduct for another 20 minutes.

9. After your aqueduct has cooled, lay the cardboard tube on the top.

10. On the bottom of the yogurt cup, poke scissors through on three sides. Cut the straw into three parts and insert into the bottom holes of the cup. This is the water tank for the Roman town. Place it under the lower end of your aqueduct.

11. Pour water into the tube at the top of your aqueduct and watch as it travels to your holding tank and out the different pipes to the parts of the town that need it. You are hired as a Roman architect!

Optional: Embellish your Roman archway with columns or scroll work on the top. Use a toothpick to etch decorative borders or use the sand dough and make heads of lions, bears or eagles on the top of the arch.

Sand Dough Recipe

Ingredients:
- 4 cups of play sand (get at any hardware store)
- 2 cups of cornstarch
- 4 teaspoons of cream of tartar

Directions:

1. Combine in a saucepan and whisk together slowly.

2. When well mixed, add 3 cups of hot water. Place the pot over medium heat and stir constantly until you cannot stir any longer.

3. When it is too stiff to stir, take off the heat and let it cool for 15 minutes. If it feels sticky at this point, put back on medium heat and stir some more. Then take off and let it cool for 15 to 20 minutes.

4. When you are able to handle it, knead it slightly and put unused dough into a re-sealable bag until it will be used.

5. Soak pan for an hour to wash out the dough residue.

Activity Project: Make a Roman Road Model

The Romans were well known for their roads. One of the most famous Roman roads was known as the Appian Way. You can make a cutaway model of a Roman road in which you can see all of the layers that went into making the final product.

Materials:
- small shoebox lid
- glue
- sand
- small pebbles or aquarium rock
- smooth, round rocks (or decorative marbles from a craft store)

Directions:

1. The first step in making a Roman road was to dig a wide ditch. The shoebox lid is going to be our ditch.

2. Then the Romans filled the ditch with sand. Brush a thin layer of glue over the entire inside surface of the shoebox lid. Then sprinkle sand over entire bottom. Let dry.

3. Next they poured small stones on top of the sand. For this step, brush a thin layer of glue over ¾ of the sand. Sprinkle small pebbles or the rock used for fish tanks over the glue.

4. Concrete was the next layer. For this layer, use the sand dough recipe from above or a mixture of glue and sand for the concrete. Optional: Add some black paint to make mixture look more like concrete. Spread the concrete over half of the surface of the shoebox lid.

5. Finally, the Romans laid smooth paving stones on top of the concrete. Glue round rocks (or marbles) one at a time over ¼ of the surface of the shoebox lid.

Activity Project: Make a Roman Chariot

Materials:

- cardboard box large enough to fit around your child
- packaging tape
- scissors
- markers
- paints
- construction paper
- glitter and anything else you may want to decorate the "chariot" with
- paper plates
- glue

Directions:

1. Use a cardboard box that will fit around your child and provide a little extra "running" room.

2. Cut out the bottom and top of the box. For handles, cut two 4-inch lines, one about 1½ inch above the other on each side of the box. Reinforce the handles with packaging tape.

3. Make two "wheels" by gluing two paper plates on the chariot, one per side.

4. Decorate your chariot.

5. Let the races begin!

CHAPTER TWENTY-NINE
Rome's War with Carthage

Encyclopedia Cross-References

Usborne Book of World History: N/A

Usborne Internet-Linked Encyclopedia: 185–187

Kingfisher Illustrated History of the World: 106, 107

Kingfisher History Encyclopedia: 62, 63

Review Questions — The Punic Wars

What city did Rome fight? *Carthage*

What did they fight over? *They wanted to trade with the same cities.*

Was it a long war or a short war? *A long war!*

Do you remember what the wars were called? *The Punic Wars*

Where did they fight—on land or on water? *Mostly on water*

What are soldiers who fight on water called? *A navy*

What did Hannibal do? *He fought the Romans with elephants.*

How did General Scipio get Hannibal out of Italy? *He attacked Carthage.*

Who won—Carthage or Rome? *Rome*

What did Hannibal do when Carthage surrendered? *He drank poison.*

Narration Exercise — The Punic Wars

"Rome and Carthage fought a long war. They fought with each other on ships. One Roman general had chickens for good luck! Then Hannibal attacked Rome with elephants. But he lost and drank poison."

OR

"Rome wanted to rule more land. So did Carthage. They fought the Punic Wars. Hannibal went into Italy with elephants. Then Scipio attacked Carthage, and Hannibal came back to fight him. But Carthage lost."

Additional History Reading

The Roman Army, by John Wilkes (Cambridge, 1973). A good illustrated guide to the arms and organization of the Roman military. (RA)

Going to War in Roman Times (Armies of the Past), by Moira Butterfield, illus. Mark Bergin (Franklin Watts, 2000). Lots of pictures with captions; describes Roman military strategy. (RA)

Hannibal, by Robert Green (Franklin Watts, 1997). The life and military exploits of the famous Carthaginian general. Really too much text for young children, but this is the only "junior biography" of Hannibal available. (RA)

Corresponding Literature Suggestions

The Young Carthaginian, by G.A. Henty (Kessinger, 2004). This historical novel, set during the times of Hannibal and the Punic Wars between Carthage and Rome, is for older children, but could be an extended read-aloud project (especially if you have an older student who could read to the younger ones). An adventure story that describes the campaigns of Hannibal in Iberia, Gaul, Cisalpine Gaul and at Rome's doorstep through the experiences of a young Carthaginian noble. (RA)

Hannibal and His 37 Elephants, by Marilyn Hirseh (Holiday House, 1977). The only available picture-book related to the Punic Wars. Unfortunately, it's **out of print; check your library.** (RA)

Corresponding Audiobook Suggestions

The Young Carthaginian, by G.A. Henty, read by Jim Weiss (Greathall Productions). The struggle between Rome and Carthage was at first a struggle for empire, and then—on the part of Carthage—a struggle for existence. Mr. Henty's classic work, *The Young Carthaginian*, tells the story of this struggle and the attempt of Hannibal to conquer Rome. Malchus, the young hero, a cousin of Hannibal, becomes involved in political intrigue and joins Hannibal in Spain and Italy, sharing for a time in his adventures. Available at www.greathall.com.

Map Work

Chapter 29: Rome's War With Carthage (Student Page 89)

1. Find **Rome** and circle it with a red crayon. Color **Italy** yellow.

2. Color the **Mediterranean Sea** with a blue crayon.

3. Find **Carthage** and circle it with a red crayon. What continent is Carthage in?

4. Draw a line showing how Hannibal and the Carthaginians got to the **Alps** by going through **North Africa**, **Spain**, and **Gaul**.

5. Now draw a line from the Alps down to Rome. This is the path that Hannibal tried to take with his elephants.

Coloring Pages

Hannibal's War Elephants (Student Page 90)

Hannibal (Student Page 91)

Projects

Craft Project: Make a Cuff Bracelet

Roman soldiers wore these bracelets to show their commitment to Rome.

Materials:
- poster board or lightweight cardboard
- aluminum foil
- permanent marker

Directions:
1. Cut the poster board so that it is about 2 inches wide and fits around the wrist of your child.

2. Cover the poster board with aluminum foil.

3. Write S-P-Q-R on the bracelet with permanent marker.

4. Staple the bracelet together so it fits your child's wrist.

Note: SPQR stood for *Senatus Populus que Romanus*, which means "The Senate and the Roman People" in Latin. Roman soldiers were supposed to remember that they served Roman citizens and the Senate.

Craft Project: Make a Coin Ring

The Romans often used money as jewelry. You can too!

Materials:
- pipe cleaner or chenille covered wire
- button with two holes
- glue
- a penny or other coin

Directions:
1. Put the pipe cleaner through the holes of the button.
2. Cut and twist together ends to fit your child's finger.
3. Then glue coin on top of the button.

Cooking Project: Hannibal's Elephant Ears

Elephant Ear Cookies

Ingredients:
- package of refrigerated biscuit dough
- cinnamon and sugar, honey, or powdered sugar

Directions:
1. Open the can of refrigerated biscuits.
2. Flatten out a little and shape dough into an elephant ear shape (scone).
3. Fry in hot oil, about one minute per side.
4. Remove from oil, and roll in cinnamon and sugar mixture.

Activity Project: Help Hannibal Cross the Alps

Using the maze on Student Page 92, help Hannibal find his way through the mountain passes to cross the Alps!

Art Project: Draw Yourself in Ancient Roman Armor

Materials:
- newsprint (from an end roll found at a newspaper printing business), or wide, white butcher paper
- black marker
- crayons
- a book with pictures of Roman soldiers (optional)

Directions:

Imagine you are called out of your ripe farm fields to help defend your country from that menace, Hannibal. You gather together your weapons. You fit your plate armor over your red tunic. Lifting your father's brightly plumed helmet over your head, you check the cheek guards. Then you reach for your javelin and rectangular shield, covered lovingly in goathide. Your family rushes around. One child brings your kit pole, which your wife has already fitted with a hide water bag and mess tins that hang from your food pack. You notice the tight knots. All is made secure for the journey. Another child ceremonially hands you your sword, sheathed securely for your travels. From under your bed, you unwrap your spiked shoes and carefully replace your hide sandals with them. The third child has been busy with your horse. So all is ready. All that is left is to say good-bye.

1. Now lie down on the paper and have your whole body traced on to the newsprint. Carefully lift yourself off.

2. With your crayons, begin dressing yourself for the battle ahead. The Roman soldiers wore a tunic, which is a long shirt that stops above the knee, has short sleeves, and is belted at the waist. Often in the pictures, the tunics are red, but you can color yours what ever color you like. But before you color it in, add the plate armor. This was a vest that crossed around the chest and stomach and was held up over the shoulders, kind of like overalls. A large belt-like strap went around the waist and held the sword and other tools the soldier would carry with him. He also would wear his shield and javelin on his back, secured over the shoulder. If the travel was long, he had a long, wooden pole, called a kit pole. It acted like a hobo-stick, only it reached the ground and was thick enough to carry a load.

3. Don't forget your spiked shoes. They looked like sandals with baseball cleats, and made a distinct sound that would strike fear in the heart of an enemy.

4. The Roman helmet was made of thick iron and had cheek guards to protect his face. They did not sport the nose guard like the Greeks did, but a Centurion did have a wide, full plume that went over the helmet's crest like a peacock's feathers spread out. Often, a soldier also had the head of a wild animal, like a lion or bear, over his helmet so that the animal's teeth rested on the soldier's forehead, making the him look fearless and ruthless. What will yours look like?

CHAPTER THIRTY
The Aryans of India

Encyclopedia Cross-References

Usborne Book of World History: 63, 83

Usborne Internet-Linked Encyclopedia: 174

Kingfisher Illustrated History of the World: 64, 65

Kingfisher History Encyclopedia: 33

Review Questions — Life on the Ganges River

What were the people who settled in ancient India called? *Aryans*

Where did they come from? *Asia*

Do you remember the names of the two big rivers that they settled near? *Ganges and Indus*

Why did they settle near the Ganges and Indus Rivers? *Because they needed water for crops and animals*

What was the name of the chief god of the Indian Aryans? *Shiva*

Why did the river-goddess Ganga get angry at Shiva? *He told her to go down to earth and give water to the people who were thirsty.*

What did Shiva do when he saw that Ganga was getting ready to jump down on the earth? *He jumped down ahead of her so that she landed on top of him.*

Which river was named after Ganga? *The Ganges*

What do we call people who believe in Shiva and Ganga? *Hindus*

Narration Exercise — Life on the Ganges River

"After the citadel cities disappeared, other people came to India. They were called Aryans. They lived near the Ganges River and the Indus River."

OR

"Once the people on earth were thirsty. Shiva told the river goddess Ganga to go down to earth. She didn't want to, so she tried to drown everyone. Shiva stopped her and she turned into the Ganges River."

Review Questions — The Castes of Ancient India

What were the four different castes of ancient India? *Priests, warriors, farmers and traders, servants*

How did you know what caste you belonged in? *You were born into it* OR *your family belonged to it.*

What was the best caste to be in? *The priests or Brahmins*

What were the people called who didn't belong to any caste? *Untouchables*

What kind of work did they do? *Dirty work: burying dead animals, cleaning streets, picking up garbage, working in the fields*

What story did the Hindus tell to explain castes? *The story of Purusha, the first man*

Narration Exercise — The Castes of Ancient India

"People in India belonged to four different groups. Some groups were better than others. People who didn't belong to any of the groups were called Untouchables. They had to do dirty work."

Review Questions — Siddhartha

Why did Siddhartha leave his palace and wander through the world? *Because he saw sick, poor, and old people*

What did Siddhartha teach all men to do? *To live good lives; to be honest, make peace, and to avoid violence*

What was Siddhartha's new name? *Buddha*

What were his followers called? *Buddhists*

Narration Exercise — Siddhartha

"Siddhartha was a prince. He lived in a great palace. Finally he saw that some people were poor and sick. He left the palace. He taught people to be good, and he was called Buddha."

Additional History Reading

The Ganges (Rivers of the World), by David Cummings (World Almanac Library, 2002). An overview of the Ganges River, one of the largest waterways in the world, valued not only for trade and irrigation, but also for its religious importance to Hindus. (RA)

The Sacred River, by Ted Lewin (Clarion, 2003). This book uses beautiful full-color illustrations to describe the Hindu pilgrimage to the Ganges. (RA)

Buddha, by Demi (Henry Holt, 1996). The story of Siddhartha's life and a brief introduction to the teachings of Buddhism. (RA)

Prince Siddhartha: The Story of Buddha, by Jonathan Landaw (Wisdom Publications, 2000). The story of Prince Siddhartha and how he became Buddha. (RA)

My Friend's Beliefs: A Young Reader's Guide to World Religions, by Hiley H. Ward (Walker Publishing, 1988). Pages 13–40 discuss Hinduism and Buddhism. (RA)

World Religions, by John Bowker (Dorling Kindersley, 1997). Pages 18–41 cover Hinduism, and pages 54–75 cover Buddhism. (RA)

India (Countries of the World), by Michael S. Dahl (Bridgestone, 1997). Focuses on the modern culture of India, with occasional glances back at the past. (RA)

Corresponding Literature Suggestions

Stories from India, by Vayu Naidu (Raintree Steck-Vaughn, 2000). Ancient Indian fairytales. (RA)

Savitri: A Tale of Ancient India, by Aaron Shepherd (Whitman, 1992). A brave and resourceful Indian princess saves her husband from death. (RA)

Buddha Stories, by Demi (Henry Holt, 1997). A collection of ten tales told by the Buddha. (RA)

The Wisdom of the Crows and Other Buddhist Tales, by Sherab Chodzin (Tricycle Press, 1998). A nice collection of Buddhist moral tales from India, Burma, Tibet, China, and Japan. (RA)

I Once Was a Monkey: Stories Buddha Told, by Jeanne Lee (Farrar, Straus and Giroux, 1999). This book covers some of the basic teachings of Buddha, through a collection of six classic tales. (RA)

Map Work

Chapter 30: The Aryans of India (Student Page 93)

1. On your map, find the **Ganges** and **Indus** Rivers and circle their names in red. Then, trace their paths with a blue crayon.

2. Notice that the Ganges River has a delta just like the Nile River does. Make sure that you traced the delta in blue.

3. Color in the area that made up the **Aryan Empire** in green. The Aryan Empire is the area inside the dashed lines.

4. Lightly shade the **Bay of Bengal** and the **Indian Ocean** in blue.

Coloring Page

The Buddha (Student Page 94)

This picture shows a statue of the Buddha.

Projects

Craft Project: Make a Rakhi

One special day in India is called *Raksha Bandhan*. This celebrates the bond of love between brothers and sisters. During this celebration the sister ties a *rakhi* (like a bracelet) on her brother's wrist. The brother promises his sister he will look after her.

Materials:
- yarn, ribbon or needlepoint floss
- cardboard or poster board cut into round shapes
- glue
- beads, sequins, glitter, foil, gel pens, and/or anything else to decorate

Directions:
1. Knot the ends of the yarn, ribbon or floss together, and divide the number of strands by three. Braid as you would braid hair. You want this to be the size of a bracelet. Attach the ends together but leave the bracelet large enough to slip over your hand.

2. Decorate a small circle of cardboard or poster board with foil, beads, sequins, etc.

3. Sew or glue the decorated circle to the middle of the braided band.

Activity Project: Color Fingernails and Lips

The ancient Indus women were the first to use lipstick. In ancient Bengal, men painted their fingernails thinking it would attract women.

Materials:
- washable lipstick
- non-toxic nail polish OR washable tempera or water colors

Directions
1. Girls: put on your lipstick! Now you look like a girl of ancient India.

2. Boys: time to paint your nails with the polish, tempera, or water colors! Remember, in ancient India, this was a sign of manhood and bravery.

Activity Project: Play Tiger Hunt

In ancient India, royalty hunted tigers for entertainment.

Materials:

- yellow construction paper or thin cardboard
- markers, paints, glitter
- yellow, black, or striped T-shirt

Directions:

1. Make a crown for the "king." Cut a strip of yellow construction paper or thin cardboard with a serrated edge, long enough to fit around child's head. Tape ends together. You can decorate the crown with your paints and art materials if you want to.

2. One child will be the "tiger" and another child the "king." If it's just you and Mom, Mom can be the tiger! The "tiger" should put on the T-shirt. The "king" should wear the crown.

3. Choose a place in the house or yard to serve as "base."

4. Now the "king" should count to ten while the "tiger" hides. Can the king find the tiger and catch him (by tagging him) before the tiger can sneak back to base?

5. If you have additional children, they should serve as the king's "beaters"—they should also try to find the tiger. When they find the tiger, they can't touch him. Only the king can catch the tiger! Instead, they should try to "herd" the tiger back towards the king so that the king can catch him.

CHAPTER THIRTY-ONE
The Mauryan Empire of India

Encyclopedia Cross-References

Usborne Book of World History: 83

Usborne Internet-Linked Encyclopedia: 175

Kingfisher Illustrated History of the World: 96, 97

Kingfisher History Encyclopedia: 57

Review Questions — The Empire United

Are cities stronger if they are independent or if they're united together? *United together*

What was the name of the Indian empire that united the cities of India together? *The Mauryan Empire*

Who was its most famous ruler? *Asoka*

What religion did he follow? *Buddhism*

Can you tell me one of the kind things he did? *He built hospitals, built animal hospitals, made laws against cruelty to animals, gave up violence, planted trees along roads, and gave up eating meat.*

Narration Exercise — The Empire United

"Cities are stronger if they're all in one country. The cities of India were all separate. Then the Mauryan Empire made them into one country. Asoka ruled the empire."

Review Questions — The Jataka Tales

Why did the hare offer to roast himself? *So that the priest wouldn't have to kill him*

Was he rewarded for his generosity? *Yes, he lived happily and was rewarded after death.*

Who lived with the hare? *An otter, a monkey, and a jackal*

Were they as generous as the hare? Why or why not? *No, because they stole the food they offered the priest.*

Narration Exercise — The Jataka Tales

Ask the child to draw a picture of the hare and the priest. If he wants to, he can also draw pictures of the otter, the jackal, and the monkey. Ask the child to describe the picture. Write the description underneath the picture.

Additional History Reading

Ancient India, by Daud Ali (Southwater, 2003). Illustrations, descriptions, and crafts all related to ancient India. (RA)

India (Countries of the World), by Michael S. Dahl (Bridgestone, 1997). A very simple introduction to modern India, with some information about India's history. (RA)

India: Festivals of the World, by Falaq Kagda (Gareth Stevens, 1997). Reviews the history and development of major Indian holidays. (RA)

A Coloring Book of Ancient India (Bellerophon Books, 1989). Uses images from ancient Indian culture. (RA and activity)

Corresponding Literature Suggestions

I Once Was a Monkey: Stories Buddha Told, by Jeanne Lee (Farrar, Straus and Giroux, 1999). Each animal story has a moral about how we should treat others. (RA)

The Monkey and the Crocodile: A Jataka Tale from India, by Paul Galdone (Clarion, 1987). A monkey manages to outwit the crocodile who decides to capture him (a retelling of one of the fables relating to Buddha). (RA)

Nine Animals and the Well, by James Rumford (Houghton Mifflin, 2003). This traditional tale from India also covers the Indian origins of our nine number signs and our zero. (RA 1–2, IR 2–4)

Map Work

Chapter 31: The Mauryan Empire of India (Student Page 95)

1. In the last chapter, you studied the Aryan Empire. The Mauryans came after the Aryans, and attempted to unite India. The two major rivers were still very important to this new empire. Find the **Ganges River** and the **Indus River**, and trace them in blue. Make sure that you trace the **Ganges Delta**.

2. The Mauryan Empire covered the whole northern part of India, and it is shown on your map as the area within the dashed lines. Shade the **Mauryan Empire** lightly in red.

3. Circle the names of the **Arabian Sea**, the **Indian Ocean**, and the **Bay of Bengal** in blue.

Coloring Page

The Jakata Tales (Student Page 96)

Projects

Cooking Project: Learn How to Make Rice

Rice is a staple food in India, as well as in China and other Asian countries. You can either make white rice or Indian Curried Rice.

<u>White Rice</u>
Ingredients:
- 2 cups cold water
- 1 cup rice

Directions:
1. Explain to your child that you make rice by using twice as much water as rice.

2. Measure the water and rice and pour into a saucepan. Bring to a boil.

3. As soon as the water boils, reduce the heat to simmer. Put a tight-fitting lid on the pot. Don't peek for 12 minutes!

<u>Indian Curried Rice</u>
Ingredients:
- 3 cups cooked rice
- 1 chopped onion
- 1 chopped green pepper
- 2 tablespoons butter
- 1 teaspoon curry powder
- 1 egg yolk

- ¼ teaspoon salt
- ⅛ to ¼ teaspoon black pepper
- ¼ teaspoon cayenne pepper

Directions:

1. Sauté onion and green pepper in butter until onions and peppers are tender.

2. Stir in curry powder, slightly beaten egg, salt, pepper and cayenne.

3. Mix into hot rice.

Game: Snakes and Ladders

Did you know that card games and the game of Chutes and Ladders both originated in ancient India?

If you have the game of Chutes and Ladders, get it out and look at it. Ancient Indians played a game like Chutes and Ladders—but they called it Snakes and Ladders! Each one of the slides in the game was a huge, scaly snake! Play the game of Chutes and Ladders, but whenever you slide down a chute, hiss like a snake.

Game: Indian Battle

Get out a pack of cards and look at the card faces. In ancient India, the king card represented the most powerful man in the country—the king of India! The jack card is his general, the man who rules his army. All the number cards are his army followers! Take out the aces and queens from your deck. Now you can play "Indian Battle"! This is best when played with four players, one for each "army" or suit of cards. But you can play two-person Indian Battle by only using two suits of cards. Whose army will win?

Play it like a normal game of *War*.

Video Viewing: The Tiger and the Brahmin by Rabbit Ears Productions (1991).

This story, told by Ben Kingsley, is a narration of the traditional Indian folktale about a well-meaning Brahmin who makes the mistake of freeing a tiger from its cage. For ages 5 and up. Try your local library; many children's departments make a point of stocking Rabbit Ears videos.

CHAPTER THIRTY-TWO
China: Writing and the Qin

Encyclopedia Cross-References

Review Questions — Calligraphy in China

What was the earliest Chinese writing called—where words looked like the things they named? *Pictograms*

What do we call later Chinese writing? *Calligraphy*

Can you tell me the names of several lines used in Chinese calligraphy? You can look back at the lesson as you answer. *Horizontal line, vertical line, dot, downward stroke, sweeping downward stroke, hook*

What kinds of hair did scribes use for their brushes? *Mouse, rabbit, sheep, wolf*

The Chinese developed a faster way to print books. What did they use? *Ink and blocks of wood*

Had anyone else ever done this? *No, the Chinese were the first.*

Narration Exercise — Calligraphy in China

"The Chinese used to use pictures for writing. Then they wrote characters instead. They didn't look as much like pictures. They used seven different lines."

OR

"At first the Chinese wrote by hand. They used special brushes made out of mouse hair, rabbit hair, and wolf hair. It took a long time. Then they figured out how to use wood blocks instead."

Review Questions — Warring States

How many "Warring States" were there in ancient China? *Six*

What Warring State conquered the rest? *Qin (pronounced "Chin")*

Where does China get its name? *From the word "Qin"*

How did Qin Zheng keep control of his new empire? *He made his rivals move into his own city, executed anyone who was planning rebellion, and had books burned.*

Did the Chinese people love their new emperor? *No; many disliked him for his cruelty.*

Narration Exercise — Warring States

"China used to be six different countries. Then the Qin conquered all the rest. China became one country, but the new emperor was cruel. China is named after the Qin."

Review Questions — The First Emperor and the Great Wall

Qin Zheng changed his name to Shi Huangdi. What does this name mean? *The First Emperor*

Why did Shi Huangdi want to build a Wall? *To keep the Mongols out*

What is the full name for the Wall he built? *The Great Wall of China*

How long is the Wall? *Almost 3000 miles, or as long as the United States is wide*

What is the Wall made out of? *Stone in some places, packed dirt in others*

Was it finished during Shi Huangdi's lifetime? *No, it took hundreds of years to finish.*

Can you still see the Wall today? *Yes*

Narration Exercise — The First Emperor and the Great Wall

"The emperor of China wanted to keep the Mongols out. So he built a huge wall. It was made out of stone and out of dirt packed hard. It is called the Great Wall of China."

Review Questions — The First Emperor's Grave

How was the tomb of Shi Huangdi discovered? *Two farmers uncovered clay pieces while digging a well.*

What was found inside the underground city? *Thousands of life-sized clay horses and soldiers*

Can you tell me two things that might be inside the burial mound? *Rivers of mercury, treasure, crossbows, stars, and planets*

Why did Shi Huangdi build such a huge city? *Because he hoped to live forever*

Narration Exercise — The First Emperor's Grave

"Shi Huangdi built an underground city. It had soldiers and horses in it, made out of clay. He is buried in the city, but no one has found his tomb yet."

Additional History Reading

Long is a Dragon: Chinese Writing for Children, by Peggy Goldstein (Pacific View Press, 1992). Explains how Chinese writing developed and demonstrates how to write seventy-five Chinese characters, using detailed instructions and examples. (RA)

The Great Wall of China, by Leonard Everett Fisher (Aladdin, 1995). A brief history of the Great Wall of China, with detailed, large pictures. (RA)

The Great Wall, by Elizabeth Mann (Mikaya Press, 1997). Covers the building of the Great Wall of China and the thousands of years of conflict that preceded it. (RA)

Ancient China (See Through History), by Brian Williams (Viking, 1996). Describes daily life in ancient China with four see-through scenes. (RA)

The Terra-cotta Army of the First Emperor of China, by William Lindesay (Odyssey Publications, 1999). Nice pictures of the Terra-cotta army. (RA)

Ancient China Treasure Chest: 2000 Years of History to Unlock and Discover, by Chao-Hui Jenny Liu (Running Press, 1996). Text would be a read-aloud. Projects include: Chinese calligraphy (brush, ink and instructions), Chinese fan, *I Ching* coins, charts, stickers, and a booklet (overview of dynasties, inventions, and principles of Taoism). Small children will need help with most of the projects. (RA and activity)

A Coloring Book of Ancient China (Bellerophon Books, 1984). Uses actual images from ancient Chinese art. (RA and activity)

Corresponding Literature Suggestions

Ten Suns: A Chinese Legend, by Eric Kimmel (Holiday House, 1998). A father, Di Jun, looks for a way to stop the destruction after his ten sons walk across the sky together causing the earth to burn from the blazing heat. (RA)

The Dragon Prince: A Chinese Beauty and the Beast Tale, by Laurence Yep (HarperCollins, 1999). A poor farmer's youngest daughter agrees to marry a fierce dragon in order to save her father's life. (RA)

The Ch'I-Lin Purse: A Collection of Ancient Chinese Stories, by Linda Fang (Farrar, Straus and Giroux, 1997). Stories of ancient China, from a number of different traditions. (RA)

Lord of the Cranes: A Chinese Tale, by Kerstin Chen (North-South Books, 2000). A traditional Chinese folktale about compassion. (RA 1–2, IR 2–4)

Da Wei's Treasure: A Chinese Tale, retold by Margaret and Raymond Chang (Margaret K. McElderry, 1999). A young Chinese man discovers a kitten who is actually a princess in disguise. (RA 1, IR 2–4)

The Lost Horse: A Chinese Folktale, by Ed Young (Silver Whistle, 1998). This tale, based in the "barbarian" lands of northern China, comes with paper puppets so that young readers can act out the story. (RA 1, IR 2–4)

Map Work

Chapter 32: China: Writing and the Qin (Student Page 97)

1. Find the **Great Wall of China**. Color it light brown.

2. On your map, find the **Qin Empire**. Remember that Qin Zeng, later known as Shi Huangdi, conquered all the Warring States until he ruled all of China. His empire, the Qin Empire, is shown within the dashed lines on your map. Shade it lightly in green.

3. Look back at the Great Wall you already colored. The Chinese built this wall to keep the Mongols out of China. Do you remember how the Great Wall was built?

3. Find the names of the **two important rivers** in the Qin Empire and circle their names in red. Then, trace the rivers in blue.

4. What **three seas** are next to China? Find them on your map, and shade them lightly in blue.

Coloring Page

The Great Wall of China (Student Page 98)

Projects

Art Project: Practice Chinese Calligraphy
Materials:
- several different sizes of watercolor paintbrushes
- black ink or tempera paint (watercolor paint will also work, but not as well)
- white paper

Directions:
1. On one piece of white paper, try making the different lines shown in the chapter. What brushes work best? How do the lines look different if they are made with smaller or larger brushes?

2. Now try combining the lines together into the characters shown in the chapter. Are you able to make similar characters? Don't try to make them small—make them as large as you want.

3. Can you make up your own characters? What do you think the character for "book" should look like? How about the character for "baby," "bread," "sun," or "egg"?

Art Project: Make the Great Wall of China

Materials:

- popsicle or craft sticks
- superglue
- yarn
- garden dirt

Directions:

1. Lay six popsicle sticks side by side on a piece of newspaper. Lay two more sticks horizontally across them (one at the top and one at the bottom) and superglue into place. (Make sure to put a dot of superglue on each stick!). Repeat three more times, so that you have four wooden "walls" made out of popsicle sticks.

2. Stand the "walls" up so that they form a box. Use a drop of superglue at each corner to hold the walls together. Wrap yarn around your wooden box and knot it to keep the walls together.

3. Set the wooden box on a newspaper, baking sheet, or other surface. Pack it full of dirt—as hard as you can! You may want to add stones, grass, or other ingredients to make the "wall" stronger.

4. When the box is full of packed dirt, lift it gently straight up. You should have a section of strong dirt wall that will stand by itself—just like the dirt sections of the Great Wall of China.

5. Experiment. Can you make another section of wall touching the first section? Can you make one on top of it?

Craft Project: Making Paper

The Chinese were among the first ancient people to use paper that is similar to the paper we use today. This project is an extensive one, but it is particularly good if you'd like to include your older children in the study of Chinese culture.

Materials:

- 2 wood picture frames (preferably flattish)
- screen (just like you use in windows)
- large tub (such as a Rubbermaid storage tub)
- blender or food processor
- paper scraps
- liquid starch (optional)
- felt
- newspapers
- scrap board for pressing (optional)

Directions:

1. Take the glass, backing, and all nails or metal off the picture frames.

2. Staple a piece of screen to the back of one; trim the edges if necessary. These two frames are officially called a mould and deckle. The size of your frame determines the size of your paper.

3. Tear your paper scraps up into small pieces. The smaller, the better.

4. Make paper pulp; construction paper is the very easiest to make into pulp. Fill your food processor or blender about ¼ full of warm water (2 or 3 cups). Slowly add about 1 cup of paper scraps. The paper turns to pulp easier if you've soaked it overnight. Don't use glossy paper or paper with very much ink on it.

5. After paper is blended with water (you should not see very many individual pieces), pour it into a tub. The tub should be larger than your frame—about 2 inches clearance on all sides minimum.

6. The thicker your pulp mixture, the easier it is to make the paper. The paper project works best if you add one tablespoon of liquid starch to a batch of pulp (a batch being about 6 to 8 cups including water) for sizing. Stir up the water-pulp mixture in the tub between every piece of paper that you make.

7. Put both of your picture frames together, with the screen in the very middle. The frames will be back to back. Slide the frames into the tub from the front. Gently rock the screen back and forth under the water and slowly bring it up to the top of the water. Pull it straight up. It will probably take a few practice runs to get the pulp distributed fairly evenly over the screen. Be careful not to make your first pieces too thick. You can add handfuls of pulp if the mixture gets too thin. Any mistakes can be recycled right back into the tub (before they dry.)

8. Now, lay down a pile of newspaper (do this outdoors—it's a wet job), and place a piece of felt (bigger than your screen/frame by about an inch) on top of the newspaper. Take the top (empty) picture frame off and carefully turn your frame/screen/paper over on top of the felt.

9. This next part can be tricky. Push your newly made paper down onto the felt, squeezing some of the water out by pressing on the screen. Lift it up, starting at one corner. The new paper should stick to the felt. Unfortunately, it may stick to the screen (this is not good!). Slightly thick paper is easiest for beginners to make. Thin paper is most difficult.

10. Now, place another piece of felt on top of your paper, so that you have a sandwich of newspaper, felt, handmade paper, felt, more newspaper. You can stack several of these sandwiches up (try not to use the slick pages of the paper or you'll have a problem with sliding), place a board on top and stand on the entire stack to squeeze out as much water as possible. Let the stack dry for about an hour. Then carefully dig the paper/felt sandwiches out, peel the felt off. Now you have damp paper.

11. Let the paper dry flat. You can speed up the drying process by ironing the paper between towels.

12. You can add all sorts of fun things to your pulp or sprinkle them onto your paper as you're removing from the tub of water—glitter, confetti, tissue paper, dried flower petals and grasses, etc.

CHAPTER THIRTY-THREE
Confucius

Encyclopedia Cross-References

Usborne Book of World History: 76

Usborne Internet-Linked Encyclopedia: 165

Kingfisher Illustrated History of the World: 73

Kingfisher History Encyclopedia: 39

Review Questions — Confucius

Who was the great teacher of ancient India? *Buddha*

Who was the great teacher of ancient China? *Confucius*

Tell me one thing that Confucius taught. *Obey people in authority, don't do anything to another person that you wouldn't want done to yourself, try to fix your mistakes, giving is more fun than getting, don't be greedy.*

When did Confucius live? *During the Period of Warring States*

Narration Exercise — Confucius

"Confucius lived in China. He taught people to obey their rulers and children to obey their parents. He had many followers."

Additional History Reading

World Religions, by John Bowker (Dorling Kindersley, 1997). Beautifully illustrated, with a section on Chinese beliefs. (RA)

Confucius: the Golden Rule, by Russell Freedman (Arthur A. Levine Books, 2002). An advanced picture-book biography which includes a brief collection of the Analects. (RA 1–3, IR 4–6)

The Life and Times of Confucius, by Kathleen Tracy (Mitchell Lane Publishers, 2005). A fairly advanced junior biography of Confucius, readable and well illustrated. Sections are suitable as read-alouds. (RA 1–3, IR 4–7)

Confucius and Ancient China, by Theodore Rowland-Entwistle (Wayland, 1986). Describes the times of Confucius and reviews his teachings. **Out of print; check your library.** (RA)

Made in China: Ideas and Inventions from Ancient China, by Suzanne Williams, illus. Andrea Fong (Pacific View Press, 1996). Covers over 3,000 years of Chinese history in about 50 pages in a more topical (rather than narrative) approach; but sections on agriculture, astronomy, and medicine, along with great illustrations, make this book useful. (IR 4–7)

Eyewitness: Ancient China, by Arthur Cotterell (DK Children, 2005). Geared toward older students, this book has great illustrations, with each chapter covering a two-page spread (one is titled "The Teachings of Confucius"). Sections will be suitable as read-alouds; the timeline across the bottom of the first several pages is also very helpful. (RA 1–3, IR 4–7)

Corresponding Literature Suggestions

The Empty Pot, by Demi (Henry Holt, 1996). This read-alone book for beginners explains the value of honesty. (IR)

Map Work

1. Look back at the map you used in the last lesson. Use a purple crayon to color in the areas that were not part of the Qin Empire.

2. Now let's make a map puzzle. Spread a thin layer of glue over the entire back side of the map. Place on a thin piece of cardboard and press down firmly. With a black marker, draw "puzzle" shaped lines on the cardboard side. Cut out the pieces. When the cutting is finished, mix up the pieces and see how quickly you can put the Qin Empire back together.

Coloring Page

Confucius, China's Wise Teacher (Student Page 99)

Projects

Activity Project: Making Tangrams

Tangrams are an ancient Chinese puzzle. There are seven pieces, and they fit together to form a square. Legend says that a man (either from the T'ang dynasty or named Tan) dropped a tile, and it broke into seven pieces. He tried to fix it by putting it back together again. The Emperor saw him trying to put the seven pieces together, later showed it to all of China, and this became a game the people in China liked to play.

To make your own tangrams you will need a 4" square of construction paper or cardboard. First, with a ruler draw 12 squares that are about 1 inch each. Your grid should look like that on Student Page 100. Next, mark the following lines on the graph. Cut on the bold lines (do not cut the grid lines). If you want to, you can color your pieces. You will now have seven pieces. Try and make a box or animal shapes with the pieces.

Cooking Project: Chinese Tea

Confucius said, "Let your palate be your guide." What is your palate? It's the part of your mouth that tells you whether something tastes good or not! Read "The Legend of Tea" and then make some simple tea. Does your palate approve?

One afternoon, very long ago, Emperor Shen Nung was enjoying a cup of boiling water. The Emperor felt that drinking very hot water made him feel better. There was a gentle breeze on this afternoon, and a few leaves from a nearby tree floated down and landed in his hot water. The Emperor thought the leaves made the water smell nice. He decided to take a sip of the water with leaves and found he enjoyed the taste. He proclaimed the leaves to be sent from heaven. This is believed to be the first cup of green tea.

Mint Tea

Ingredients:
- fresh or dried mint leaves
- boiling water
- tea cup

Directions:

1. Pour boiling water into teacup and have your child add a few mint leaves. Let steep 3–5 minutes then remove mint leaves.

2. Let cool slightly and drink.

Note: Most children seem to prefer mint herb tea to black or green tea. You can often buy fresh mint in the produce section of a grocery store. Another option is to buy some loose tea. Put it into an infusing basket, add it to the water, and steep. See if you can find some Chinese tea at the store.

CHAPTER THIRTY-FOUR
The Rise of Julius Caesar

Encyclopedia Cross-References

Usborne Book of World History: 87
Usborne Internet-Linked Encyclopedia: 185

Kingfisher Illustrated History of the World: 115
Kingfisher History Encyclopedia: 63

Review Questions — Caesar is Kidnapped

What city was Julius Caesar from? *Rome*

Who did Julius Caesar's family say they were descended from? *Romulus*

Why did the people of Rome like Caesar? *He was a good speaker; he threw parties for people; he was brave; he defeated the pirates.*

The pirates told Caesar that they wanted a lot of money from his relatives before they would let him go. What did Caesar tell them? *That he was worth more than that*

What did Caesar do when the pirates let him go? *He gathered an army together, hunted down the pirates, and defeated them.*

Narration Exercise — Caesar is Kidnapped

"Julius Caesar was from an important family. He lived in Rome. He was captured by pirates, but when they set him free he punished them. "

OR

"Julius Caesar was captured by pirates. Pirates sailed on the sea and stole things. Julius Caesar told the pirates to let him go. Finally they did."

Review Questions — The Consuls of Rome

What did a consul do? *Governed (or ruled) Rome*

What country did Caesar govern, before he became a consul? *Spain*

Why did Caesar weep when he read the story of Alexander the Great? *Because he hadn't accomplished anything great*

Did Caesar become a consul? *Yes*

Once Caesar became consul, how many consuls were there? *Three*

The three consuls were called the "triumvirate." What does "tri" mean? *Three*

Narration Exercise — The Consuls of Rome

"Caesar wanted to be important in Rome. He went to Spain, but he didn't like it there. Finally he got to be a consul in Rome."

OR

"Consuls ruled Rome. Caesar wanted to be a consul. Finally he got to be one. There were two other consuls, too."

Review Questions — Caesar and the Senate

What did the Senators think Caesar wanted to be? *King of Rome*

What was Caesar doing that made the Senators angry? *He ignored them and did whatever he wanted.*

What did Cincinnatus do when the people wanted him to be king? *He went back to his fields.*

Do you think Caesar was like Cincinnatus? *No*

Narration Exercise — Caesar and the Senate

"The Senate didn't want Caesar to be king. They thought he should be like Cincinnatus. Cincinnatus didn't want to be king of Rome."
OR
"The people of Rome liked Caesar. But the Senate didn't. They were men who ran Rome. They thought Caesar wanted to be king."

Additional History Reading

Julius Caesar, Great Dictator of Rome, by Richard Platt (DK Publishing, 2001). Spectacular illustrations, pull-out sections, and easy-to-read narrative about the rise to power of Julius Caesar. (RA)

A Pirate's Life for Me, by Julie Thompson and Brownie Macintosh (Charlesbridge Publishing, 1996). A fun, fact filled book about all kinds of pirates. (RA)

Great Pirate Activity Book, by Deri Robins (Kingfisher Books, 1995). Instructions for making games, models, and recipes are included along with many pirate facts in this activity book. (RA)

The Legionary (The Roman World series), by Peter Connolly (Oxford University Press Children's Books, 1998). A detailed, nicely illustrated description of the legionary's duties, equipment, and lifestyle. (RA)

The Life and Times of Julius Caesar (Biography from Ancient Civilizations series), by Jim Whiting (Mitchell Lane Publishers, 2005). A fairly advanced junior biography of Julius Caesar, readable and well illustrated. Sections are suitable as read-alouds. (RA 1–3, IR 4–7)

Corresponding Literature Suggestions

Famous Men of Rome, by John Haaren and A.B. Poland (Greenleaf Press, 1989). Stories of famous Roman figures, including Cincinnatus and Caesar. (RA)

The Wadjet Eye, by Jill Rubalcaba (Clarion, 2000). The story of Damon, a medical student living in Egypt, who journeys to Spain to locate his father, who is serving in the Roman army led by Julius Caesar. Written for slightly older children; a good read-aloud project over several weeks, particularly if an older student can read to the younger child. (RA)

Map Work

Chapter 34: The Rise of Julius Caesar (Student Page 101)

1. On your map, find the **Mediterranean Sea** and color it blue. Then, color the **islands** in the sea pink. Do you remember what happened to Julius Caesar in the Mediterranean Sea?

2. Find the **Tiber River** and trace it in blue.

3. Find **Rome** and circle it in red.

4. The consuls made Julius Caesar a leader of the colony of Spain. Find **Spain** on your map. Use a dotted line and draw a route that Caesar and his men might have taken from Rome to Spain.

Art Project: Make a Roman Mosaic

A Roman mosaic was made by pressing small pieces of stone into plaster or cement in the shape of a picture. Romans often used mosaics to decorate the floors of their homes, instead of carpets. You can make your mosaic in the pattern of a sun, flower, or cloud, or just make an interesting design.

Materials:
- poster board or heavy construction paper
- a variety of dried beans (you can also use squares of colored paper)
- glue
- pencil, for drawing outline

Directions:
1. Draw the outline of your picture on the poster board or construction paper. Erase and redraw until you have it just right.

2. Squeeze out a line of thin glue onto the pencil lines.

3. Lay beans or colored paper squares along the lines of glue.

4. Now fill in the middle of your picture. You can arrange the beans or colored paper squares into patterns to complete your mosaic!

Activity Project: Play the Ransom Caesar Game

Materials:
- 2 copies of pirate game board (Student Page 102)
- 2 pennies
- a handful of beans

Directions:
1. Each player hides Julius Caesar (the penny) on their game board. Don't let your opponent see your game board!

2. Taking turns, pick a row letter and a column number (for example, R3). Call the number out to your opponent.

3. If your opponent's penny is on that number, you've found Caesar! But if it isn't, mark that square on your own board with a bean, so that you'll remember not to call it again.

4. The first person to rescue Julius Caesar from the pirate wins.

Craft Project: Make a Crown of Leaves

Roman leaders liked to wear crowns on their heads. This was to show their importance or rank in society. The crowns were made from leaves and formed into the shape of a wreath. Julius Caesar liked to wear wreaths of gold leaves.

Materials:
- ¾" wide strip of posterboard, long enough to fit around child's head
- leaves (real, fake, or made from construction paper)
- glue
- scissors

Directions:
1. Form the posterboard into a circle that will fit on child's head. Tape or glue into place.

2. Glue leaves onto crown form and let dry.

CHAPTER THIRTY-FIVE
Caesar the Hero

Encyclopedia Cross-References

Usborne Book of World History: 84, 85, 87, 115

Usborne Internet-Linked Encyclopedia: 182, 183, 185

Kingfisher Illustrated History of the World: 112, 113,

Kingfisher History Encyclopedia: 63, 68, 69

Review Questions — Caesar Fights the Celts

Why were Caesar's soldiers so loyal to him? *He treated them well, paid them money, and made sure they had plenty of food to eat.*

What country did Caesar want to conquer? *Britain*

What do we call the people who lived in Britain? *Celts*

Did Caesar ever completely conquer Britain. *No*

What did he tell the people of Rome about his wars with the Celts? *That he was winning*

Do you remember the name of the book Caesar wrote about his wars? *The Gallic Wars*

Narration Exercise — Caesar Fights the Celts

"Caesar wanted to conquer Britain. It was hard because the Celts were very good fighters. He told the Romans that he was winning, but he didn't win all his battles."

Review Questions — Caesar Crosses the Rubicon

Which senator married Caesar's daughter and then became jealous of Caesar? *Pompey*

When Caesar heard that he was going to be arrested, what did he do? *He marched his army towards Rome.*

What river did Caesar cross over with his army? *The Rubicon*

Did Pompey and the Senators fight against Caesar? *No, their soldiers ran away.*

Was Caesar the king yet? *No, but he was very powerful.*

What does "crossing the Rubicon" still mean? *Doing something you can't undo*

Narration Exercise — Caesar Crosses the Rubicon

"The Senators made Pompey jealous of Caesar. Pompey tried to arrest Caesar. But Caesar marched into Rome with his army, and Pompey and the Senators ran away."

Review Questions — Caesar and Cleopatra

What country did Pompey run to? *Egypt*

What queen ruled Egypt? *Cleopatra*

How did Cleopatra and her brother try to make friends with Caesar? *They killed Pompey.*

Why did Cleopatra want Caesar to be on her side? *She wanted to get rid of her brother and rule Egypt all alone.*

Did Caesar help her rule Egypt alone? *Yes, he did.*

What does *"Veni, Vidi, Vici"* mean? *I came, I saw, I conquered.*

What language is this in? *Latin*

Narration Exercise — Caesar and Cleopatra

"Pompey went to Egypt. Caesar went after him. Cleopatra was the queen of Egypt. She got Caesar to stay and help her in Egypt."

Review Questions — The Death of Caesar

When Caesar became dictator, what could he do? *Anything he wanted*

Can you name one thing that Caesar did when he became dictator? *He took power away from the Senate; he could declare war, pass laws, and raise taxes; he made money with his picture on it; he paid for gladiator fighting and chariot racing.*

What did Caesar want to be called? *King Caesar*

Who did he want to be king after him? *His nephew Octavian*

Why did the Senate decide to kill Caesar? *They were afraid of his power; they didn't want him to pass his power on to another king.*

Can you remember one strange thing that happened to Caesar on the fifteenth of March? *His horses were crying; a fortune-teller told him to be careful; his wife had a strange dream.*

What did Caesar say when he died? *Et tu, Brute?*

What does this mean? *You, too, Brutus?*

Narration Exercise — The Death of Caesar

"Caesar became a dictator. He could do whatever he wanted. But he wanted to be called 'king.' So the Senators decided to kill Caesar. They stabbed him to death."

Additional History Reading

The Romans, by Peter Hicks (Thomas Learning, 1995). Illustrates the culture and history of ancient Rome. (RA)

Roman Numerals I to MM, by Arthur Geisert (Sagebrush, 2001). Introduces Roman numerals; by counting pigs in the illustrations, the reader can practice Roman math! (RA)

Cleopatra: The Queen of Kings, by Fiona MacDonald (DK Publishing, 2001). Another in the Dorling Kindersley series "DK Discoveries"; beautiful pictures and interesting narrative. (RA)

Cleopatra, by Diane Stanley (HarperTrophy, 1997). Slightly more detailed account of Cleopatra's life. (RA)

The Celts (See Through History), by Hazel Mary Martell (Viking, 1996). A colorful and interesting guide to ancient Celtic culture. (RA)

Corresponding Literature Suggestions

"Julius Caesar," from *Tales from Shakespeare*, by Marcia Williams (Candlewick Press, 2004). Retells Shakespeare's famous play in eye-appealing, comic-book format. (RA, IR for strong readers)

Shakespeare Stories II, by Leon Garfield (Houghton Mifflin, 1998). A read-aloud, story version of Shakespeare's play. (RA)

Cleopatra: The Queen of Dreams, by Haydn Middleton (Oxford University Press Children's Books, 1998). The story of Cleopatra. (RA)

Rome Antics, by David Macaulay (Houghton Mifflin, 1997). A pigeon carrying an important message takes the reader on a unique tour, which includes both ancient and modern parts of the city of Rome. (RA)

Map Work

Chapter 35: Caesar the Hero (Student Page 103)

1. On your map, find **Britain** and color it with a red crayon.

2. Trace the **Rubicon River** in blue.

3. Find **Egypt** and circle it in red. Then, trace the **Nile River** in blue.

4. Draw a line from **Britain** down to Rome, to show the route Caesar might have taken when he returned to Rome with his army. Make sure that your line crosses the **Rubicon River**!

5. Now draw another line from Rome down to the **Nile Delta**. This route might be the one Caesar would have taken when he went down to Egypt to see Cleopatra.

Coloring Page

Julius Caesar (Student Page 104)

Projects

Activity Project: Measure Your Height

The Romans were afraid of the Celts because they were so tall. How tall are you?

Materials:

- pen
- paper
- scissors
- measuring tape

Directions:

1. Romans used different measurements than we do. A foot was the actual length of each individual's foot—from heel to toe. On a piece of paper, draw and cut out a model of your foot.

2. Using a measuring tape, see how tall you are.

3. Now, using your foot measurement, see how tall you are.

4. Measure mom or dad's foot. Compare your height using all three measurements. Are they the same?

Craft Project: Make Caesar's Flag

The flag bearer jumped into the water to fight the Celts and immediately the remaining soldiers followed. The flag, also known as a *signum*, was a symbol that reminded the soldiers of their purpose. The flag was not to be destroyed or captured by the enemy. Choose a flag to make:

Flag #1
Materials:

- dowel
- felt
- glue
- scissors
- permanent markers

- glitter, sequins, other decorations

Directions:
1. Cut a large rectangle out of the felt.

2. Glue the flag to the dowel by placing the dowel on the middle of the flag, running the dowel parallel to the long sides of the rectangle. Let dry.

3. Use the permanent markers to draw a symbol on the flag. What will your symbol be?

4. Decorate the flag with glitter and sequins.

Flag #2
Materials:
- wrapping paper tube
- piece of cardboard, 1½" x 8"
- ribbons, streamers, or yarn
- decorations such as aluminum foil, cardboard or fun foam shapes, fake jewels

Directions:
1. Glue the strip of cardboard near the top of the tube. Attach streamers to the edges of the strip.

2. Using your imagination, decorate the rest of the tube anyway you would like. Be sure and leave an empty space in order to hold the flag in your hand.

Activity Project: Mint Your Own Coins

Julius Caesar was the first politician to place his likeness on the coins of Rome. Prior to that time, coins were decorated with the pictures of animals, ships, buildings, and pictures of the gods. Many coins were minted to commemorate a special event, such a Caesar winning the Gallic Wars. Today you will make coins that will commemorate something special that has happened in your life, such as learning to read or ride a bike.

Materials:
- air-drying clay or Sculpey (at a craft store)
- rolling pin, sculpting tool, sharpened pencil or toothpick
- round plastic lids (hair spray, starch) in assorted sizes (round biscuit and cookie cutters would also work).
- copper, silver and gold metallic paint
- paint brush

Directions:
1. Roll out the air-drying clay into a rectangle that is about ¼"—½" thick. Use the varying sizes of plastic tops or cookie cutters to cut out your coins. It might be easier for the children to work with larger, rather than smaller, circles.

2. Use the sculpting tool, pencil or toothpick to draw a picture on your clay circle. If it is to commemorate the day you learned to ride a two-wheel bike, don't forget to add the year you did it in.

3. Place the coins aside and allow them to dry completely.

4. When the coins have dried, take your different colored paints and paint each coin. This will need to be done in a two-step process: paint one side, let dry, paint the other side.

Activity Project: Learn the Roman Numerals
Materials:
- 15 blank index cards
- black marker

Directions:

1. On side one, write the Arabic numbers 1, 2, 3, 4, 5, 6, 7, 8, 9, 10, 50, 100, 500, and 1000.

2. On side two, write each corresponding Roman numeral: I, II, III, IV, V, VI, VII, VIII, IX, X, L, C, D, and M respectively.

3. After the cards have finished being made, turn them over Roman numeral face up and see if you can guess the correct value for each card.

4. When you have learned the Roman numerals well, use them to write out the ages of all your family members. Be sure to include grandma and grandpa, since their ages will probably use the L (50) numeral.

CHAPTER THIRTY-SIX
The First Roman Prince

Encyclopedia Cross-References

Usborne Book of World History: 87–89   *Kingfisher Illustrated History of the World*: 118, 119
Usborne Internet-Linked Encyclopedia: 185–191   *Kingfisher History Encyclopedia*: 64–67

Review Questions — The First Roman Prince

Who was Octavian's uncle? *Julius Caesar*

How did Octavian make himself popular with the people of Rome? *He threw a big party with Caesar's money; he gave presents and money to the poor families.*

Did Octavian ask to be king? *No, he said that he would quit.*

What title did the Senate give Octavian? *First Citizen, or "princeps"*

What was Octavian's new name? *Augustus Caesar*

Which month is named after Augustus Caesar? *August*

Which month is named after Julius Caesar? *July*

Narration Exercise — The First Roman Prince

"Octavian was Caesar's nephew. The people of Rome liked him because he was generous. He said that he would not be king, but the Senate wanted him to rule. They gave him a title that means 'prince.'"

Additional History Reading

Augustus and Imperial Rome, by Miriam Greenblatt (Benchmark, 1999). Covers Augustus Caesar and his role as the first Roman emperor. (RA)

The Story of Clocks and Calendars: Marking a Millenium, by Guilio Maestro (HarperTrophy, 2004). Discusses the evolution of the calendar. (RA)

The Ancient Romans, by Allison Lassieur (Franklin Watts, 2004). A colorful guide to the Roman empire after Augustus, with the focus on daily life. (RA 1–3, IR 4–6)

Cleopatra, by Struan Reid (Heinemann, 2002). This biography of Cleopatra also covers events in the Roman and Egyptian empires during her time. (RA 1–3, IR 3–5)

Corresponding Literature Suggestions

Sun-day, Moon-day: How the Week Was Made, by Cherry Gilchrist (Barefoot Books, 1998). Presents the stories behind the names of the days of the week. (RA)

Shakespeare Stories II, by Leon Garfield (Houghton Mifflin, 1995). Tells the play of Antony and Cleopatra in a story format. (RA)

Map Work

Chapter 36: The First Roman Prince (Student Page 105)

1. On your map, color in green the area that made up the **Roman Empire** when Julius Caesar was killed. The dashed lines on your map show you the borders of the Empire.

2. What is the name of the **sea** that the Roman Empire surrounded? Find this sea on your map, and shade it lightly in blue.

3. Find Cleopatra's home of **Egypt** on your map, and mark it with an X.

Coloring Page

Augustus Caesar (Student Page 106)

This picture of Augustus Caesar is based on a marble statue located in the Vatican Museum in Rome.

Projects

Art Project: Make a Mosaic Calendar
Materials:
- 13" x 20" piece of stiff poster board
- old glossy magazines, colored mylar, or construction paper
- scissors
- glue stick
- white glue
- paint brush
- 8½" x 11" monthly planner sheets (available at office supply store) or blank sheet of paper

Directions:
1. Lay your piece of poster board flat on the table. Take one sheet from the monthly planner pad and center it and glue it down 1" from the bottom of the board. (If you can't find the monthly planner sheets, take a piece of blank paper and, using a ruler, draw a grid containing 5 rows and 7 columns.)

2. Write the name of the month and the number of days on your sheet.

3. Now for the fun part. Take old glossy magazines and cut colorful pages in small squares. Use the pieces to make any design that you like in the space above the calendar. You can make a face design, animals or flowers, whatever you like. When you have laid out your design, use the glue stick to glue it all into place.

4. When everything has been glued in place and allowed to dry completely, mix 2 parts white glue to 1 part water. This will make a varnish. Use the paint brush to spread the varnish over the entire surface of the mosaic, and let it dry.

5. To hang your calendar, make a small hole in the center at the top of the board and hang on a nail.

Craft Project: Make a Roman Toga

A toga was a very complicated outfit to wear and was usually only worn on very special or important occasions. Traditionally the toga was 2 ½ times as long as the person was tall and about 2 times as wide as the person. Slaves were forbidden from ever wearing a toga, because the toga was considered to be a sign of power and prestige. Only the most important people of the Roman Empire were allowed to use the color purple.
Materials:
- one old white sheet
- 3 yards of wide purple ribbon
- double-sided tape
- length of cord
- one of Dad's t-shirts

Directions:

1. Fold the sheet in half lengthwise. Sew, or use the double-sided tape to attach the purple ribbon along one side of the long edge. Trim away any excess ribbon.

2. Put on Dad's t-shirt and use a piece of cord to tie a belt around your waist.

3. Have mom stand behind you, holding the toga by the long straight edge. Have her drape a quarter of the toga over your left shoulder and arm. Push the toga up your arm, so that your hand is free.

4. Bring the rest of the toga around your body, making sure that you go under your right arm. Gather a couple of folds in the toga and tuck them into the waistband securely.

5. Last of all, fold the remaining loose fabric over your left arm. You will need to keep your left arm close to your body to hold it in position. Don't forget to wear the laurel wreath from Chapter 35 and a pair of sandals for the full effect!

CHAPTER THIRTY-SEVEN
The Beginning of Christianity

Encyclopedia Cross-References

Usborne Book of World History: 90
Usborne Internet-Linked Encyclopedia: 192, 193

Kingfisher Illustrated History of the World: 124–129
Kingfisher History Encyclopedia: 72

Review Questions — The Birth of Jesus

What do we call the time of peace and safety in the Roman empire? *The Pax Romana*

What is the other name for the land of Judea? *Canaan*

According to the story from the Gospel of Luke, where was Jesus born? *In Bethlehem*

What holiday celebrates the birth of Jesus? *Christmas*

Who came running to see Jesus after he was born? *Shepherds*

How did they know he had been born? *Angels told them.*

Narration Exercise — The Birth of Jesus

"Canaan was also called Judea. Rome ruled it. Mary lived in Judea. She had Jesus in Bethlehem."

OR

"Jesus was born in Bethlehem. His mother was named Mary. Shepherds came to see him because angels told them to. "

Review Questions — Jesus Crucified and Resurrected

What is Jesus' most famous teaching called? *The Sermon on the Mount*

Do you remember any of the things Jesus taught? *Poor people are blessed; merciful people are blessed; peaceful people are blessed; don't fight back; love your enemies; don't judge other people.*

Why did the Romans get worried about Jesus? *They thought that the Jews would obey Jesus instead of Augustus Caesar.*

What does the Gospel of Luke say happened after Jesus was buried? *He rose from the dead.*

What are followers of Jesus called? *Christians*

Narration Exercise — Jesus Crucified and Resurrected

"Jesus taught people and many followed him. The Romans were afraid that people wouldn't listen to the emperor. They put Jesus to death, but he rose from the dead."

OR

"Jesus was put to death because the Romans didn't want him teaching the people any more. The Gospel says that he rose from the dead. People who believe in Jesus are called Christians."

Additional History Reading

DK Read and Listen: First Bible Story Book, by Mary Hoffman (DK Publishing, 2000). A simplified biblical account. (RA)

The Bible, whichever version your family prefers (try the New International Version for up-to-date language). The story of the birth of Jesus is found in Matthew 1:18–2:18 and Luke 2:1–20; the Beatitudes are found in Matthew 5:1–12; and the story of the death and resurrection of Jesus is found in Matthew 26:47–28:20, Mark 14:43–16:20, Luke 22:47–24:53, and John 18:1–21:25.

The Jesus Story, by Mary Batchelor (Lion Children's, 1999). With detailed illustrations, this book presents the biblical story of Jesus with historical background information. Features include Roman dress, soldiers, architecture, maps, and ships. Also highlights Jewish religious practices of that time regarding marriages, farming, the calendar, and more. (RA)

Corresponding Literature Suggestions

The Very First Christmas, by Paul Maier (Concordia Publishing House, 1998). Following the Luke narrative, this beautifully illustrated look at the first Christmas draws readers into each scene. (RA)

The Parables of Jesus, by Tomie dePaola (Holiday House, 1995). Straightforward retellings of Jesus' parables. (RA)

The Miracles of Jesus, by Tomie dePaola (Holiday House, 1996). Simple, one-page stories about the miracles of Jesus. (RA)

The Very First Easter, by Paul Maier (Concordia Publishing House, 2004). Full-page illustrations and a simple story. (RA)

The Tell-me Stories, Volume I, by Ella K. Lindvall (Moody Press, 2000). Short narratives of the parables Jesus told. (RA)

Jesus is Born, by Claudia Courtney (Concordia Publishing House, 1998). This book and many others by this author are written for the beginning reader and focus on a certain phonetic sound. Titles also include *Rise and Shine: The Story of Easter; Little is Big: Jesus Fed the 5,000; Blow! Jesus Calms the Storm*; and more. (IR)

Map Work

Chapter 37: The Beginning of Christianity (Student Page 107)

1. Find the **Mediterranean Sea** on your map. Color it in blue.

2. Judea was near the coast of the Mediterranean Sea. Jesus was born in Bethlehem, which is in Judea. Circle **Bethlehem** in yellow.

3. Jesus was crucified in Jerusalem. Find **Jerusalem** on your map, and circle it in green.

Coloring Page

The Life of Jesus (Student Page 108)

Projects

Craft Project: Make a Mosaic Cross
The cross became the symbol of eternal life for the people who followed the teachings of Jesus.
Materials for simple mosaic cross:
- cardboard, 9" x 12"
- scissors
- glue
- small square bits of construction paper or tissue paper

Materials for a more complicated mosaic cross:
- cardboard, 9" x 12"
- scissors
- three ceramic tiles (color or colors of your choice)
- paper bag
- hammer
- caulk (tube)
- piping (optional)

Directions:

1. Cut the piece of cardboard into the shape of a cross.

2. Put the tiles into the paper bag and break them into desired sizes with the hammer. Squirt the caulk in small areas on the cardboard and immediately put the broken tiles on the caulk in desired pattern. Continue in this manner, doing small areas until entire cardboard is covered. If you're using the decorative piping, squirt the caulk around the edge of the cross and quickly cover the caulk with the piping to make a finished edge.

   OR

   Spread glue over the surface of the cross. Arrange your construction or tissue paper squares to cover the glue.

   (Special thanks to Sally Keller for project idea and instructions)

Craft Project: Make a Pendant (With a Secret Pocket!)
Materials:
- polymer clay such as Sculpey, light colored
- pencil or pen
- spoon and table knife
- leather necklace cord
- three large beads, your choice of color (optional)
- photocopy of one of the symbols of Jesus and the corresponding verse (Student Page 109)
- glass pie plate

Directions:

1. Symbols are used to remind us of special things we want or need to remember. They can be symbols that keep us safe, like the yellow lines in the road that tell us it is dangerous to pass in that area, or symbols that help us to know where to go, like the symbols for the ladies or men's bathrooms at a restaurant. The people who followed Jesus heard him talk about who he was. Jesus used word pictures that helped the people remember. There are a few of them on Student Page 109.

2. Preheat your oven to 250 degrees. Decide which symbol and verse you want on your pendant. Copy (or scan) it, cutting around the picture and the verse so they are separated.

3. Knead ¼ of the rectangle of clay (it comes packaged in a small rectangle). Roll it out a little larger then the symbol is. Using the end of a pencil, make a hole at the top of your pendant or make a loop on the top. Use a table knife to make the edges smooth, if you want.

4. Place the copied (or scanned) symbol on one side of your pendant rectangle, face down. Rub the back of this paper with a spoon. This is to make sure that there are no air bubbles and the copy is completely touching the clay. Slowly flip your pendant over and on to a glass pie plate. Wrap some more clay around a pencil or pen, sliding it off, forming a small sleeve or pocket. On the back side, attach the clay pocket. It

will be a tiny hiding place. Roll up a small piece of foil and fit it carefully into the sleeve in the back while you're cooking it. This will help the pocket to keep its shape. After you've cooked your pendant, you can roll up the verse and hide it behind in this secret place. Look under your pendant and check to see if your symbol is still placed correctly.

5. Bake for 20 minutes. Let it cool well before touching. It will not feel completely "cooked" right after you pull it out of the oven. However, if it still feels too soft five minutes later, place back in the oven and cook longer.

6. Hang your leather cord around your neck to determine how long you want it to be, adding 3 inches to the amount to account for the knots. Cut and then fold the length in half. Slip the folded looped edge through your pendant's hole just a little ways. Make sure you thread it front to back. Then bring the ends through the loop just on through the hole. Tighten it and make sure it is secure. Slip three large beads down the cord to the pendant. Tie a knot after the last one. Then secure the cord at the end by knotting them together.

7. Slip around your neck and slide your verse into its secret place.

Art Project: The Night With a Brilliant Star
Materials:
- wipe-off or washable crayons OR white board or washable markers
- clean window (sliding glass doors work great!)

Directions:
1. The night Jesus was born offered much excitement! On a big window, recreate the story in a picture of the night Jesus was born with your crayons or markers. Don't forget the shepherds, angels, sheep, Mary, Joseph, and the baby.

2. The crayons or markers will come right off with a damp cloth whenever you are done with it.

Activity Project: Make a "Life of Jesus" Puzzle
Materials:
- Coloring Page
- sheet of thin cardboard
- glue
- scissors
- pencil

Directions:
1. After coloring the picture, spread glue over the back of it. Stick it onto the cardboard sheet and let it dry.

2. Turn the cardboard sheet over and draw a pattern of puzzle pieces on the back.

3. Cut out the pieces along the lines. Now try to reassemble your puzzle!

NOTE: If someone in the family has experience with woodworking equipment and owns a jigsaw, you can also make a puzzle by gluing the picture onto a thin sheet of wood and cutting it into pieces with the jigsaw.

CHAPTER THIRTY-EIGHT
The End of the Ancient Jewish Nation

Encyclopedia Cross-References

Usborne Book of World History: 90

Kingfisher Illustrated History of the World: 110, 111

Usborne Internet-Linked Encyclopedia: N/A

Kingfisher History Encyclopedia: 61

Review Questions — The End of the Ancient Jewish Nation

What Persian king let the Jews go back to their home? *Cyrus*

Who ruled over the Jews then? *The Romans*

Why did the Jews attack the Romans? *They didn't want to pay taxes and obey the Romans.*

What city did the Romans destroy? *Jerusalem*

What did the Romans do the Temple? *They burned it and pulled the stones apart to get the gold and silver inside.*

What happened to the Jewish people then? *They were scattered through all the countries of the world.*

Narration Exercise — The End of the Ancient Jewish Nation

"The Romans made the Jews pay taxes and obey them, so the Jews attacked them. Then the Romans burned Jerusalem and knocked the Temple down. The Jews had to leave their country and didn't come back for a long time."

Additional History Reading

Israel, by Kristen Thoennes (Bridgestone, 1999). A young child's history of Israel. (RA)

First I Say the Shema (Hear, O Israel!), by Molly Cone (URJ Press, 1988). A simple introduction to Judaism. (RA)

Israel in Pictures (Visual Geography Series), by Steve Feinstein (Lerner, 1988). You won't want to read the text to young children, but this book will give them plenty of chances to look at the scenery of Israel. (RA)

Masada, by Neil Waldman (Morrow, 1998). Tells the story of the Jewish revolt against the Romans at the fortress of Masada. This book was designed to be acceptable to younger students, but the story of Masada is a sad and violent one, so be sure to preview it. (RA)

Corresponding Literature Suggestions

Celebrate! Stories of the Jewish Holidays, by Gilda Berger (Scholastic, 2002). Covers the basics of Jewish history through the stories of the holidays. (RA)

Festival of Lights: The Story of Hanukah, by Maida Silverman (Aladdin, 1999). An illustrated account of the Maccabean revolt in the first century. (RA)

Jason's Miracle: A Hanukkah Story, by Beryl Lieff Benderly (Whitman & Co., 2000). Twelve-year-old Jason has ambivalent feelings about Hanukkah until he finds himself transported back to the time of the Maccabean revolt in Judea. (RA)

Shabbat, by Miriam Nerlove (Whitman & Co., 2000). Soft-toned watercolors show a happy traditional family observing Shabbat, the Jewish Sabbath. (IR)

Journeys with Elijah: 8 Tales of the Prophet, by Barbara Diamond Goldin (Gulliver Books, 1999). Presents eight stories about the Old Testament prophet Elijah, set in a variety of time periods and in places all over the world where Jews have lived. (RA)

Miriam's Cup: A Passover Story, by Fran Manushkin (Scholastic, 2006). A Jewish mother preparing for Passover tells her young children the story of Miriam. (RA)

Map Work

Chapter 38: The End of the Ancient Jewish Nation (Student Page 110)

1. On your map, use a green pencil to show the route Abraham took when he left Haran and went to live in Canaan as God instructed him to do.

2. Find **Jerusalem** and circle it with a red pencil. Do you remember what the Romans did to the Temple in Jerusalem?

3. Trace the **Tigris River** and **Euphrates River** in blue.

4. Color the area between the rivers green. Do you remember what this was called? It was called **Mesopotamia**, because it was between the rivers.

Coloring Page

The Star of David (Student Page 111)

Today, the Star of David is the most common symbol for the Jewish people. You can color this star any color you want!

The Star of David is on the flag of the modern Jewish nation, Israel. The upper and lower stripes of the flag and the star are all blue.

Projects

Craft Project: Make a Shabbat "Sand Art" Candle Holder

The word Sabbath comes from the Hebrew word "Shabbat," and means to rest. Shabbat is a weekly celebration; it begins at sun down on Friday, with the lighting of the candles and ends at sun down on Saturday. The lighting of the Shabbat candles is a signal that people should set aside their everyday problems and worries and start taking the time to enjoy the company of their family and friends over a good meal.

Even though you might not be Jewish, you can still make your family's meals a special celebration; a time to enjoy each other and give thanks. Maybe your family could start the tradition of lighting a candle to signal that "family time" has begun. The directions below are for making sand art candlestick holders for your family's table.

Materials:
- sand, plastic bags, food coloring
- 2 baby food jars

Directions:
1. Divide the sand into a different bag for each color. Add several drops of food coloring into each bag, close the plastic bag tightly and knead the color into the sand. Add additional food coloring if you would like to darken the color.

2. Use a spoon to slowly sprinkle the colored sand into the jars, one layer at a time. When you have finished layering the colored sand, carefully push a tapered candle through the sand to the bottom of the jar. The sand will hold the candle firmly.

Craft Project: Make Your Own Dreidel

Hanukkah means "dedication." It is an eight-day holiday that celebrates the victory of Judah Maccabee and his followers over the Syrian King Antiochus. King Antiochus commanded the Jews not to worship God, and dirtied the Temple in Jerusalem. After Judah Maccabee was victorious, his people cleaned the temple and started to rededicate it to God. But they only found enough pure oil to light the menorah for one day. Then a miracle happened, and the oil burned for eight days instead. This is why Hanukkah is celebrated for an eight-day period, so that the Jewish people will never forget the miracle that happened there.

A traditional game played during this holiday is called Dreidel. The Hebrew letters written on each side of the square top stand for the words "A great miracle happened there."

There is an old legend as to why this game is played during Hanukkah. Even though King Antiochus forbade the Jews to study their Bible, which is called the Torah, young Jewish boys would gather together and study it anyway. When they heard soldiers approaching, the boys would hide their Bibles, take out their tops and pretend that they were playing games instead.

Materials:
- paper
- scissors
- glue
- markers and pencil
- dreidel pattern (Student Page 112)

Directions:
1. Cut out the dreidel. If you like, use colored markers to decorate.

2. Fold along each of the solid lines. This will make it easier to glue the tabs down when you shape the dreidel. Place glue on all of the tabs and form into a four-sided top.

3. Insert a pencil in the middle of the X at the top of the dreidel. Get ready to play!

Game instructions:
1. All players need to start out with 10–15 pieces of candy. Each player puts one piece of candy in the middle (or the pot) to start the game off.

2. Then each player takes a turn spinning the dreidel and does what each letter stands for. The 'N' stands for *nisht* and means "nothing." If you land on this you do nothing and pass the dreidel on to the next player. The 'G" stands for *ganz* and means "all." If you land on this you get to take everything that is in the pot. The 'H' stands for *halb* and means "half." If you land on 'H', you get to take half of the candy out of the pot (take an extra one if there is an odd number of candy in the pot). The 'S' stands for *shtel* and means "to put in." When you land on this, you must add a piece of your candy to the pot.

3. When there is only one piece of candy or none left in the pot, each player must add a piece of candy to the pot so the game can continue. The game ends when one person has all the candy.

Cooking Project: Make Hanukkah Latkes

Latkes, or potato pancakes, are another Jewish tradition at Hanukkah. Latkes became part of the tradition, because they are fried in oil, and that helps remind the Jewish people that a little jar of oil burned miraculously for eight days so very long ago. Instructions are on the next page.

Latkes

Ingredients:

- 4 large potatoes, peeled, grated and well drained
- 1 medium onion grated
- 2 beaten eggs
- 1½ teaspoons of salt
- dash of white pepper
- 2 tablespoons all-purpose flour
- vegetable oil

Directions:

1. In a large bowl, combine the potatoes, onions, eggs, salt, pepper, and flour.

2. Heat 1" of oil in a 12" skillet. When the oil is hot, slowly drop a heaping tablespoon of the potato mixture into the oil. For a crisper latke, gently flatten with the back of a spoon. Fry over medium heat for about 3–4 minutes on each side, or until the pancakes are golden brown and crispy.

3. Drain the cooked latkes on paper towels and set them aside in a warm oven. Finish frying the rest of the batter. You may need to add extra oil between batches.

4. When the cooking is completed, sprinkle the hot latkes with sugar or cinnamon, and serve with applesauce, jam, or sour cream.

CHAPTER THIRTY-NINE
Rome and the Christians

Encyclopedia Cross-References

Review Questions — Nero, the Evil Emperor

Where was Nero when Rome burned? *At a party, at a house in the country*

Did he come back to Rome when he heard about the fire? *No, he stayed in the country a little while longer.*

Did Nero help the families who lost their homes? *No*

What did he do instead? *He decided to build a bigger palace where the fire had burned.*

What did the people of Rome think about this? *They were angry with Nero.*

Whom did Nero blame for the fire? *The Christians*

Narration Exercise — Nero, the Evil Emperor

"Nero was a bad emperor. He thought he was a good musician. When Rome burned down, he decided to build a bigger palace. He blamed the Christians for the fire."

OR

"A big fire burned down the poor part of Rome. It burned down some of the rich part too. The emperor Nero blamed Christians for starting the fire. He had them arrested."

Review Questions — Christians in the Catacombs

What man were Romans supposed to worship? *The emperor*

Did Christians worship the emperor? *No*

How were Christians punished? *They were put in prison or forced to fight wild animals.*

Where did Christians have their meetings? *Underground, in secret passages*

What were those secret passages called? *Catacombs*

What secret symbol did the Christians use? *The symbol of a fish*

Narration Exercise — Christians in the Catacombs

"Christians were supposed to worship the emperor, but they said that they wouldn't. Some of the emperors had them arrested or made them fight animals. So the Christians met in secret places called catacombs."

Review Questions — The Emperor Is a Christian!

What god did Constantine worship at first? *Apollo*

Why did he stop persecuting Christians? *He didn't think people should be put in jail because of the god they worshipped.*

What did he see a vision of? *A cross made out of light*

Do you remember what the words underneath the cross said? *By this sign, you will be victor.*

What battle did Constantine's army win? *The Battle of Milvian Bridge*

What happened to Constantine after the victory? *He became a Christian* OR *He built a new capital city.*

Constantine built a new capital city and named it after himself. Do you remember what it was called? *Constantinople*

Narration Exercise — The Emperor is a Christian!

"Roman emperors persecuted Christians. But Constantine thought that was wrong. He said that Christians should be left alone. Then he had a vision of a cross and became a Christian too."

OR

"Constantine and his army were going to a battle. They were very tired and discouraged. Then Constantine saw a cross in the sky. He put the cross on his soldiers' shields, and they won the battle. Then Constantine became a Christian."

Additional History Reading

I Wonder Why Romans Wore Togas? And Other Questions About Ancient Rome, by Fiona MacDonald (Kingfisher, 1997). A good basic review of Roman culture from its beginnings to its final days. (RA)

The Roman Record: Hot News from the Swirling Mists of Time, by Paul Dowswell (EDC Publications, 1998). A slightly tongue-in-cheek look at Roman history, set up like a tabloid sheet. (RA)

A Coloring Book of Ancient Rome (Bellerophon, 1988). Uses actual images from Roman art and architecture. (RA and activity)

Pompeii: Lost and Found, by Mary Pope Osborne, illus. Bonnie Christensen (Knopf Books for Young Readers, 2006). Osborne describes what life would have been like in Pompeii around 79 AD. (RA 2–3, IR 4–5)

Bodies from the Ash: Life and Death in Ancient Pompeii, by James M. Deem (Houghton Mifflin, 2005). Deem aims his retelling of the story toward older students. Parents should preview this book because of the excellent yet graphic photographs of the plaster casts. (IR 4–7)

Corresponding Literature Suggestions

Pompeii ... Buried Alive, by Edith Kunhardt (Random House, 1987). A simple retelling of the fateful days in 79 AD when Mt. Vesuvius erupted and the people in the ancient town of Pompeii perished. (IR for most readers, RA for beginners)

Mystery of the Roman Ransom, by Henry Winterfeld (Odyssey Classics, 2002). The purchase of a slave for their teacher leads a group of Roman schoolboys into a dangerous intrigue. A good book, but intended for slightly older readers; this would be a good, long read-aloud project, especially if older children can read to the younger students.

Corresponding Audiobook Suggestions

Beric the Briton, by G.A. Henty, read by Jim Weiss (Greathall Productions). Beric, a dashing young British chieftain, must fight for liberty from the forests of his homeland, where he defies legendary Roman legions, to the Roman Colosseum, where he must employ gladiatorial skills to defend a persecuted Christian girl. G.A. Henty provides fascinating details of life in a Roman villa, in the imperial palace, and in the villages of the tribal Britons; and accurately shows the strengths that allowed the Romans to conquer their empire and the weaknesses that would end it. Available at www.greathall.com.

Map Work

Chapter 39: Rome and the Christians (Student Page 113)

1. At the time of Nero, the Roman Empire was still very large. On your map, use a green pencil to color in the area that made up the **Roman Empire**. The dashed lines on your map show the borders of the Roman Empire.

2. Color the rest of the land on your map with a red pencil. This shows you the land around the Mediterranean Sea that was not part of the Roman Empire.

3. Shade the seas and oceans on your map lightly in blue.

4. Can you find **Rome**, in Italy, on your map? Some of the catacombs you read about—the ones the Christians hid in—were in Rome.

Coloring Page

The Catacombs Beneath Rome (Student Page 114)

Projects

Art Project: Make Nero's New Crown

Nero was the first emperor to wear a crown with points on it. During his reign, he went mad and started believing that he was a living god. He had the crown fashioned to resemble the one worn by Jupiter, king of the Roman gods. This new style was used by most kings thereafter and is still used to this day.

Materials:
- gold-colored poster board or construction paper
- measuring tape, ruler, pencil, scissors, and tape
- optional: glue, glitter, plastic beads, and jewels

Directions:

1. Measure around your head with a measuring tape, then cut a 3" wide strip of poster board the same length.

2. On the inside of the crown, draw a straight line 1" from the bottom. This line will be used as a guide when laying out the saw tooth (/\/\/\/\) pattern at the top of the crown.

3. With a ruler, draw the lines for your teeth. Start in the middle and work out towards each edge. After the lines have been drawn, have Mom cut the pattern out.

4. If you would like to add more decoration to your crown, this is the time to do it. Otherwise, fold the points down towards the outside. Use the guideline from step 2, to make the folds even. When the crown ends are joined together with tape, this will give the effect of a sun burst.

Craft Project: Make a Salt Dough Map of Italy

Materials:
- thin cardboard or posterboard
- white flour, salt, and water
- pencil and paints
- "I" encyclopedia, or globe with geographical features marked on it

Directions:

1. On the cardboard, draw an outline of Italy. You can use the map from Chapter 27 as a pattern.

2. Mix two parts flour with two parts salt to approximately one part water. Add the water a little at a time until a thick paste has formed.

3. Spread the dough onto the outline.

4. Consult your encyclopedia or globe. Do you see the mountains of Italy? Make peaks where the mountain ranges belong.

5. Dry thoroughly and then paint. Don't forget to paint in the Rubicon and the Tiber!

Activity Project: Make a Secret Symbol

The Christians in Rome used the fish as their secret symbol. Make a secret symbol for your family.

Materials:
- paper
- crayons or pencils
- tape
- scissors

Directions:

1. Decide what your family symbol will be. It could have to do with your last name, like this:

   Long—a long line
   Rainey—rain drop
   Wise—owl
   Johnson—a man ("John") and his little boy ("son")
   Smith—a hammer (like a blacksmith uses)

   It could have to do with where you live, for example:

   trees
   cactus
   seashore
   mountains or hills

   It could be a favorite hobby, for example:

   music—musical note
   baseball—ball

2. Draw your symbol on several pieces of paper.

3. Cut your symbol out and leave it around the house (tape it to the bathroom mirror or to your father's dresser). In ancient Rome, the Christians drew a fish symbol to let other Christians know that they were present. What happens when your parents find your symbol? Do they know what it means?

Activity Project: Make a Catacomb

Materials:
- sheets
- flashlight
- secret symbol from previous project
- tape

Directions:

1. Make a catacomb (or cave) using sheets draped over tables and chairs.

2. Tape your family symbol signs on the walls of the catacomb.

3. Using your flashlight, pretend you are visiting the Roman catacombs and locate the signs. Optional: Invite extended family and friends over. See if they can identify what the signs mean.

Craft Project: Make Your Own Lyre
Materials:

- cardboard egg carton (a half-dozen carton can also be used)
- 4 feet of pencil-thick dowel
- scissors, paintbrush, paints, pipe cleaners
- rubber bands or fishing line
- hot glue gun

Directions:

1. Remove and discard the lid from your egg carton, then cut the carton in half. This will leave you with a rectangular six-egg section that will be used as the body of the lyre. Turning the carton bottom side up, use your paints to decorate the lyre body and allow it to dry completely.

2. Place your carton painted side up. Use a pair of scissors to punch a hole on the outside bottom of the top two eggcups. These holes should be made in the middle of each cup. Insert a length of dowelling through these holes, having it extend about a ¼" on either side of carton.

3. To make the lyre's neck, turn the carton painted side down. Take a 12" length of dowelling and attach it to the short dowel at each side of the carton. The dowels should angle out a bit, instead of being straight up and down. Do this using a hot glue gun and a length of pipe cleaner. Let this dry completely before continuing.

4. Attach another 12-inch dowel horizontally across the lyre neck dowels, about 1 ½" from the top. This will make a triangular shape. Again, do this with a hot glue gun and a length of pipe cleaner. Once the glue has dried, the child can decorate the dowels with paint.

5. When the paint has dried, string the lyre, by attaching 7 lengths of fishing line (or rubber bands that have been cut in half) from the top dowel to the smaller dowel secured in the egg carton. The picture above gives an example of how your lyre should look.

Craft Project: Make Constantine's Shield
Materials:

- cardboard
- scissors
- glue
- stapler (use brads if cardboard is too thick)
- construction paper
- black marker

Directions:

1. Cut out a large rectangle or circle from the cardboard for the shield. Cut a long strip of cardboard to use as a strap to carry the shield.

2. Constantine ordered all of his soldiers to put the monogram for Christ on their shields. The monogram for Christ is *Chi Rho*, which are the first two letters, in Greek, of the word "Christ." These Greek letters look like the letters "X" and "P" in the English alphabet. Make an X P on shield.

3. Cut out designs in the construction paper and decorate the rest of the shield. Attach strap to back of shield. Let dry.

Cooking Project: Make an Edible Shield Cheesecake

<u>Cheesecake</u>

Ingredients:

- 1 graham cracker pie crust
- 2 8 oz. packages cream cheese (do not use low-fat)
- 1 14 oz. can sweetened condensed milk
- 2–3 capfuls of lemon juice concentrate

Directions:

1. Mix cream cheese, condensed milk, and lemon juice together. Pour into crust. Refrigerate at least 2 hours.

2. On top, using cherries, strawberries or some other topping, design the monogram for Christ. Enjoy!

CHAPTER FORTY
Rome Begins to Weaken

Encyclopedia Cross-References

Usborne Book of World History: 90, 91

Usborne Internet-Linked Encyclopedia: 194

Kingfisher Illustrated History of the World: 140, 141

Kingfisher History Encyclopedia: 80, 81

Review Questions — The British Rebellion

Do you remember the names of two strong, powerful leaders of Rome? *Julius Caesar and Caesar Augustus*

Were the emperors after them strong too? *No, many were weak.*

Who lived in Britain? *The Celts*

Did Rome control all of Britain? *No, only part of it.*

Who was the leader of the rebellious Celts in our story? *Boadicea*

Why were the Romans embarrassed to be beaten by Boadicea? *Because she was a woman*

Do you remember any of the strange things that were supposed to have happened when the Celts were attacking the Romans? Acceptable answers include: *The statue of Victory fell face down, the sea turned red, a ghost town in ruins was seen near Londinium, yells came from an empty theatre.*

Were there more Romans or more Celts? *Celts*

Why did the Romans win? *They obeyed their general and fought together.*

Narration Exercise — The British Rebellion

"The Romans tried to rule Britain. But the people who lived there didn't like the Romans. They were Celts. Their leader was a woman. The Celts fought Rome, but they lost."

OR

"The Celts lived in Britain. Their leader was named Boadicea. She led them against Rome. They lost, but Rome had to leave Britain anyway."

Review Questions — Rome Divided in Two

Why couldn't the Roman soldiers defend all the borders of Rome? *It was too big!*

How did the emperor Diocletian try to protect the huge empire of Rome? *He divided it into two pieces.*

What were the two parts of the Roman empire called? *The Western Roman Empire and the Eastern Roman Empire*

What city was the capital of the Western Roman Empire? *Rome*

What city was the capital of the Eastern Roman Empire? You can look on your map as you answer. *Constantinople*

Which city got to be rich and powerful? *Constantinople*

Which city grew poor and shabby? *Rome*

Who invaded the Western Roman Empire? *Barbarians*

Narration Exercise — Rome Divided in Two

"Rome got too big for one emperor. So it was split into two parts. The two parts were the Eastern Roman Empire and the Western Roman Empire. Barbarians invaded the west."

OR

"Rome got so big that it split into two parts. Rome was the capital of the west part. Constantinople was the capital of the east part. The east got richer and the west got poorer."

Additional History Reading

The Celts (See Through History series), by Hazel Mary Martell (Viking, 1996). Transparent panels peel away so that you can see inside Celtic buildings. (RA)

Raiders of the North: Discover the Dramatic World of the Celts and Vikings, by Philip Steele (Southwater Publishers, 2001). Focuses on the warlike nature of the Celts. (RA)

Life in Celtic Times, by A.G. Smith (Dover, 1997). Focuses on the culture of the ancient Celts. (RA)

The Ancient Celts, by Patricia Calvert (Franklin Watts, 2005). An excellent guide to the Celts during Roman times, with many illustrations and a good clear explanation of the earliest Celtic tribes and their origins. (RA 1–3, IR 3–6)

Corresponding Literature Suggestions

Celtic Fairy Tales, by Joseph Jacobs (Kessinger, 2003). A standard collection of wonderful tales. (RA)

Celtic Fairy Tales, by Neil Philip (Viking, 1999). A more recent collection, beautifully illustrated in the style of the *Book of Kells*, with gold-leaf borders. (RA)

Celtic Memories, by Caitlin Matthews (Barefoot, 2003). Twelve traditional Celtic tales, suitable for reading aloud. (RA 1–3, IR 3–5)

Map Work

Chapter 40: Rome Begins to Weaken (Student Page 115)

1. On your map, color the **Eastern Roman Empire** yellow. East is *right* on your map.

2. Do you remember the capital city of the Eastern Roman Empire? It was Constantinople. Find **Constantinople** on your map.

3. Color the **Western Roman Empire** blue. West is to your left.

4. Do you remember the capital city of the Western Roman Empire? It was Rome. Find **Rome** on your map.

5. Which half of the Roman Empire became the richer one? Which became the poorer, weaker one?

Coloring Page

Boadicea in Her Chariot (Student Page 116)

Projects

Activity Project: North, South, East, West

The Roman Empire was divided into two sections, the Eastern Roman Empire and the Western Roman Empire. Can you find east and west?

Materials:
- chalk
- a sunny day

Directions:

1. Outside in an open area, draw a large circle in chalk. Early in the morning, stand in center of circle and face the sun. Mark an E for east on the side of the circle that you are facing.

2. West is behind you. Turn all the way around and face west. Mark a W on that side of the circle.

3. Now turn so that the E is on your right hand, and the W is on your left. You are facing north. Mark an N on the north side of the circle.

4. Now south is behind you. Turn completely around and mark an S on the circle behind you.

(NOTE: this activity will not be precisely accurate, but you can come close!)

Craft Project: Design a Celtic Border

The Celtic people were known for beautiful, intricate patterns, like the pattern around the border of your coloring picture. You can design a border too!

Materials:

- white paper and crayons or markers
  OR
- white cloth and fabric markers

Directions:

1. Practice making one or more of the designs below on a scrap piece of paper.

2. Draw a border around your paper or cloth. Have your parent help you to make this border about 4 inches wide.

3. Draw your design over and over again in a line around your border. You can alternate two or more designs, if you want to. Your Celtic border should look a little bit like the border around the picture of Boadicea in her chariot.

Activity Project: Have a Celtic Feast

The Celts had great feasts for their warriors to celebrate victories in battles. Borrow some traditional Celtic music from the library, appoint someone to be the "bard" (the person who tells stories or poems about the Celtic heroes), have them narrate the story of Boadicea or another Celtic tale, and enjoy some simple food. Be sure to eat it with your hands! No silverware allowed!

roasted chicken
wine (better use grape juice!)
berries
plain bread with no butter

CHAPTER FORTY-ONE
The Attacking Barbarians

Encyclopedia Cross-References

Usborne Book of World History: 90–93

Usborne Internet-Linked Encyclopedia: 194, 195

Kingfisher Illustrated History of the World: 142–145

Kingfisher History Encyclopedia: 80–83

Review Questions — Attila the Hun

What do we call the barbarians who came from central Asia? *Huns*

Who was their leader? *Attila*

Who was Honoria? *The sister of the Western Roman Emperor*

Why did she send Attila a letter, offering to marry him? *Because she wanted to get away from the Roman court*

What did Attila do when he got the letter? *He invaded Italy.*

Why did Attila agree to leave Italy? *The Western Roman Emperor paid him to leave.*

Narration Exercise — Attila the Hun

"Attila the Hun was the leader of the Huns. He tried to conquer the Western Roman Empire, but the Emperor paid him to leave. He died of a nosebleed."

OR

"The Huns were barbarians. Their leader was Attila. The Emperor's sister wanted to marry him, but she didn't. Attila came all the way to Italy."

Review Questions — Stilicho, Roman and Barbarian

What barbarian tribe invaded the Western Roman Empire? *The Visigoths*

How long did it take them to fight the barbarians? *Years and years*

Were the Romans able to beat the Visigoths? *No*

How did they finally convince the Visigoths to go away? *The Romans paid them 4000 pounds of gold.*

Why were people suspicious of Stilicho? *Because his father was a barbarian*

Was he a good Roman, or not? *Yes, he was.*

What happened to him? *He was executed.*

Narration Exercise — Stilicho, Roman and Barbarian

"The Visigoths invaded Rome. Stilicho fought against them. He had to pay them to leave. But the Romans had him killed."

OR

"Stilicho was part barbarian and part Roman. He fought the Visigoths. But people didn't like him because he was a barbarian. He was executed."

Review Questions — The Coming of the Visigoths

What was the first barbarian tribe to invade the city of Rome? *The Visigoths*

What was the second tribe? *The Vandals*

Which tribe was worse? *The Vandals*

Why didn't the Visigoths burn the churches of Rome? *Because some of them were Christian*

Where was the Emperor when Rome was invaded? *He had gone away to a city in a swamp.*

Why didn't the Eastern Roman Emperor send help? *He was afraid of the barbarians invading his own city.*

Narration Exercise — The Coming of the Visigoths

"The Visigoths invaded Rome and took gold. Then the Vandals came and destroyed Rome. They were worse." OR

"Barbarians invaded Rome. The Eastern Roman Emperor wouldn't help. The Western Roman Emperor ran away to a swamp where he was safe."

Additional History Reading

Note: Many of the previously recommended titles also contain sections on the barbarian invasions.

Ten Kings: And the Worlds They Ruled, by Milton Metzger (Orchard, 2002). Brief and interesting biographical sketches of ten rulers, from Hammurabi through Peter the Great of Russia. Includes Attila the Hun. The tone is aimed towards upper elementary-school students. **Out of print; check your local library.** (RA 3–4, IR 4–6)

Corresponding Literature Suggestions

Why Are You Calling Me a Barbarian? by Birgitta Petren (J. Paul Getty Museum Publications, 2000). A Roman child makes friends with the child of a barbarian. (RA)

Map Work

Chapter 41: The Attacking Barbarians (Student Page 117)

1. Look back at your map from the last chapter. The Huns attacked the Roman Empires from the area north of the Black Sea. (North is *up* on your map.) Find "**HUNS**" in this area on your map. Draw an arrow from the word HUNS to the border of the Western Roman Empire (to the north of Rome).

2. The Visigoths came from the area we now call Germany. Find "**VISIGOTHS**" on your map. Draw a line from VISIGOTHS down to Rome.

3. The Vandals came from France and north Africa. Find "**VANDALS**" next to France, and find Africa on your map. Draw lines from the VANDALS down to Rome.

Coloring Page

A Visigoth Invader (Student Page 118)

Projects

Craft Project: Make Barbarian Bracelets

The barbarians often wore thick, heavy jewelry. These bracelets served as armor as well as decoration—they could stop a sword!

Materials:

- aluminum foil
- posterboard or thin cardboard
- glue or tape
- scissors
- measuring tape

Directions:

1. Measure around the upper part of your arm.

2. Cut a length of cardboard or posterboard 3 inch wide and as long as your arm measurement, plus two extra inches.

3. Cover the cardboard or posterboard strip with aluminum foil. Tape the foil on the inside to secure it.

4. Bend the foil-covered strip into a circle. Overlap it 1 inch on each end. Tape the ends securely.

5. Push the bracelet onto your upper arm until it stays firmly.

6. Repeat for your arm above the elbow and your forearm. Now you have three bracelets—you look like a barbarian!

Activity Project: Reassemble a Roman Pot

When the barbarians invaded, they destroyed much of Rome—they broke everything they could get their hands on! Centuries later, archaeologists dug in the ruins of Rome to find out more about the invasion. They had to put back together the things that the barbarians broke! Try to be an archaeologist and reassemble a Roman artifact.

Materials:

- pot or dish that your mother will let you break (NOT glass—pottery is best; an old flowerpot works very well. Be sure not to look at it! Ask your mother to choose it herself.)
- glue

Directions:

1. Archaeologists don't know what their artifacts will look like—all they see are the ruined pieces! So don't look at the dish or pot. Ask your mother to take it away and break it. She should be careful to pick out tiny splinters that might hurt you. Ask her to put the pieces into a paper bag.

2. Now it's your turn to figure out how the pot looked before the "barbarian" broke it! Can you reassemble the pieces with your glue? Ask your mother whether your reassembled pot or dish looks like the original.

Art Project: Draw a Picture of Attila the Hun

The great historian Edward Gibbon wrote this description of Attila the Hun in his book *The Decline and Fall of the Roman Empire*. Listen: "[Attila had] a large head, a swarthy complexion, small, deep-seated eyes, a flat nose, a few hairs in the place of a beard, broad shoulders, and a short square body, of a nervous strength, though of a disproportioned form. The haughty step and demeanour of the king of the Huns expressed the consciousness of his superiority above the rest of mankind; and he had a custom of fiercely rolling his eyes, as if he wished to enjoy the terror which he inspired."

Can you draw a picture of Attila that fits this description?

CHAPTER FORTY-TWO
The End of Rome

Encyclopedia Cross-References

Usborne Book of World History: 90–93
Usborne Internet-Linked Encyclopedia: 194, 195

Kingfisher Illustrated History of the World: 142–145
Kingfisher History Encyclopedia: 80–83

Review Questions — The Last Roman Emperor

Why did the Roman people call Romulus Augustus "Little disgrace"? *They didn't want to obey a child who was also a barbarian.*

How old was he when he became Emperor? *Six*

What happened to him, after he was removed from the throne? *He was sent to live in another city.*

Was there another Roman Emperor after him? *No. He was the last Roman emperor.*

What happened to the Western Roman Empire? *It disappeared. Barbarians lived there.*

What happened to the Eastern Roman Empire? *It was called the "Byzantine Empire."*

Narration Exercise — The Last Roman Emperor

"The last Roman emperor was only six years old. After he left his throne, there were no more emperors. That was the end of the Roman empire."

OR

"The Western Roman Empire ended and barbarian lived there. The Eastern Roman Empire was called a different name. The last Roman emperor was only six. He was called 'Little Disgrace'."

Review Questions — The Gifts of Rome

Can you tell me three things that we got from the Romans? *Books, swimming pools, coins, names of months, names of planets*

Can you tell me two words that come from Latin? *Flower, P.S., ship, library, family, refrigerator* (Names of months and planets are also acceptable.)

Narration Exercise — The Gifts of Rome

"The Roman Empire is gone, but we still use Roman words. We also use Roman things like books and swimming pools."

OR

"The Romans spoke Latin. Some of our English words come from Latin, like flower, navy, and ship."

Additional History Reading

Ancient Rome: See Through History, by Simon James (Viking, 1992). Peel-away sheets reveal the insides of Roman buildings. (RA)

Science in Ancient Rome, by Jacqueline L. Harris (Franklin Watts, 1998). Overview of the scientific advances made during the Roman era. (RA)

Corresponding Literature Suggestions

Cattus Petasatus: The Cat in the Hat in Latin, by Dr. Seuss and Jennifer Morish Tunberg (Bolchazy Carducci, 2000). Just for fun, look through this book together and see if you can spot familiar words that are almost the same in Latin as in English. English borrowed those words from Latin! (RA)

Quomodo Invidiosulus Nomine Grinchus Christi Natalem Abrogaverit: How the Grinch Stole Christmas in Latin, by Dr. Seuss and Terence O. Tunberg (Bolchazy Carducci, 1998). Try the same experiment with this familiar book. (RA)

Virent Ova! Viret Perna!!: Green Eggs and Ham in Latin, by Dr. Seuss and Terence O. Tunberg (Bolchazy Carucci, 2003). One more for fun. (RA)

Map Work

Chapter 42: The End of Rome (Student Page 119)

1. Let's review what we've learned. On your map, can you identify the continents of **North America, South America, Europe, Asia,** and **Africa?**

2. Can you find the **Mediterranean Sea?**

3. Where is **Italy?**

4. Where is **Britain?**

5. Where is **China?**

6. Where is **India?**

7. Where is the **Nile River?**

8. Where is **Central America?**

Projects

Craft Project: Make the Emperor's Scepter
Materials:
- length of dowel
- tennis ball
- spray paint
- glue
- jewels (or other decorations)

Directions

1. (Parent) Using a sharp knife, cut a small hole in the tennis ball.

2. Slide dowel into the tennis ball. The fit should be snug. If too loose, hot glue in place.

3. Take it outside and lay on newspaper. Spray paint one side and let dry. Turn over and paint the other side.

4. Decorate with jewels or other decorations.

(Optional) Attach a star or other design instead of a tennis ball.

Craft Project: Make a "Gifts of Rome" Collage

Materials:

- posterboard
- scissors
- glue
- magazines
- crayons or markers

Directions:

Make a collage depicting the gifts of Rome. Use the list in *The Story of the World*. Cut pictures out of magazines, print pictures from clipart or the Internet, or draw pictures.

Activity Project: Have a Roman Party

You have just completed your year of Ancient History and it is time to celebrate! A great way of doing that would be to have a Roman party. Roman parties were very elaborate affairs. Guests would sit on couches and share food that had been set on a table between them. Many different courses were served at these feasts, sometimes as many as 40. How could anyone eat that much food at one time? Romans also loved drinking wine while they ate their meals, but I think we will have grape juice or sparkling cider instead!

Make this a grand affair by gathering all of your saved projects from previous chapters and displaying them on a separate table. Be sure to invite some guests.

Directions:

1. Prepare a place for the feast.

2. Plan and make the food.

3. Dress up in your toga (Chapter 38), crown (Chapter 35), and scepter (Chapter 42).

The type of food you might have are breads, salads, a meat dish, fresh fruit, and desserts. You can also make honeyed dates—a classic Mediterranean dish.

<u>Honeyed Dates</u>

Materials and Ingredients:

- chopping board
- frying pan
- food processor or grinder
- pitted dates
- walnuts, pecans, and almonds
- ½ cup of honey

Directions:

1. Carefully slit open the side of each date. Be careful not to cut all the way through the date.

2. Use the food processor or grinder to chop the nuts into fine pieces. Stuff a small amount of the nut mixture into each date.

3. Pour some salt on the chopping board and lightly roll each date in it. Make sure that you don't use too much salt.

4. On low heat, melt the honey in the frying pan. Lightly fry the dates for about 5 minutes, turning them with a spoon while they cook.

5. Place the fried dates on a serving dish and sprinkle with more of the chopped nuts.

Chapter 1: The Earliest People

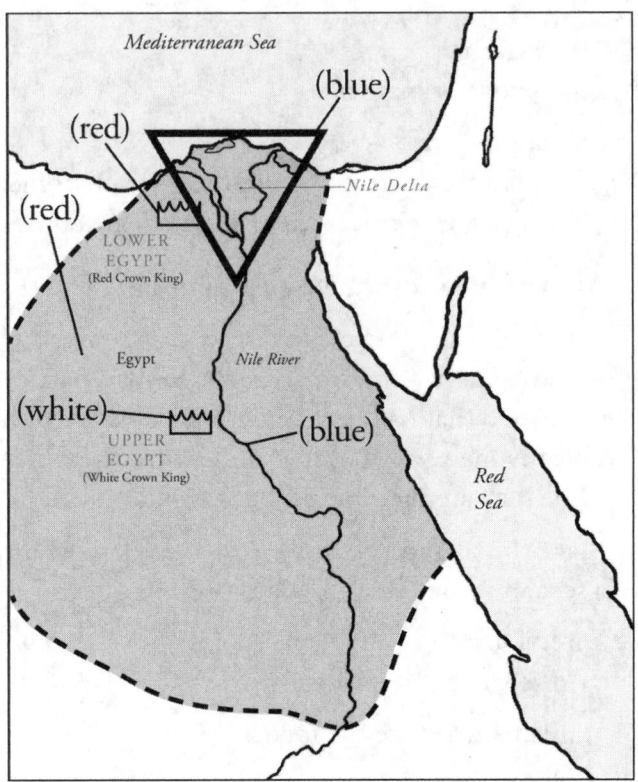

Chapter 2: Egyptians Lived on the Nile River

Chapter 3: The First Writing

Chapter 4: The Old Kingdom of Egypt

Chapter 5: The First Sumerian Dictator

Chapter 6: The Jewish People

Chapter 7: Hammurabi and the Babylonians

Chapter 8: The Assyrians

Chapter 9: The First Cities of India

Chapter 10: The Far East: Ancient China

Chapter 11: Ancient Africa

Chapter 12: The Middle Kingdom of Egypt

Chapter 13: The New Kingdom of Egypt

Chapter 14: The Israelites Leave Egypt

Chapter 15: The Phoenicians

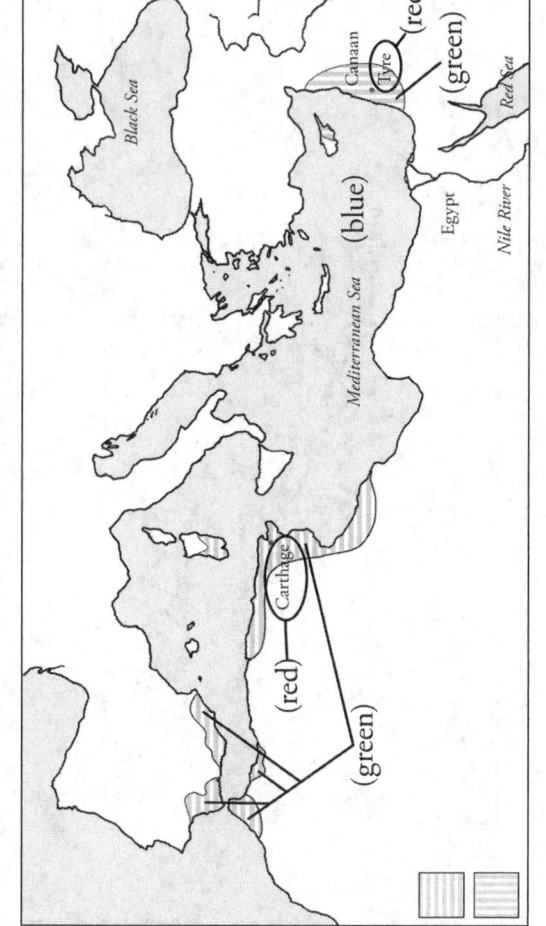

Chapter 16: The Return of Assyria

Chapter 17: Babylon Takes Over Again

Chapter 18: Life in Early Crete

Chapter 19: The Early Greeks

Chapter 20: Greece Gets Civilized Again

Chapter 21: The Medes and the Persians

Chapter 22: Sparta and Athens

Chapter 23: The Greek Gods

Chapter 24: The Wars of the Greeks

Chapter 25: Alexander the Great

(blue)

Indus River

Arabian Sea

(red)

Caspian Sea

(blue)

Tigris River

Persian Gulf

Euphrates River

(red)

Red Sea

Black Sea

Alexandria

Mediterranean Sea

Nile River

Egypt

(blue)

Chapter 26: The People of the Americas

(North America = third color)

(Central America = second color)

(South America = favorite color)

Chapter 27: The Rise of Rome

Rome

(blue)

(red)

Sicily

Mediterranean Sea

Chapter 28: The Roman Empire

Rome

(blue)

(red)

Sicily

Mediterranean Sea

Chapter 29: Rome's War With Carthage

(red)
Gaul
the Alps
Spain
Italy
Rome
(red)
Mediterranean Sea
Carthage
(red)

Chapter 30: The Aryans of India

(red)
Indus River
(green)
(red)
Ganges River
(blue)
India
(blue)
Arabian Sea
Bay of Bengal
(blue)
(blue)
INDIAN OCEAN

Chapter 31: The Mauryan Empire of India

(red)
Indus River
(green)
(red)
Ganges River
(blue)
India
(blue)
Arabian Sea
Bay of Bengal
(blue)
(blue)
INDIAN OCEAN

Chapter 32: China: Writing and the Qin

Yellow Sea (blue)
East China Sea (blue)
(blue)
South China Sea (blue)
(red)
Yellow River
(blue)
Yangtze River
(red)
(green)
China
(brown)
The Great Wall

Chapter 34: The Rise of Julius Caesar

Gaul

Spain

the Alps

(blue)

Tiber River

Rome

(red)

(pink)

(pink)

(pink)

(pink)

Mediterranean Sea

(blue)

Chapter 35: Caesar the Hero

(red)

Britain

Gaul

Spain

the Alps

(blue)

Rubicon River

Tiber River

Rome

Mediterranean Sea

(red)

Egypt

(blue)

Nile River

Chapter 36: The First Roman Prince

(green)

Rome

Mediterranean Sea

(blue)

X·Egypt

Chapter 37: The Beginning of Christianity

Mediterranean Sea

(blue)

Nazareth

Jerusalem

Bethlehem

(green)

(yellow)

Chapter 38: The End of the Ancient Jewish Nation

Chapter 39: Rome and the Christians

Chapter 40: Rome Begins to Weaken

Chapter 41: The Attacking Barbarians

Chapter 42: The End of Rome

The Story of the World
Activity Book, Volume One

Student Pages

WELL-
TRAINED
MIND
PRESS

www.welltrainedmind.com

$11.95
ISBN 978-1-933339-15-3
51195>

9 781933 339153

A Note to Parents (Preview Notice)

Please preview the coloring pages for chapters 17, 20, and 28 (Student Pages 50, 58, and 87), to make sure that they are appropriate for your family.

The History of My Family

by _____

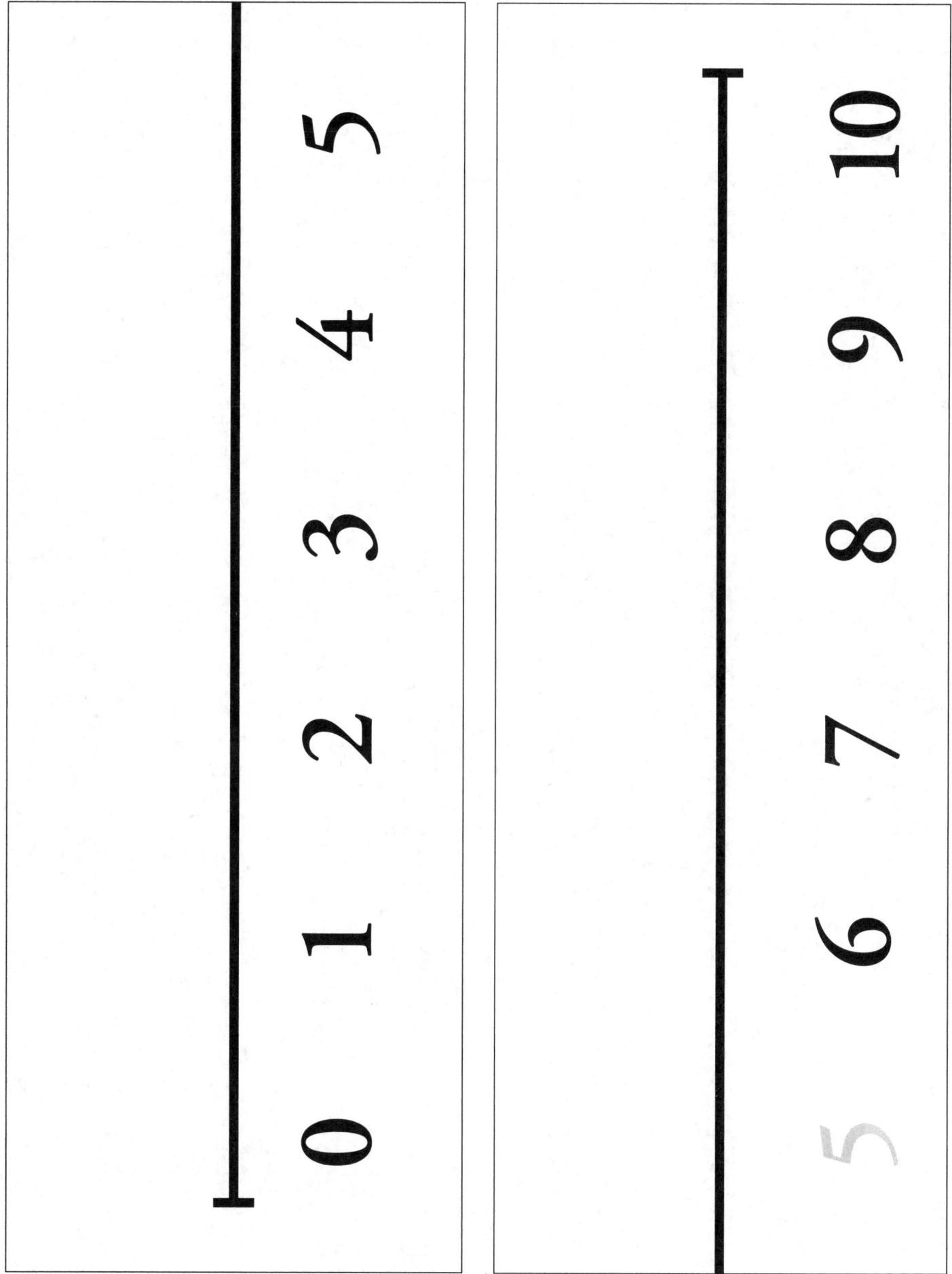

Name _____

Date _____

Chapter 2: Egyptians Lived on the Nile River

Mediterranean Sea

Nile Delta

LOWER
EGYPT
(Red Crown King)

Egypt

Nile River

UPPER
EGYPT
(White Crown King)

*Red
Sea*

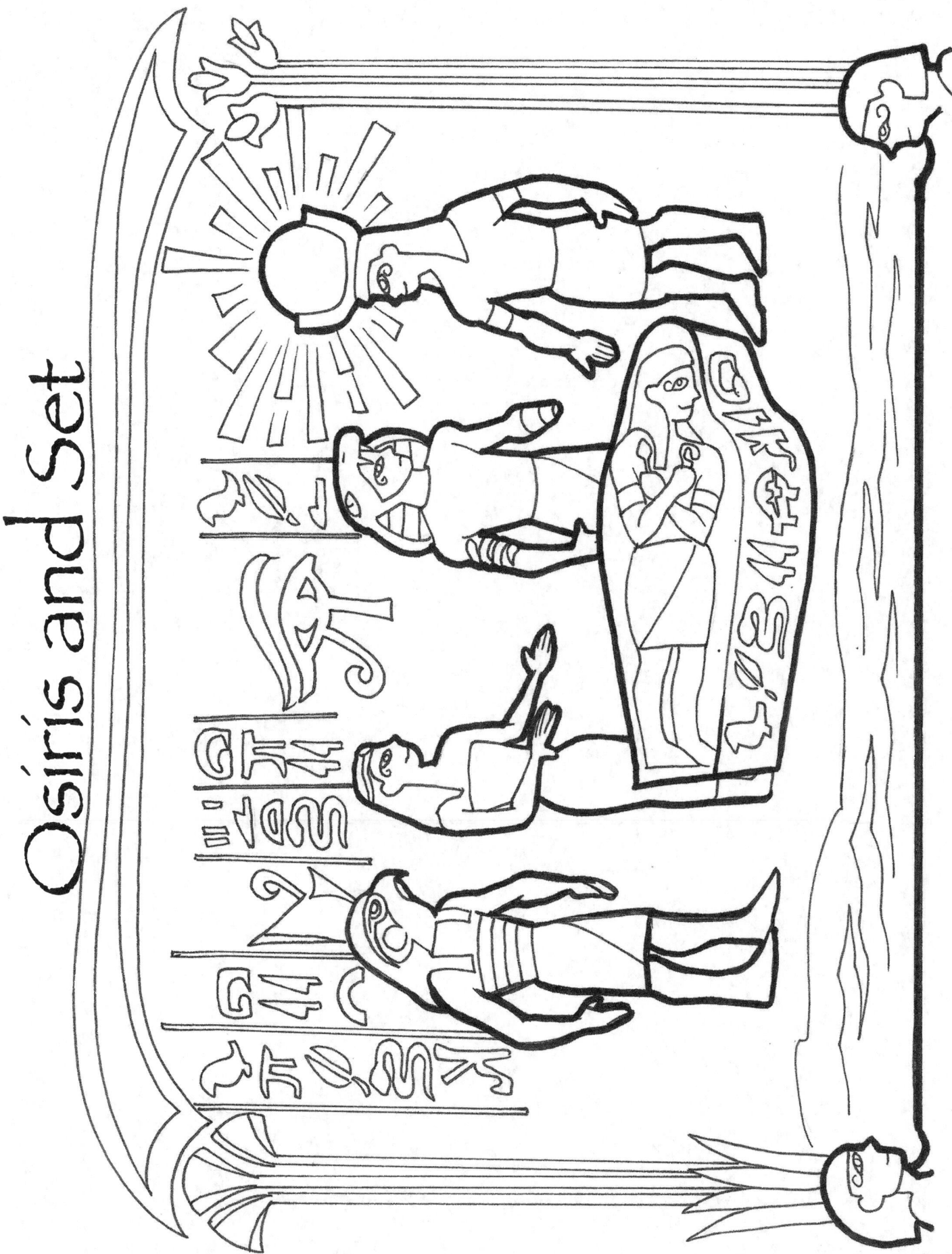

Osiris and Set

Chapter 3: The First Writing

Carving Hieroglyphs

Cuneiform Chart

Hieroglyph Chart

Chapter 4: The Old Kingdom of Egypt

The Pyramids of Egypt

Name _____

Date _____

Chapter 5: The First Sumerian Dictator

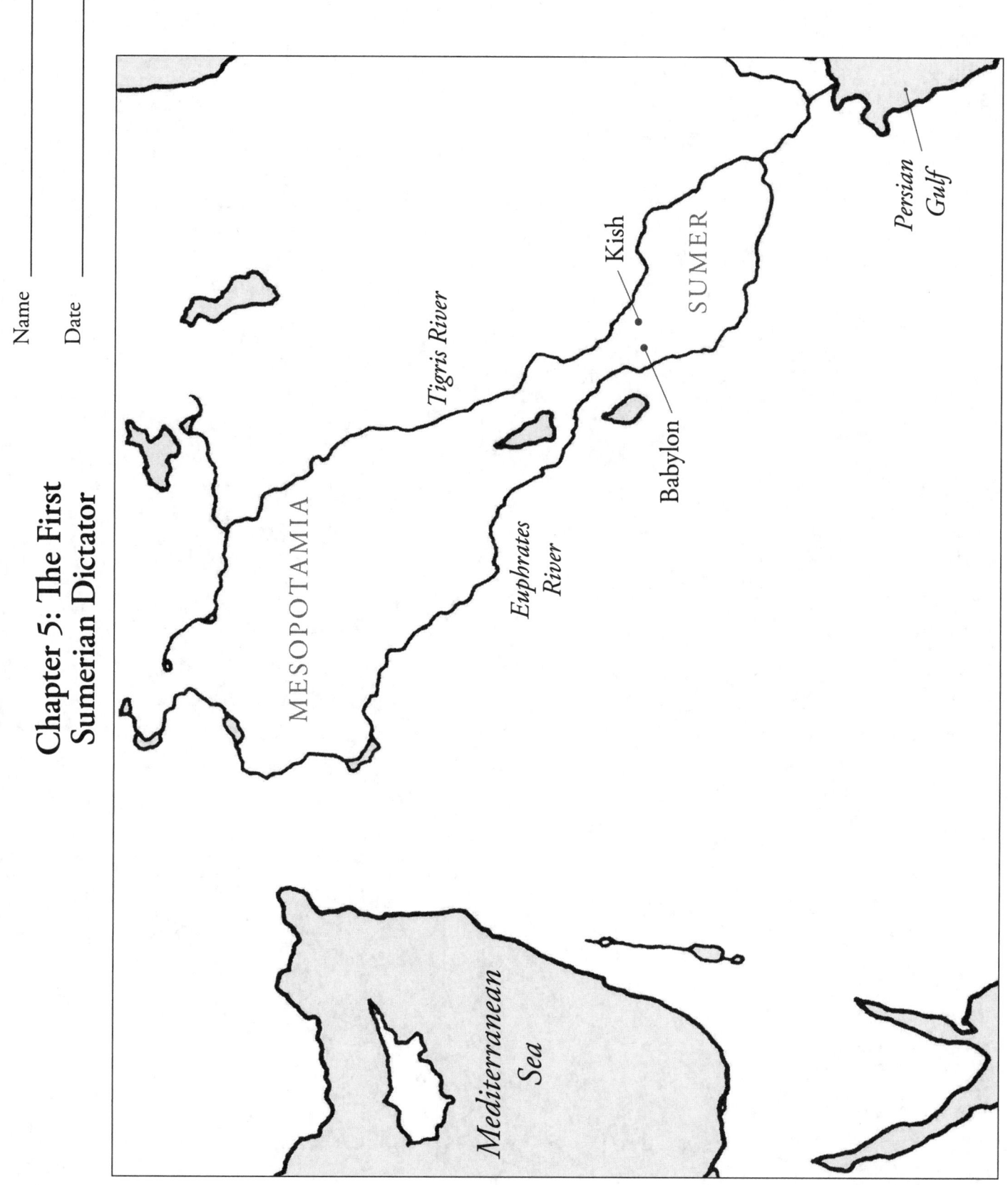

MESOPOTAMIA

Tigris River

Euphrates River

Kish

Babylon

SUMER

Persian Gulf

Mediterranean Sea

Sargon
King of Mesopotamia

Sumerian Inventions Word Search

Find the following hidden words:
wheel, shaduf, clock, pottery, hour, numbers,
minute, calendar, cuneiforms, sumer

N	E	M	R	V	S	U	M	E	R	J	P
G	R	A	N	H	H	A	R	F	N	B	R
A	W	E	U	Y	A	A	L	N	K	T	I
E	H	I	M	I	D	R	P	C	S	T	A
K	E	N	B	N	U	E	O	E	S	C	E
Z	E	G	E	F	F	L	T	S	O	I	M
O	L	L	R	R	C	U	T	H	S	P	L
E	A	L	S	T	N	N	E	G	N	H	T
C	U	N	E	I	F	O	R	M	S	V	R
Z	T	T	M	T	C	U	Y	E	C	O	H
N	H	M	P	G	O	R	E	U	D	S	E
F	D	E	E	H	O	S	U	E	K	G	S

Chapter 6: The Jewish People

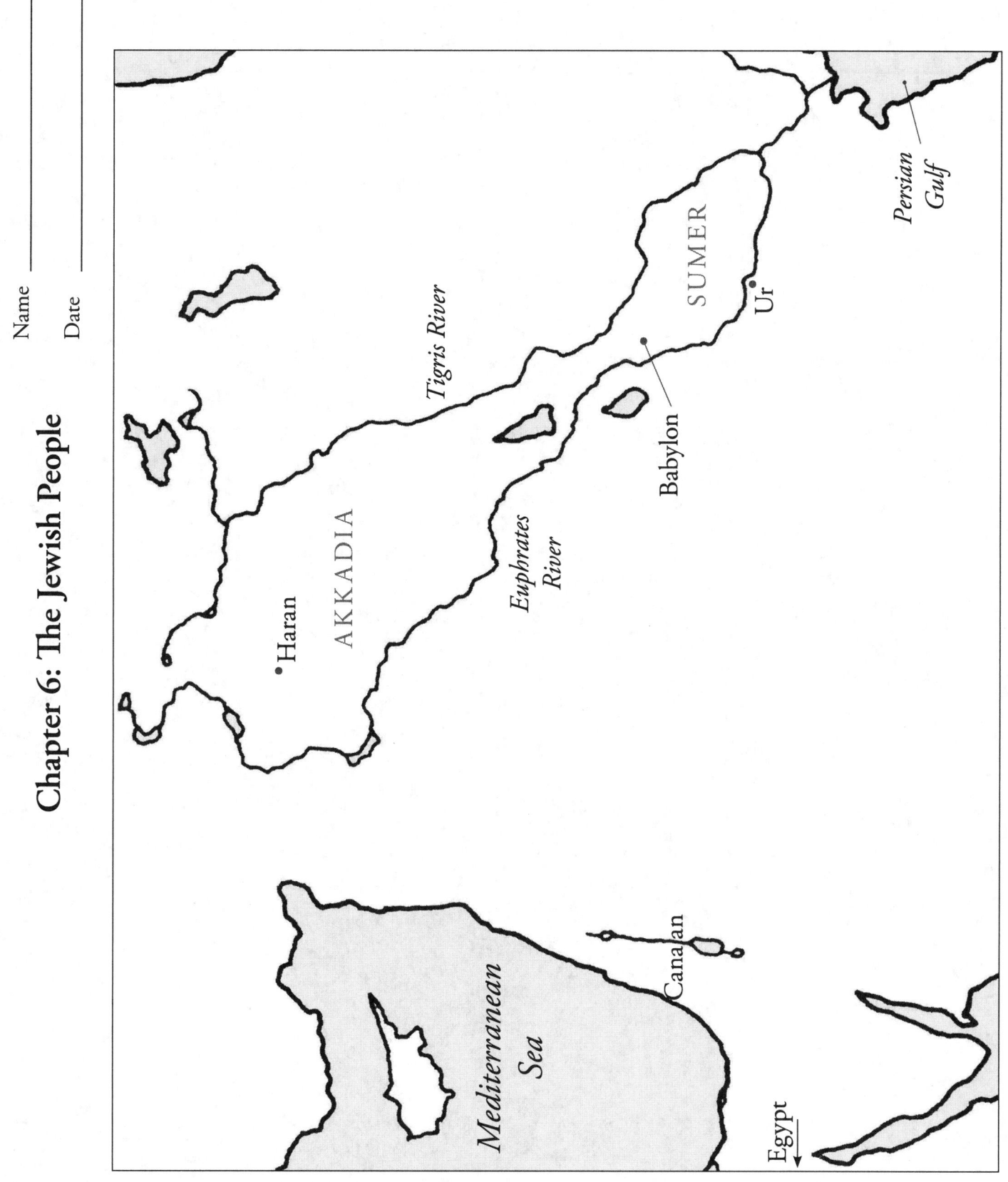

Name _____

Date _____

The Jewish People Word Search

Directions:

1. Solve the following clues, and write the answers in the spaces provided.
2. All the answer words from the clues are in the word search and run from left to right, top to bottom, or diagonally. Find them now.

Clues:

1. Sargon the Great was a ruler of this river-side city-state where Terah and his family first lived. _ _
2. The name of Abram's father. _ _ _ _ _
3. The threat of war with Babylon caused Terah to decide to move from his hometown. He and his family moved to what merchant town? _ _ _ _ _
4. Once they moved, Abram looked after the sheep, goats and cattle. What is another name for cattle? _ _ _ _
5. When Terah died, Abram was advised by his one god to move to this new location. _ _ _ _ _ _
6. Abram's new-found god renamed both Abram and his wife. Abram's wife was renamed this. _ _ _ _ _
7. Abram's new name was this. _ _ _ _ _ _ _
8. Abram laughed at his god when he was told he would have a baby with his wife. When she did have that baby, they named him this, because it means "laughter." _ _ _ _ _
9. Their son, had a son named this. _ _ _ _ _
10. Jacob had twelve sons. Which was his favorite? _ _ _ _ _ _
11. Jacob made this special, colorful piece of clothing for his favorite son. _ _ _ _
12. Because of the envy his brothers felt, they sold Joseph to be this. _ _ _ _ _
13. Joseph was taken to this country. _ _ _ _ _
14. While in prison, Joseph demonstrated his ability to tell the meaning of something we think about while we're sleeping. He knew what a _ _ _ _ _ meant.
15. Later, someone had a dream about seven fat cows that were eaten by seven thin cows. Who had this dream? _ _ _ _ _ _ _
16. Joseph knew the Pharaoh's dream meant that seven good years would be followed by seven years of famine. To help the people, he suggested they collect this in each of the seven good years, so there would be enough during the dry years. _ _ _ _ _

The Jewish People Word Search

```
J A C O B E T S M D R E A M F
C B A O L R R I N R U T X C G
R R N X A B E F E E L Y B O A
E A A K R T Z U D P E G Y P T
T H A R A N C H G H R N C E E
T A N R S F D J P A T I V B R
H M S L A V E O S R I H S Y A
I S A A C O W S A A U W R O H
N S A R A H P E R O G R A I N
D Y V G X W R P H H D I K F P
R O Y E Q I O H L F P A G E Y
```

If you have difficulty answering the clues on the previous page, see if you can find the right word from this list: ABRAHAM, CANAAN, COAT, COWS, DREAM, EGYPT, GRAIN, HARAN, ISAAC, JACOB, JOSEPH, PHARAOH, SARAH, SLAVE, TERAH, UR

Joseph: Lost and Found

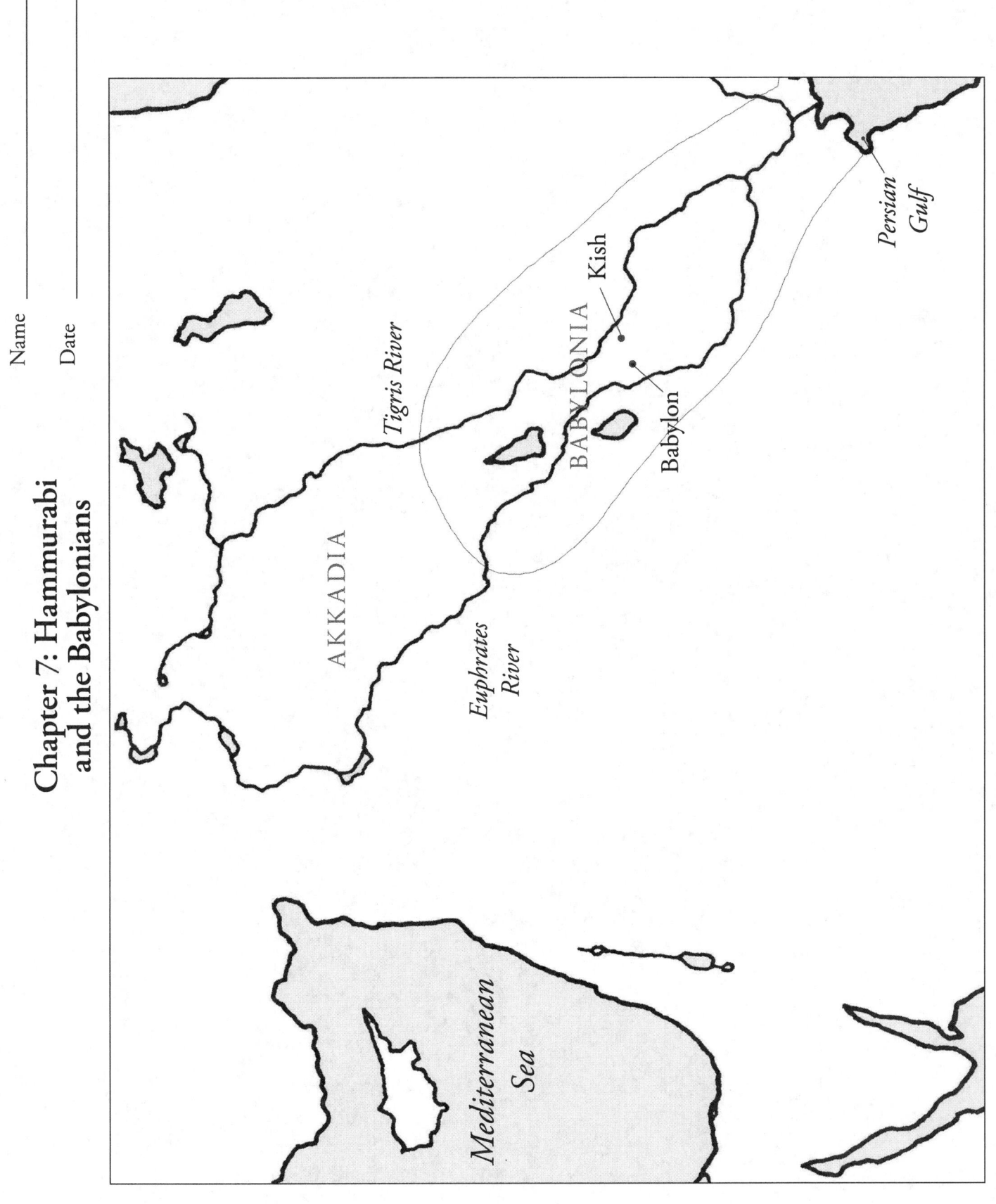

Name _____

Date _____

Chapter 7: Hammurabi and the Babylonians

Persian Gulf

Kish

BABYLONIA

Babylon

Tigris River

Euphrates River

AKKADIA

Mediterranean Sea

The Ziggurat of Ur

Crossword Puzzle: Name That Place

Across

3.   The name Sargon called his new kingdom

4.   The town Abraham was from

6.   The name of one of the first cities in the world

Down

1.   The name of Hammurabi's city

2.   Not the Euphrates River; the other one

5.   The name of the city where Sargon first lived

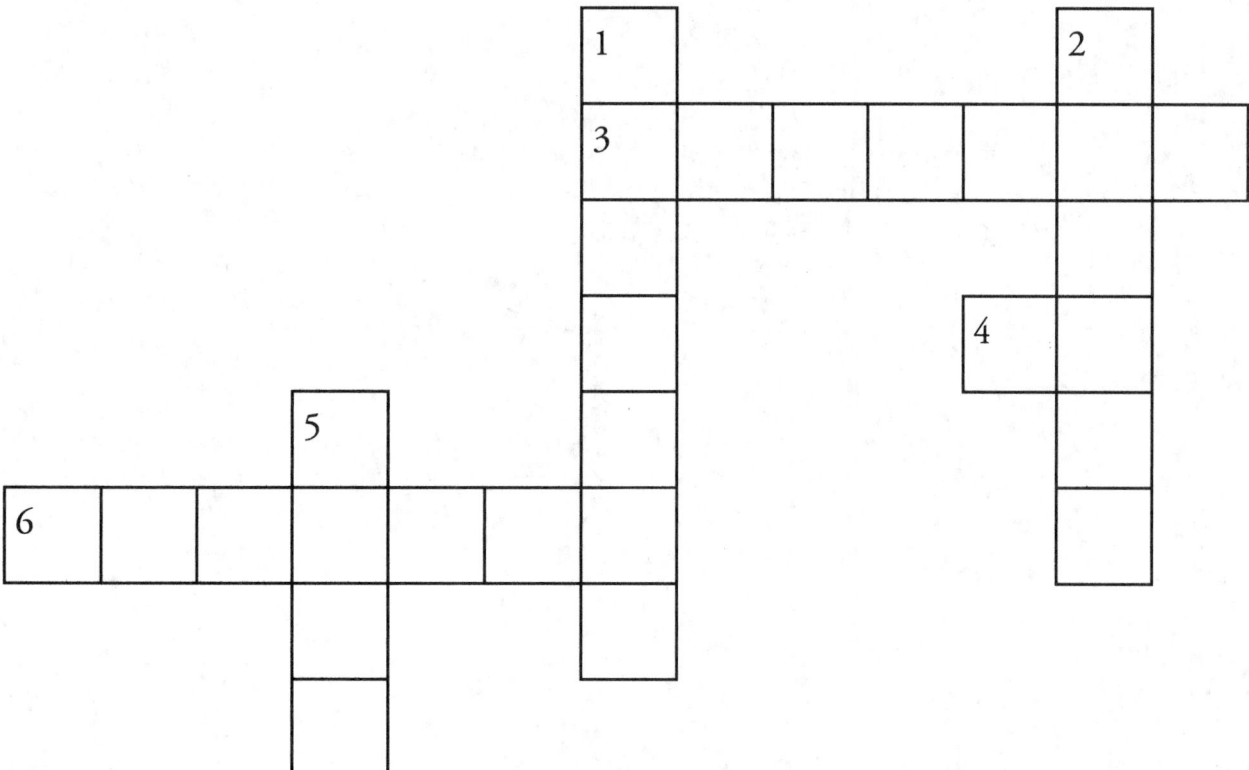

Chapter 8: The Assyrians

GILGAMESH AND THE LION

Chapter 9: The First Cities of India

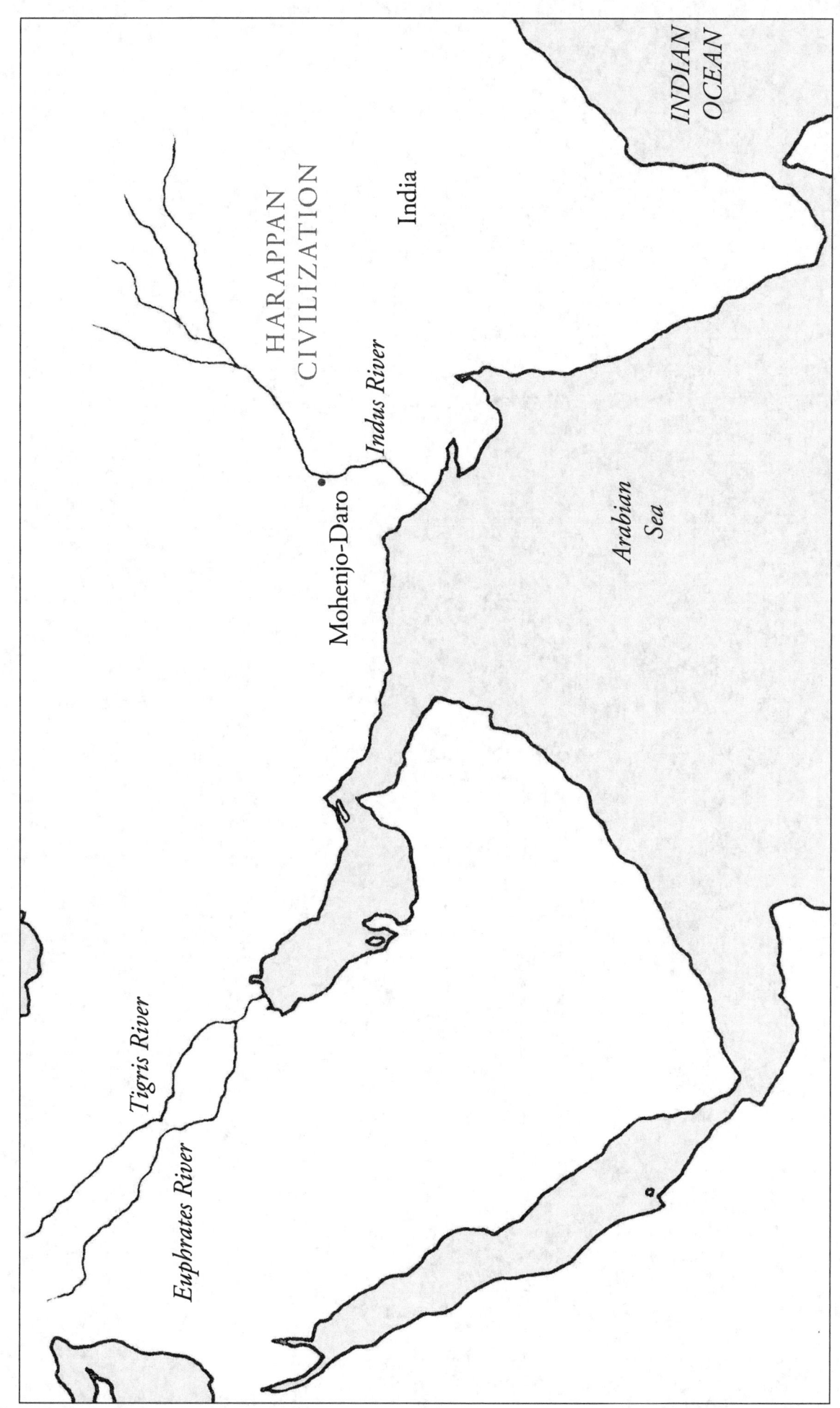

INDIAN OCEAN

HARAPPAN CIVILIZATION

India

Indus River

Mohenjo-Daro

Arabian Sea

Tigris River

Euphrates River

A Ceremonial Mask

A Statue From Mohenjo-Daro

Chapter 10: The Far East: Ancient China

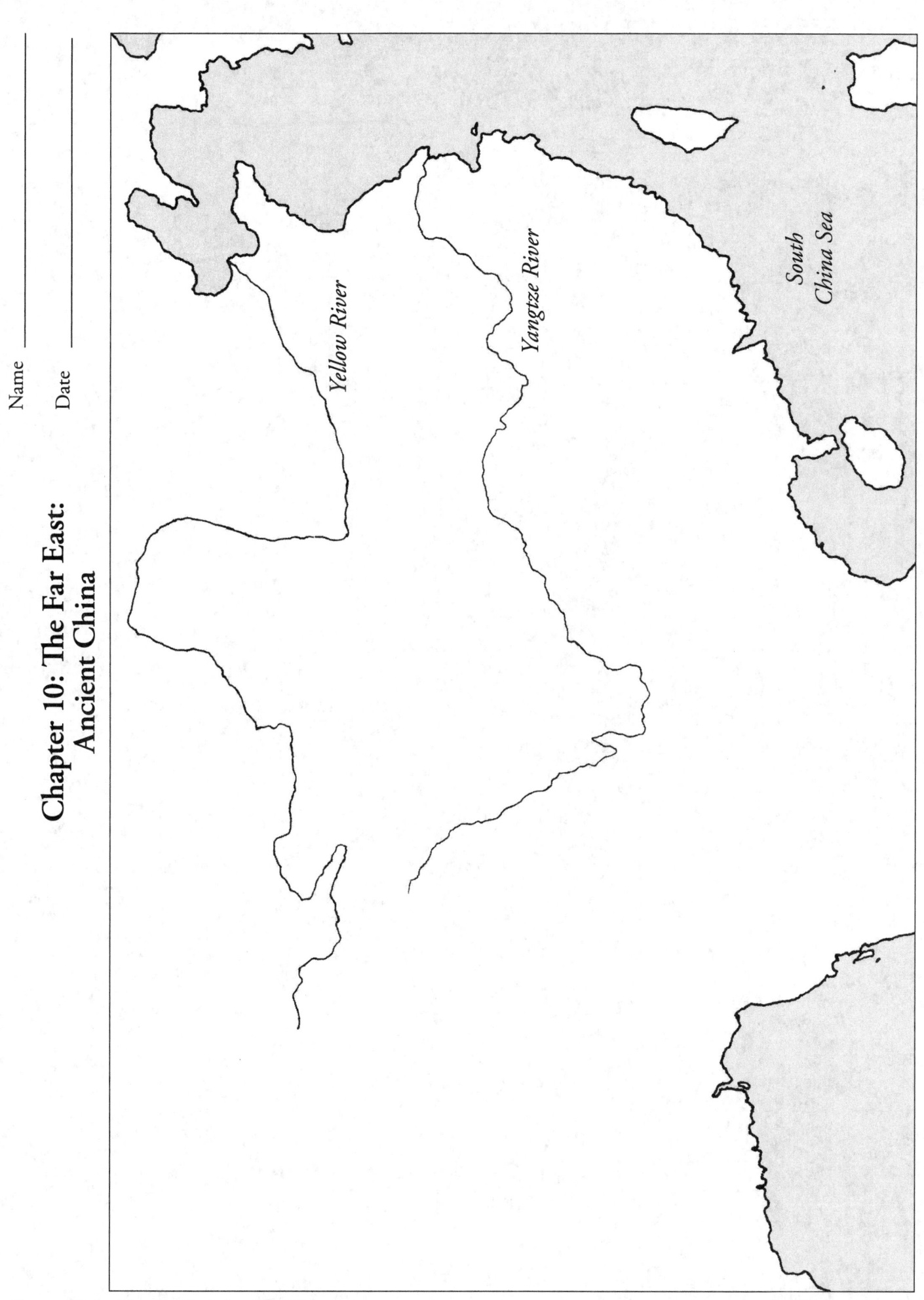

Yellow River

Yangtze River

South China Sea

Chin and His Father

Chapter 11: Ancient Africa

Name _____

Date _____

Chapter 12: The Middle Kingdom of Egypt

Hyksos Jewelry

Chapter 13: The New Kingdom of Egypt

The Mask of King Tut

Chapter 14: The Israelites Leave Egypt

Moses Leads the Israelites Across the Red Sea

Moses and the Ten Plagues

Moses and the Ten Plagues
sticker pages

Pharaoh
Read what he thought about the whole adventure in Exodus 5:1-9.

Plague 1
The Hebrew God changed the mighty Nile into blood. Read Exodus 7:14-24. Color the Nile red.

Moses
Read about whose idea this all was and how Moses felt about it in Exodus 2-4.

Plague 2
The Hebrew God sent a plague of frogs! Read Exodus 7:25-8:15.

Plague 3
The Hebrew God sent a plague of gnats! Read Exodus 8:16-19.

Moses and the Ten Plagues
sticker pages

Plague 5
The Hebrew God sent a plague on the Egyptian livestock! Read Exodus 9:1-7.

Plague 4
The Hebrew God sent a plague of flies! Read Exodus 8:20-32.

Plague 6
The Hebrew God sent a plague on the Egyptian people! Read Exodus 9:8-12.

(When you cut out this sticker, place it on top of Pharaoh, matching the top and bottom parts.)

Moses and the Ten Plagues
sticker pages

Plague 7
The Hebrew God sent a plague of hail. thunder, and lightning!
Read Exodus 9:13-34.

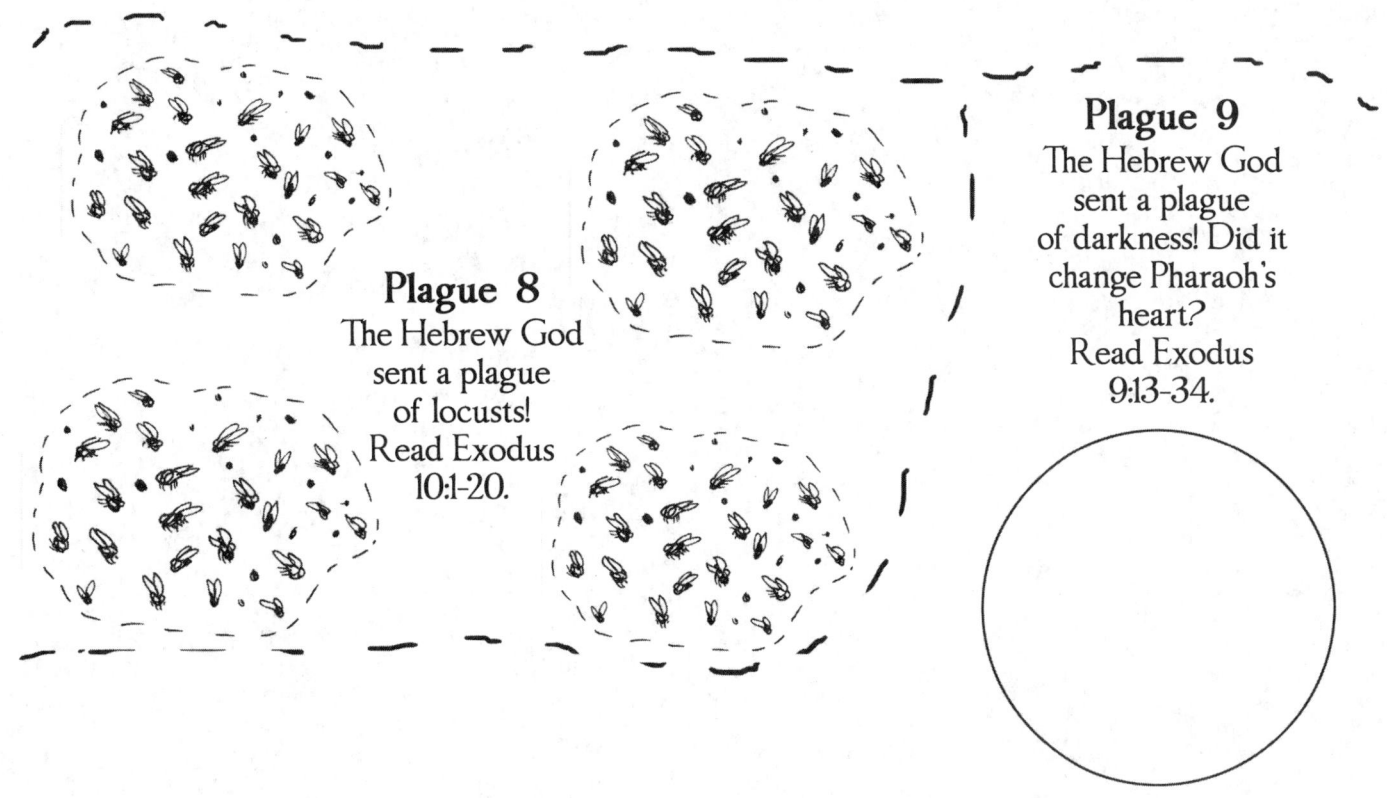

Plague 8
The Hebrew God sent a plague of locusts! Read Exodus 10:1-20.

Plague 9
The Hebrew God sent a plague of darkness! Did it change Pharaoh's heart?
Read Exodus 9:13-34.

Name _____

Date _____

Chapter 15: The Phoenicians

A Phoenician Ship

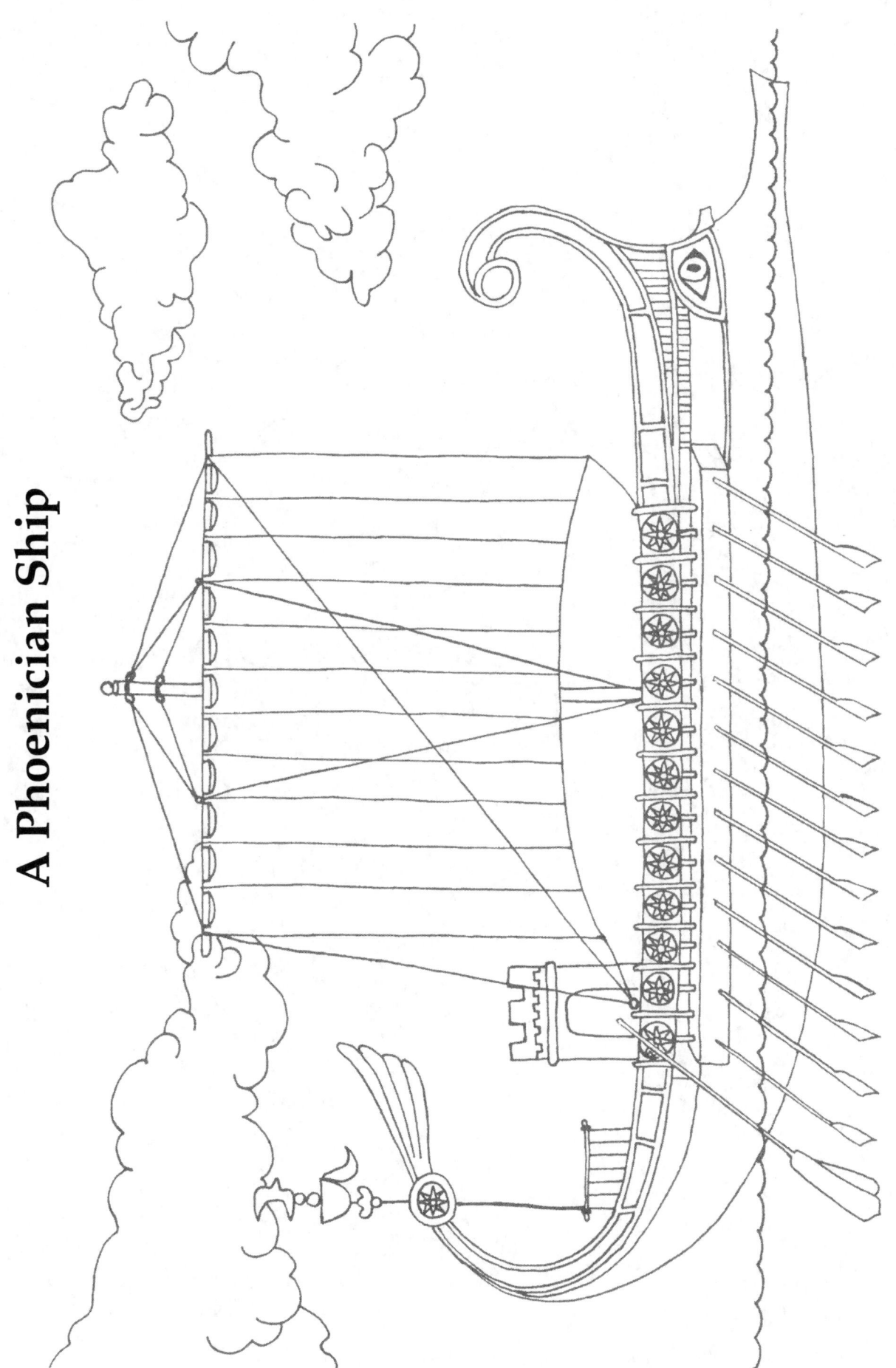

Name _____

Date _____

Chapter 16: The Return of Assyria

A Bas Relief From Ancient Assyria

Chapter 17: Babylon Takes Over Again

Marduk and Tiamat

Chapter 18: Life in Early Crete

ASIA MINOR

Aegean Sea

Thebes

Athens

Mycenae

Greece

Sparta

Thera

Crete

Mediterranean Sea

Bull Jumper

Theseus and the Minotaur

Name _____

Date _____

Chapter 19: The Early Greeks

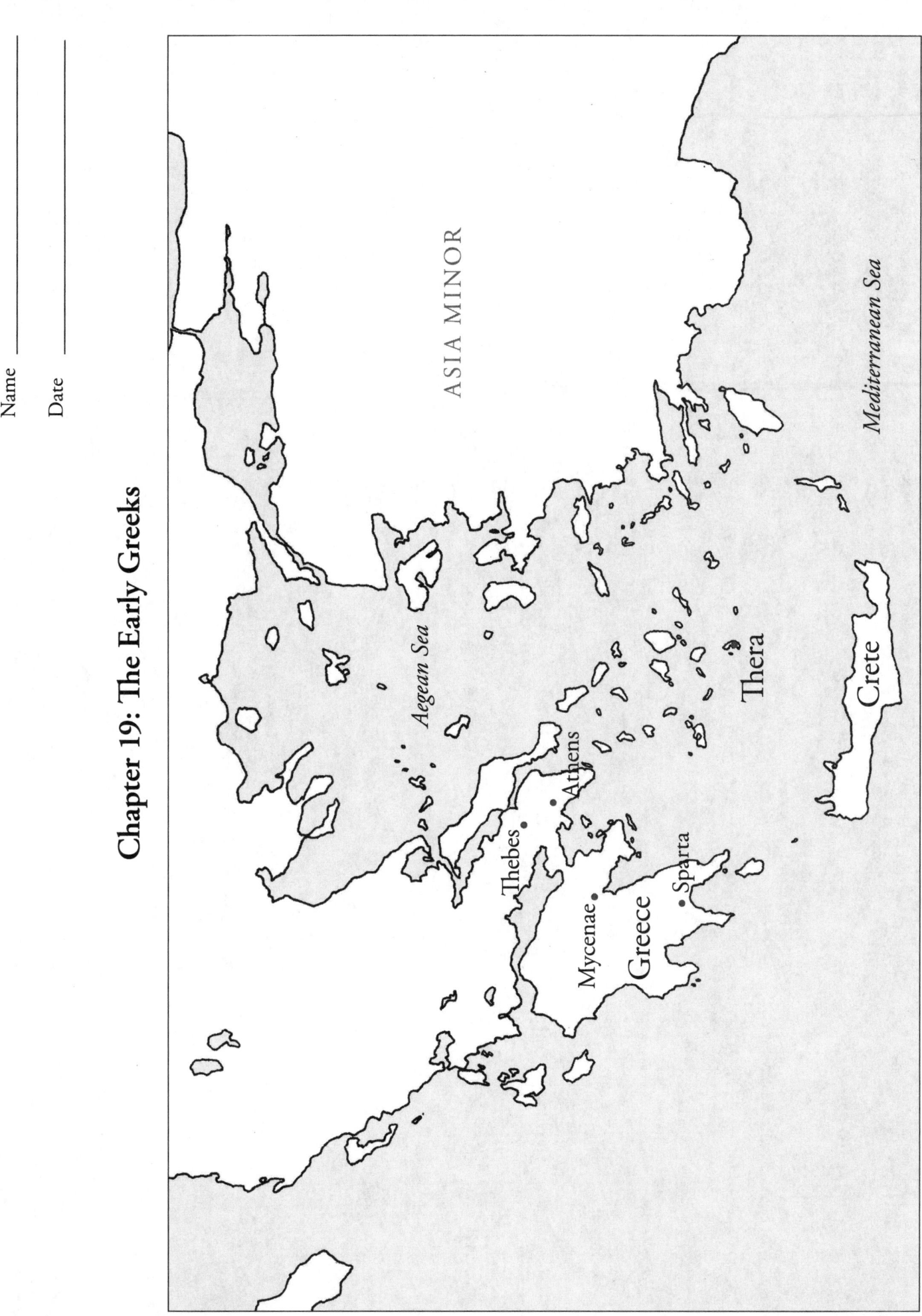

ASIA MINOR

Mediterranean Sea

Aegean Sea

Thebes

Athens

Mycenae

Greece

Sparta

Thera

Crete

Greek War Chariot

A Grecian Vase

Name _____

Date _____

Chapter 20: Greece Gets Civilized Again

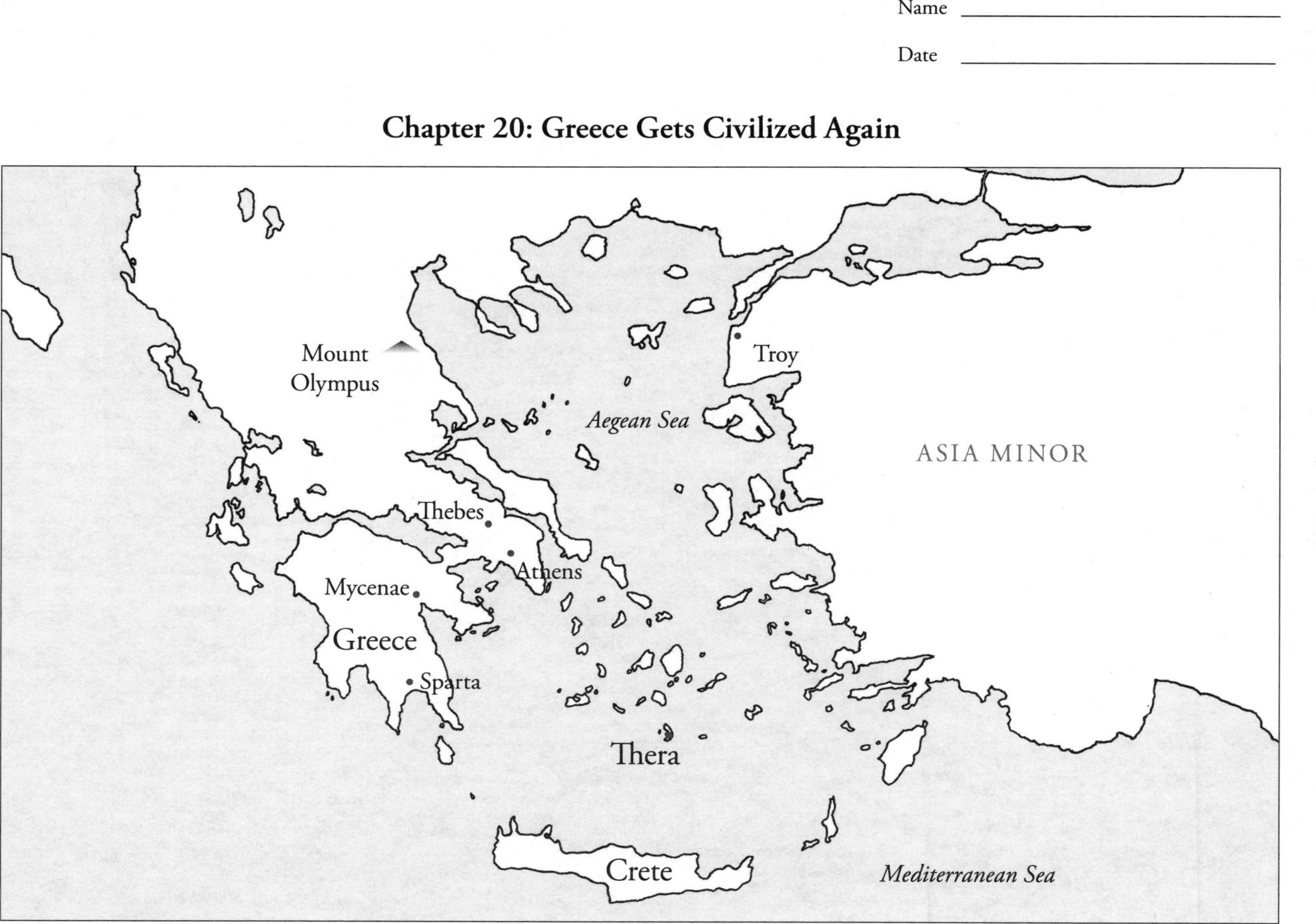

Mount Olympus

Troy

Aegean Sea

ASIA MINOR

Thebes

Athens

Mycenae

Greece

Sparta

Thera

Crete

Mediterranean Sea

The Cyclops

Greek Alphabet

Using the Greek alphabet to the right, write your name in Greek.

_____

_____

_____

_____

English	Capital	Lower-Case
A	Α	α
B	Β	β
G	Γ	γ
D	Δ	δ
E (short)	Ε	ε
Z	Ζ	ζ
E (long)	Η	η
Th	Θ	θ
I	Ι	ι
K	Κ	κ
L	Λ	λ
M	Μ	μ
N	Ν	ν
CH	Ξ	ξ
O (short)	Ο	ο
P	Π	π
R	Ρ	ρ
S	Σ	σ
T	Τ	τ
U	Υ	υ
Ph	Φ	φ
X	Χ	χ
PS	Ψ	ψ
O (long)	Ω	ω

Chapter 21: The Medes and the Persians

HARAPPAN CIVILIZATION

Indus River

Arabian Sea

Persian Gulf

Caspian Sea

Tigris River

Euphrates River

Canaan

Black Sea

Mediterranean Sea

Red Sea

Nile River

Egypt

Greece

Cyrus the Great

START HERE

⚐ You find an old cuneiform treasure map of the Fertile Crescent. Go 3 spaces ahead!

⸫ Tell where the 12 Jewish tribes get their names! (See Ch. 6) Do you know? Go 2 spaces ahead!

☆ Can you remember the first Sumerian Dictator? Sargon! He is the first to unite the cities of Mesopotamia. Say "Sargon" three times and advance 2 spaces!

⚡ CITY STATES AT WAR! Go back 3 spaces!

☽ Name the two main rivers in Mesopotamia and move 3 spaces.

✕ Hammurabi, King of Babylon conquers Mesopotamia. Move ahead 1 space!

☼ Hammurabi puts his laws in stone. Can you name one? (See Ch. 7) Go ahead 3 spaces!

☾ Yikes! Up north, another king is building the Assyrian empire: Shamshi-Adad! Move back 2 spaces!

✛ Babylonians discover that the Earth goes all the way around the sun. They name that rotation "one year." Move 1 space ahead!

◈ Shamshi-Adad conquers another city. His son gets to rule it! He gives a party to celebrate! Advance 4 spaces!

CONQUER MESOPOTAMIA

☺ Cyrus lets the Jews go back to their homes. The Jews call him, "The Anointed of the Lord." Move 6 spaces ahead!

☼ Cyrus the Great gains the Persian throne and leads the Persians against the Medes. Is he a good king? (See Ch. 21) Advance 4 spaces! Cheer for Cyrus the Great!

𐀏 Assyrians take land back and attack everyone! So, Babylon makes friends with the Medes. Now Babylon and the Medes are in charge! Go ahead 3.

♆ The Babylonians and the Medes are getting very proud! But who is the next nation to take over? (See Ch. 21) Go 2 spaces back!

☏ Nebuchadnezzar's beautiful wife wants to return home to Persia. What does he build for her? (See Ch. 17) Got the answer? Advance 4 spaces!

☷ Nebuchadnezzar the Great rebuilds Babylon. Advance 6!

⚒ Oh, no! Ashurbanipal is scaring everyone! Go back 1 space!

⚡ Babylon wants revenge! Now they rule Mesopotamia! They destroy the library at Ninevah. Go back 3 spaces!

✖ Shamshi-Adad dies. His sons start fighting and don't keep Assyria united. Do you know who conquers them? (See Ch. 8) If you can say the name of their conqueror, go five spaces forward!

〜 Who is Gilgamesh? Explain, and move 3 spaces ahead!

𐀏𐀏 The Assyrians rebel against their masters, the Babylonians! They rage up and down the Tigris and Euphrates Rivers, and invade Canaan and scatter the Jews. And one of the greatest Assyrian kings of all, Ashurbanipal, leads his soldiers all the way down to Egypt to take it over! Move forward 6 spaces.

⚊ What does Ashurbanipal build in Ninevah? (See Ch. 16) Move 3 spaces.

FINISH!

Name _____

Date _____

Chapter 22: Sparta and Athens

A Spartan Warrior

GREEK STICKERS

Greek Paper Dolls

Greek Paper Dolls
outfits

Greek Paper Dolls

outfit and accessories

Chapter 23: The Greek Gods

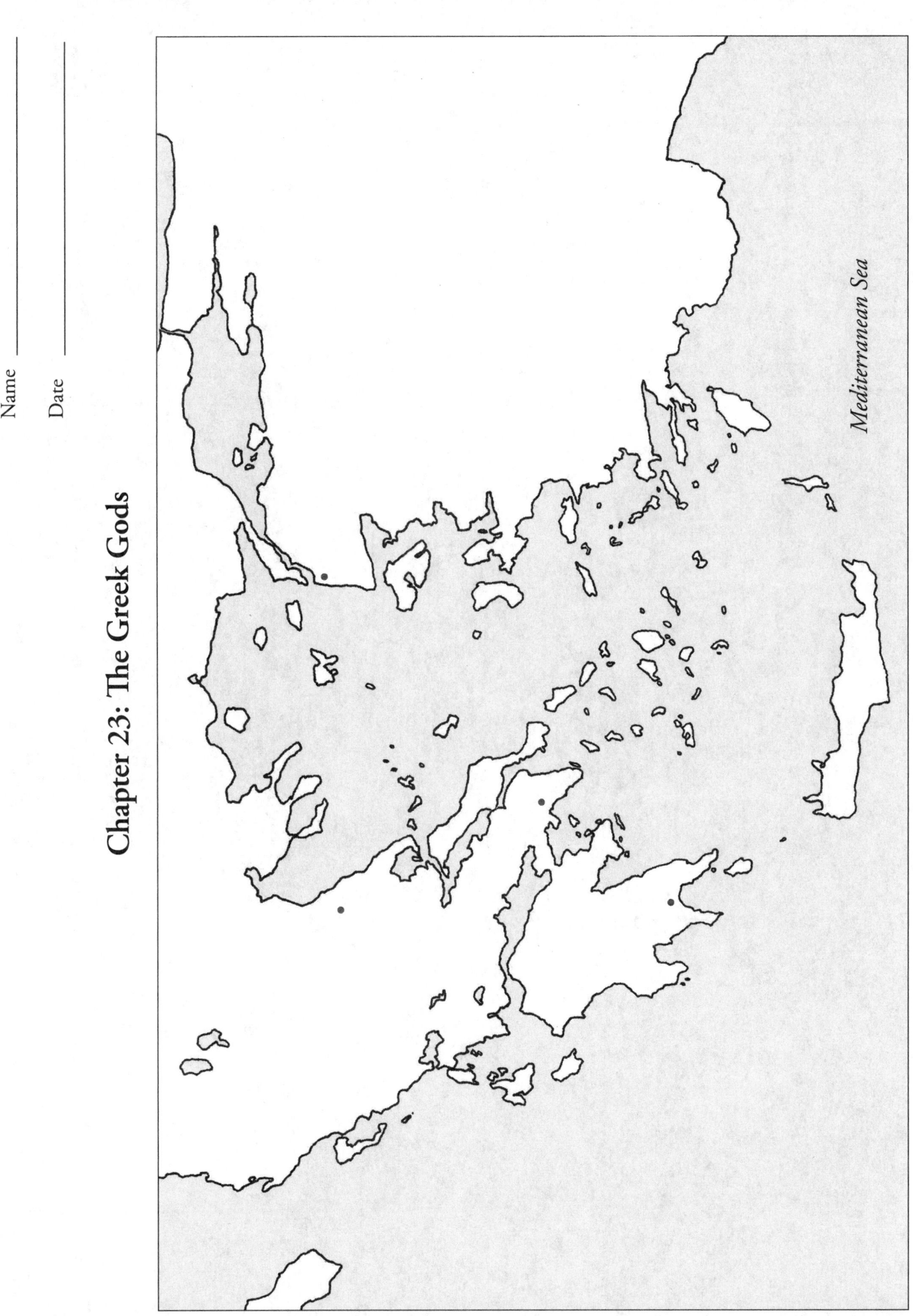

Mediterranean Sea

Aphrodite and Zeus

The Gods and Goddesses of Greece

Greek Name	Roman / Latin Name	Description
Zeus	Jupiter, Jove	Chief of the Gods and Goddesses
Hera	Juno	Protector of Marriage
Poseidon	Neptune	Ruler of the Sea
Hades	Pluto	God of the Underworld and Precious Metals
Athena	Minerva	Goddess of the City, Education, Science, and War
Apollo	Apollo	God of Sun, Truth, Music, and Healing
Artemis	Diana	Goddess of Wild Things, Chief Huntress
Aphrodite	Venus	Goddess of Love and Beauty
Hermes	Mercury	God of Commerce and the Marketplace
Ares	Mars	God of War
Hephaestus	Vulcan	God of Fire and Blacksmiths
Hestia	Vesta	Goddess of Hearth and Home
Eros	Cupid	God of Love
Persephone	Persipina	Goddess of the Springtime
Demeter	Ceres	Goddess of the Earth, the Harvest, and Corn
Dionysus	Bacchus	God of Wine, Grapes, and Merriment
Pan	Faunus	God of Sheep and Flocks
Selene	Luna	Goddess of the Moon
Helios	Sol	God of the Sun
Eris	Discordia	Goddess of Discord
Hypnos	Somnus	God of Sleep
Nike	Victoria	Goddess of Victory
Phosphor	Lucifer	Light-bearer; the star that brings in the day

Greek Gods and Goddesses Wordsearch

Find these words from the story of the Golden Apple in the wordsearch below. Words are only across or down.

Mount Olympus	Aphrodite	Eris	Athena
Greece	Paris	Zeus	Troy
Hera	Beautiful	Apple	Helen

```
G  S  P  A  P  H  R  O  D  I  T  E
R  Z  I  P  F  E  Q  L  O  O  K  X
E  A  H  P  G  O  T  W  G  H  Z  A
E  U  W  L  Z  E  R  I  S  E  E  T
C  S  M  E  B  V  O  X  I  L  Y  H
E  X  J  R  E  D  Y  P  N  E  M  E
Y  K  I  Z  A  P  L  J  G  N  O  N
B  J  M  S  U  T  S  U  N  R  M  A
M  O  U  N  T  O  L  Y  M  P  U  S
B  P  T  E  I  Y  C  T  O  Y  S  C
O  W  P  J  F  P  A  R  I  S  I  F
Y  O  U  R  U  Z  Q  M  X  B  T  G
H  E  R  A  L  O  N  G  Z  E  U  S
```

Chapter 24: The Wars of the Greeks

Persian Empire

Mediterranean Sea

Aegean Sea

Marathon

Athens

Salamis

Sparta

Greece

The Parthenon

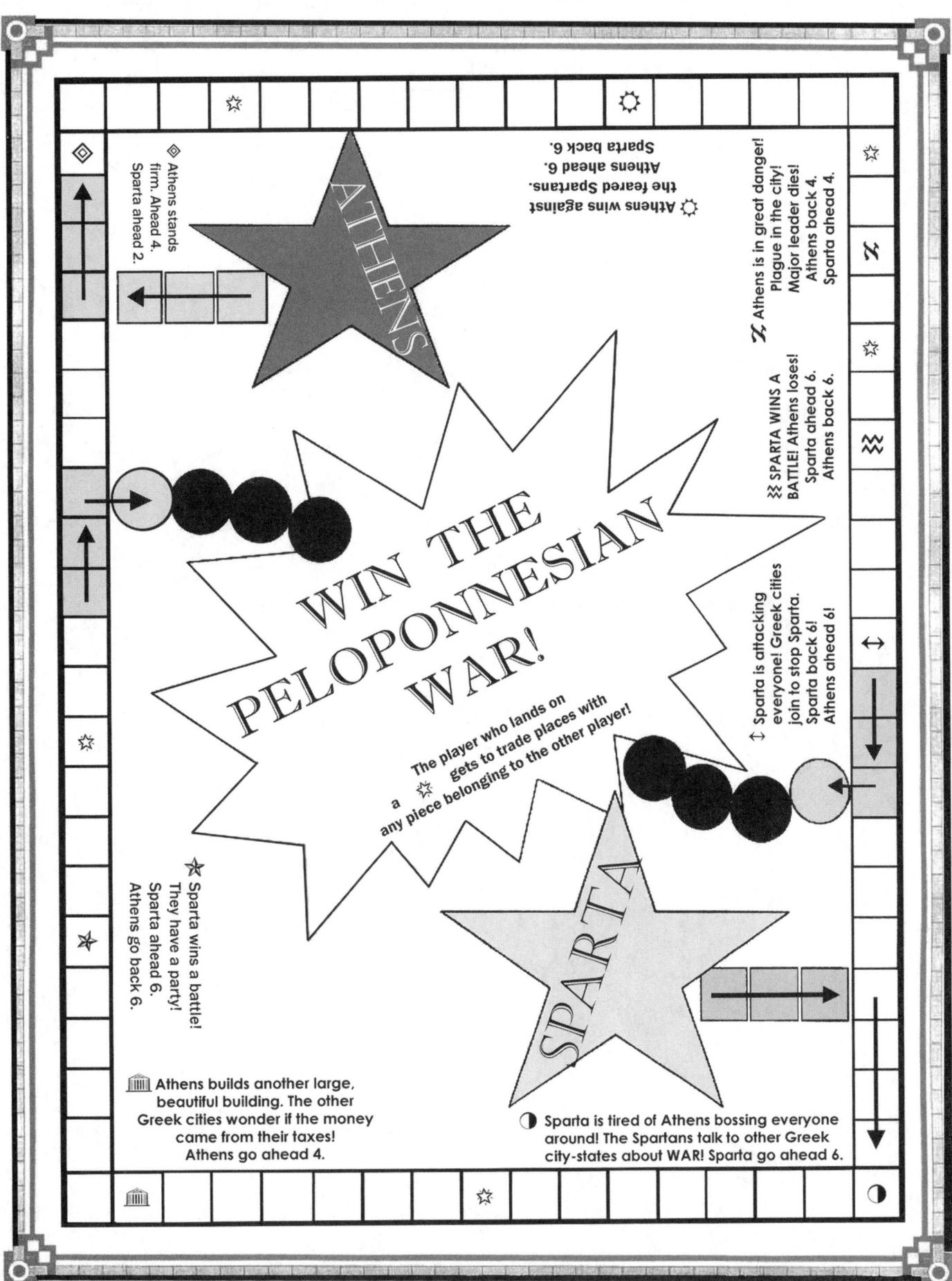

WIN THE PELOPONNESIAN WAR!

The player who lands on a ☆ gets to trade places with any piece belonging to the other player!

ATHENS

SPARTA

◈ Athens stands firm. Ahead 4. Sparta ahead 2.

Sparta back 6.
Athens ahead 6.
☼ Athens wins against the feared Spartans.

𝒵 Athens is in great danger! Plague in the city! Major leader dies! Athens back 4. Sparta ahead 4.

≈ SPARTA WINS A BATTLE! Athens loses! Sparta ahead 6. Athens back 6.

↕ Sparta is attacking everyone! Greek cities join to stop Sparta. Sparta back 6! Athens ahead 6!

☆ Sparta wins a battle! They have a party! Sparta ahead 6. Athens go back 6.

🏛 Athens builds another large, beautiful building. The other Greek cities wonder if the money came from their taxes! Athens go ahead 4.

◐ Sparta is tired of Athens bossing everyone around! The Spartans talk to other Greek city-states about WAR! Sparta go ahead 6.

Name _____

Date _____

Chapter 25: Alexander the Great

Alexander the Great and Bucephalus

Tie a Gordian Knot

A Bowline

Step One   *Step Two*   *Step Three*

A Sheet Bend

Step One   *Step Two*

Bucephalus Stick Horse

cut out

attach to broomstick

The Pharos Lighthouse

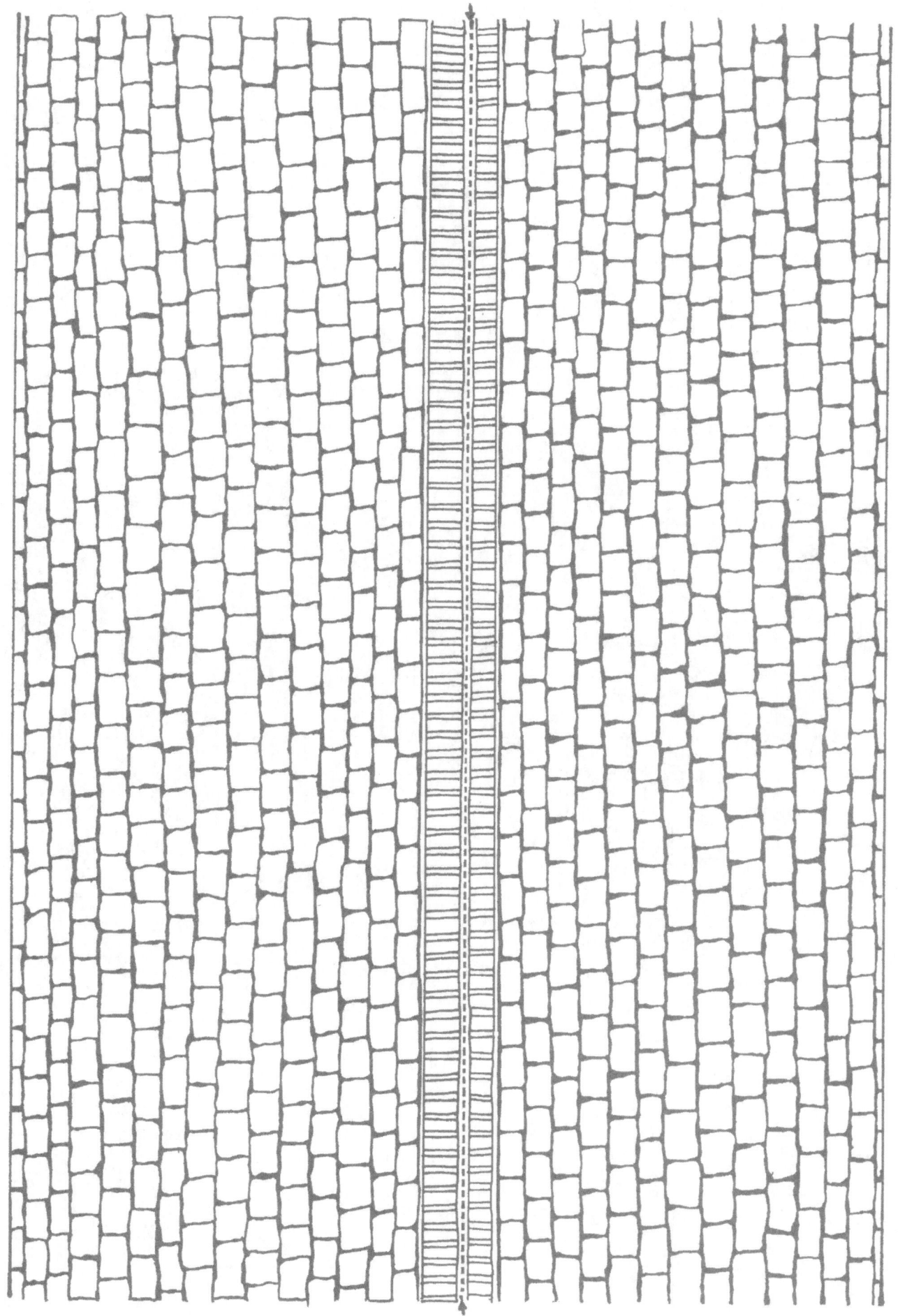

Make two photocopies of this template. Use both to wrap around the potato chip can.

Alexander the Great Game

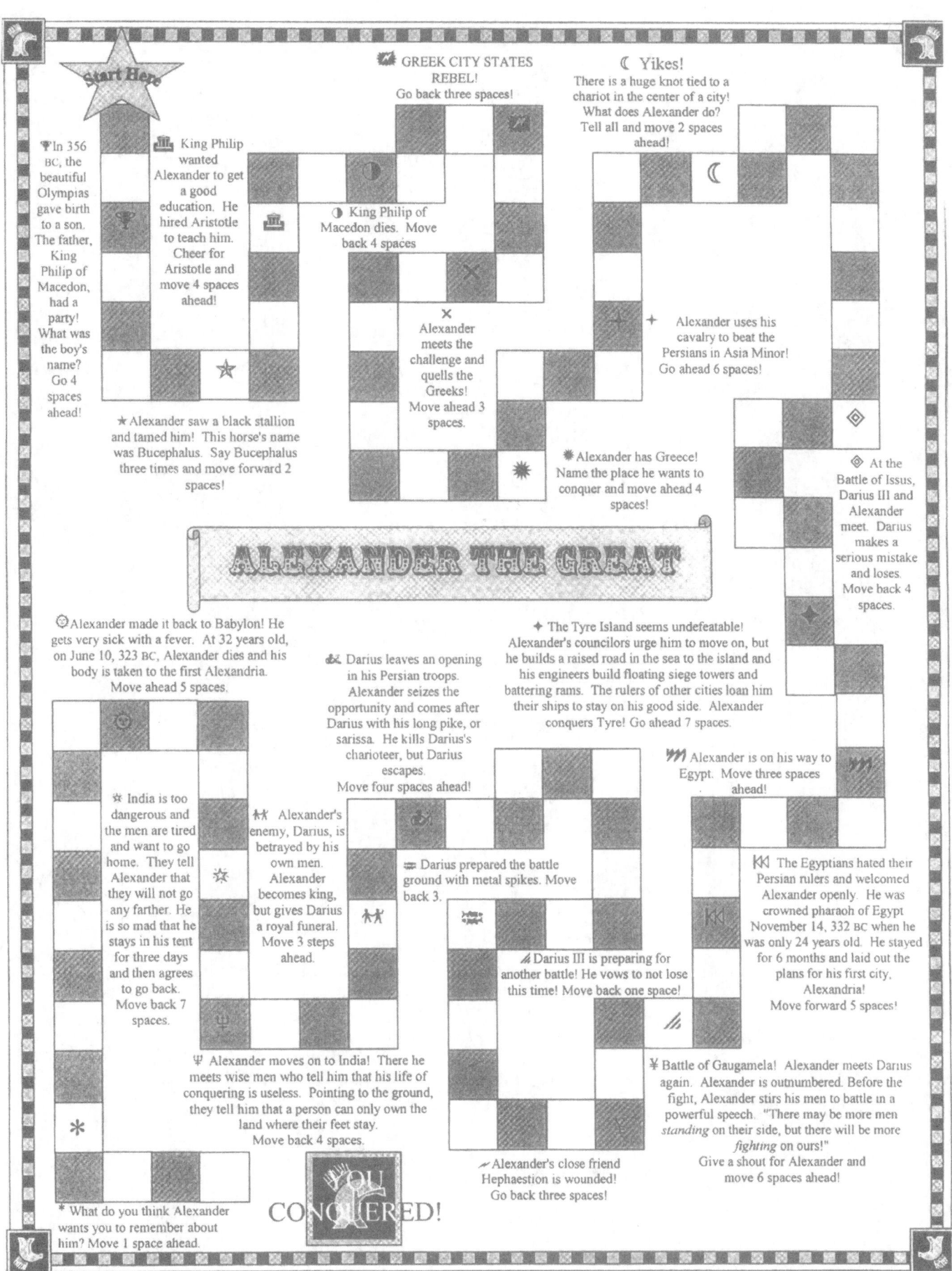

Name _____

Date _____

Chapter 26: The People of the Americas

Rabbit Shoots the Sun

Chapter 27: The Rise of Rome

Rome

Sicily

Mediterranean Sea

Name _____

Date _____

ROMULUS
and
REMUS

Chapter 28: The Roman Empire

Rome

Italy

Sicily

Mediterranean Sea

Gladiators in the Arena

Aqueduct Template

Name _____

Date _____

Chapter 29: Rome's War With Carthage

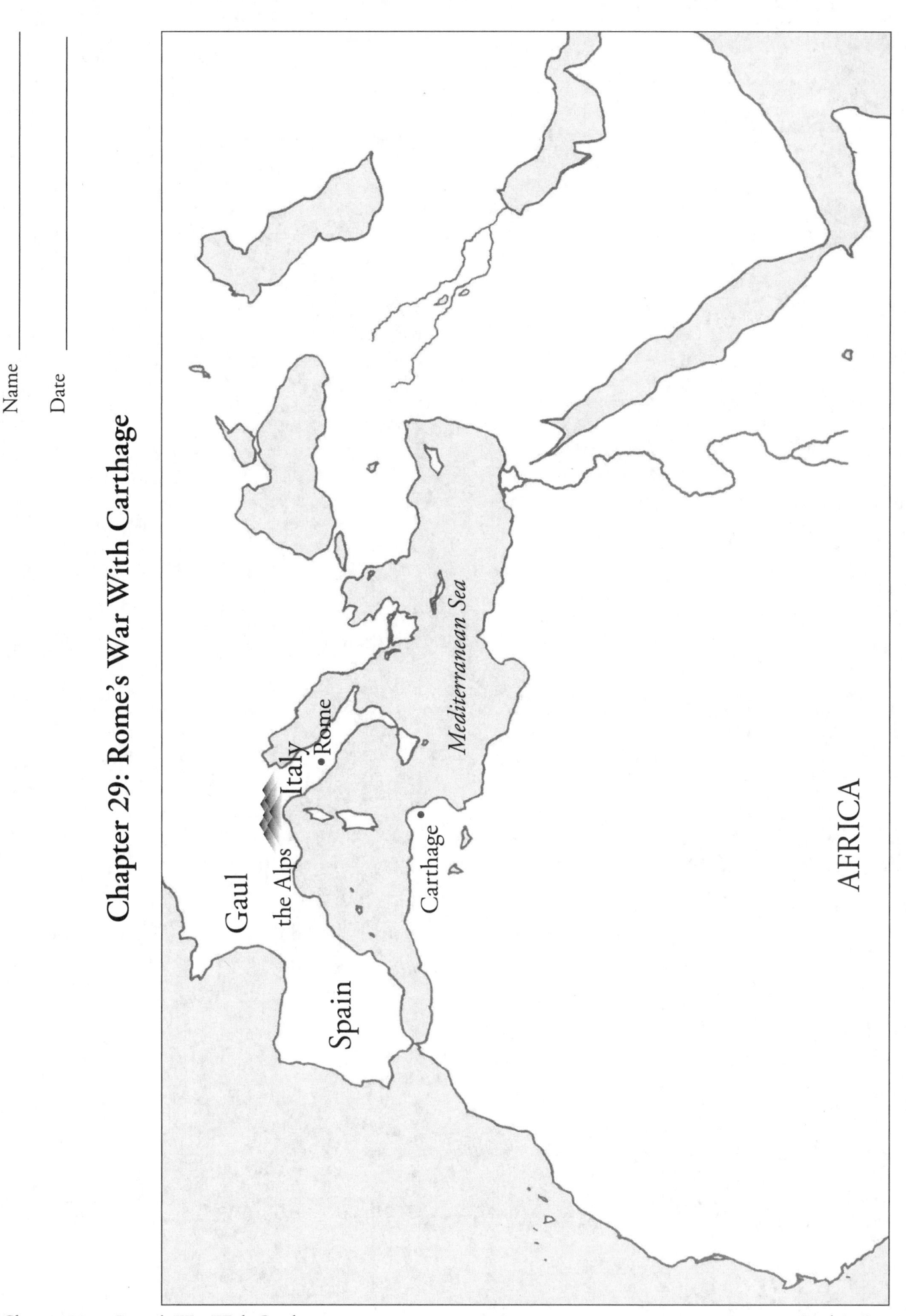

Gaul

the Alps

Italy

•Rome

Spain

Carthage•

Mediterranean Sea

AFRICA

Hannibal's War Elephants

HANNIBAL

Help Hannibal cross the Alps

Name _____

Date _____

Chapter 30: The Aryans of India

The Buddha

Chapter 31: The Mauryan Empire of India

The Jataka Tales

Name _____

Date _____

Chapter 32: China: Writing and the Qin

The Great Wall

The Great Wall of China

Confucius
China's Wise Teacher

Tangrams

Name _____

Date _____

Chapter 34: The Rise of Julius Caesar

Gaul

the Alps

Spain

Tiber River

Rome

Mediterranean Sea

Play the "Ransom Caesar" Game!

	1	2	3	4
P				
I				
R				
A				
T				
E				

- -

	1	2	3	4
P				
I				
R				
A				
T				
E				

Name _____

Date _____

Chapter 35: Caesar the Hero

Britain

Gaul

Spain

the Alps

Rubicon River

Tiber River

Rome

Mediterranean Sea

Egypt

Nile River

Julius Caesar

Chapter 36: The First Roman Prince

Augustus Caesar
THE FIRST ROMAN PRINCE

Chapter 37: The Beginning of Christianity

The Life of Jesus

Chapter 38: The End of the Ancient Jewish Nation

Haran

Tigris River

Euphrates River

Canaan

Jerusalem

Mediterranean Sea

The Star of David

The Flag of Modern Israel

Make Your Own Dreidel

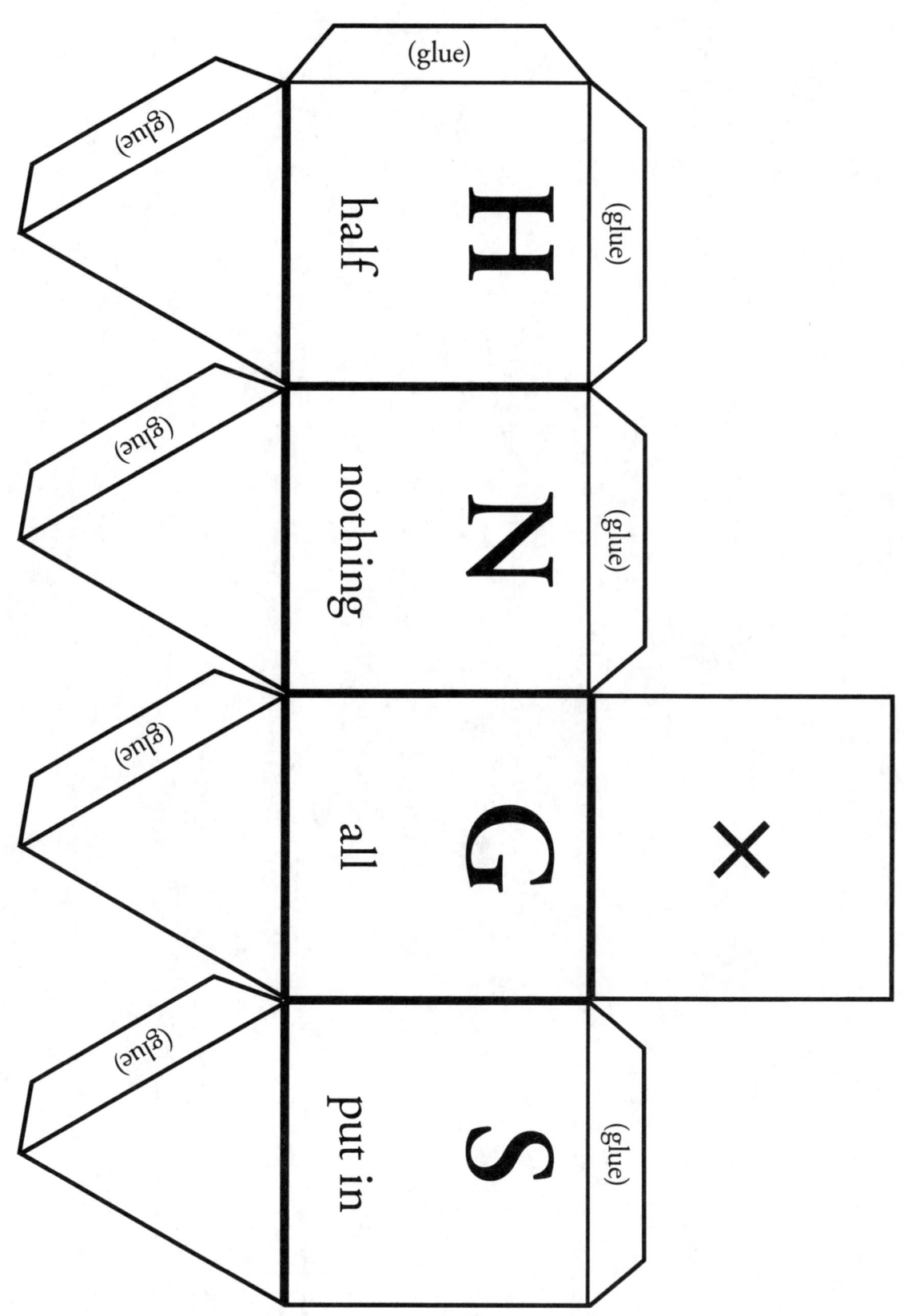

Name _____

Date _____

Chapter 39: Rome and the Christians

The Catacombs

Chapter 40: Rome Begins to Weaken

Constantinople

Nile River

Egypt

Mediterranean Sea

Rome

Boadicea

Chapter 41: The Attacking Barbarians

HUNS

VISIGOTHS

VANDALS

Black Sea

Constantinople

Mediterranean Sea

Rome

Nile River

Egypt

Africa

A VISIGOTH INVADER

Chapter 42: The End of Rome

Review Cards

The Jewish People   6   SOTW1

Abraham did what God told him to do. He had a son: Isaac. Isaac had a son named Jacob. Jacob had 12 sons! These 12 sons all had families of their own. Abraham's family was getting larger and larger. These 12 sons name the 12 tribes of the Jewish people.

Hammurabi / Babylonians   7   SOTW1

Hammurabi was a great king of Babylon. He didn't want people to obey him just because his army was strong. He wanted his empire to be governed by just laws. He wrote down all the laws in stone. They are the first set of written laws we know of.

The Assyrians   8   SOTW1

The Assyrians, a powerful kingdom from the north, took over much of Mesopotamia. Both the Babylonians and the Assyrians told stories about a great, mythical king named Gilgamesh. He was half god and half man, able to lift huge stones with one hand and leap over high walls.

The First Cities of India   9   SOTW1

The cities in the Indus Valley were built around huge circular mounds called *citadels*. Each citadel had a stronghold in it—a place to go in case enemies attacked. All around the citadel people build their houses our of mud bricks.

Ancient China   10   SOTW1

Empress Lei Zu and her court made the wonderful cloth called silk, discovered when a cocoon had dropped into her tea. They fed the silk worms mulberry leaves and waited for the precious threads of silk. China soon became famous for its silk, made only there!

Ancient Africa   11   SOTW1

Long ago, the Sahara Desert was a fertile place full of water and trees. But then something happened. Rain did not fall, grass died, and the ground dried up. The people of the Sahara went south where they settled around lakes and rivers and began a new life.

Review Cards

The Middle Kingdom — 12 — SOTW1

Egyptians were overrun by the Hyksos from Canaan. They hated their Hyksos kings! Finally, a group of Egyptian princes, using the weapons of the Hyksos such as the sickle-shaped swords and chariots, drove out the Hyksos. Egypt became stronger than ever!

The New Kingdom of Egypt — 13 — SOTW1

After the Egyptians kicked out the Hyksos, Egypt became more powerful. This is called the *Golden Age of Egypt*. Many pharaohs came and went. But four of the most important ones include Thutmose I, Hatshepsut, Amenhotep, and Tutankhamen.

The Israelites Leave Egypt — 14 — SOTW1

This part of Israel's history is called the Exodus. Moses led the Jewish people away from slavery in Egypt, where they were serving the pharaoh. The Israelites moved back to Canaan and lived there for many years. In time, they became a powerful kingdom in their own right.

The Phoenicians — 15 — SOTW1

Northern Canaan wasn't a good place to grow food. So the Phoenicians put boats in the water and became the best sailors in the ancient world. They made beautiful purple cloth and blown glass. Carthage was founded by Dido, a famous Phoenician princess.

The Return of Assyria — 16 — SOTW1

The Assyrians rebelled against their masters, the Babylonians. One of the greatest Assyrian kings, Ashurbanipal, led the strong army as far as Egypt, making his nation rich. But he was not happy until he collected all the clay tablets, forming the world's first library.

Babylon Takes Over Again! — 17 — SOTW1

Now the Babylonians wanted revenge! Their empire was almost as big as the Assyrians'. One Babylonian king was such a famous ruler that he was known as "Nebuchadnezzar the Great." He built a beautiful mountain with gardens for his Persian wife.

Review Cards

Life in Early Crete 18 SOTW1	**The Early Greeks** 19 SOTW1

Life in Early Crete   18   SOTW1

Crete is a long, skinny island in the Mediterranean Sea. The Minoans who lived there entertained themselves by leaping over bulls! They were also known for their ship-building. They made the seas safe. But they mysteriously disappeared.

The Early Greeks   19   SOTW1

Crete was then taken over by the Mycenaeans from Greece. They were great fighters because they had bronze weapons and chariots. But the Barbarians and Dorians defeated them. These people didn't keep records so we call this time the Greek Dark Ages.

Greece Gets Civilized   20   SOTW1

The longer the barbarians lived in Greece, the more civilized they became. They no longer wandered around looking for cities to attack. Instead, they settled into villages. They became Greeks. They used their own alphabet and began to write down stories about themselves.

The Medes and Persians   21   SOTW1

The Babylonians and the Medes destroyed Assyria, but they weren't in charge long! A new nation gained control under the leadership of Cyrus the Great. He was a strong warrior, but he was also a good and fair king. He was called "The Anointed of the Lord" by the Jews.

Sparta and Athens   22   SOTW1

The Greeks all spoke the same language, dressed the same, and worshipped the same. But the Greeks didn't all obey a single king. Instead, each Greek city made its own laws. Each had its own army. Each city had its own way of living. They liked independence.

The Greek Gods   23   SOTW1

The Greeks believed in a whole family of gods. They were polytheists. Sometimes the gods were helpful. Other times they were cruel, such as the time the chief god, Zeus, made a golden apple that started a horrible war down on earth.

Review Cards

The Wars of the Greeks   24   SOTW1

The Persians wanted Greece. The Athenians and the Spartans were furious! They decided to stop fighting each other and defend themselves against the Persians. The war lasted 60 years. The Greeks finally won. Then they started fighting each other again!

Alexander the Great   25   SOTW1

Alexander had always been an unusual boy. Even as a child, he was strong and brave. Nothing scared him. He fought the Persians and took over their whole territory! He learned how to use elephants in combat. He also built cities and gave them his name.

The People of the Americas   26   SOTW1

The Olmecs were the first civilization in Central America. They built a city on top of a hill. At the center they built a pyramid of dirt and clay. On top of that they built their temple, with the heads of their gods around it. They carried every bit of the dirt up in baskets!

The Rise of Rome   27   SOTW1

At first, Rome was just a tiny village in the hills of Italy. But as it began to grow, it fought other kingdoms. From the Etruscans the Romans learned about Greek gods, painting and music, and the customs of kings, like *togas* and *fasces*, carried to show how powerful a king was.

The Roman Empire   28   SOTW1

The Romans needed more land so they attacked their neighbors. The more land they got, the richer they became. The cities grew larger and the people needed more fresh water. So they designed special channels for water called *aqueducts*. They also built many roads.

Rome's War with Carthage   29   SOTW1

Carthage and Rome both wanted to control the trade at sea. A war broke out between them. Hannibal, from Carthage, planned a fantastic assault. He traveled over the Alps with elephants for a surprise attack. It almost worked!

Review Cards

The Aryans of India 30 SOTW1

The Aryans brought in the caste system and the poor in India suffered. One man, Siddhartha, gave up his rich life to find an answer to poverty and sadness. He saw that anyone can find happiness by leading a good life. He was known as the Buddha.

The Mauryan Empire 31 SOTW1

The most famous Mauryan emperor was named Asoka. He conquered many cities in a war that killed thousands. When he saw the suffering the war caused, he decided to try and bring people in through honesty, truthfulness, and mercy. He followed Buddha.

China: Writing and the Qin 32 SOTW1

The warring state to the east was called Qin. Its warlord, Qin Zheng had an army of a million. He conquered all, ruling all of China. He moved his enemies close to him, built roads, melted down weapons, and punished severely. He built the Great Wall against the Mongols.

Confucius 33 SOTW1

At the same time that Buddha was teaching in India, another man in China was teaching the Chinese people that they too could be happy even if poor. He taught his followers to be peaceful, honest, and kind—to avoid any kind of violence, even to animals or insects.

The Rise of Julius Caesar 34 SOTW1

Julius Caesar wanted to be consul, but was sent to govern the Romans in Spain. He was not happy, but worked hard and was popular with the people of Rome. He went back and convinced the other consuls that he should be a consul as well. Soon the people forgot the other consuls.

Caesar the Hero 35 SOTW1

Caesar set out to be a great war hero. The Senate didn't like it. Caesar became more and more powerful. He got rid of his enemies and declared himself dictator. He also established who his heir would be. The Senate finally carried out a plan to kill him.

Review Cards

The First Roman Prince   36   SOTW1

Caesar's nephew, Octavian, was only nineteen when Caesar died. He inherited all of Caesar's money and threw a big party for ten days in Caesar's honor. When he saw how popular he was, he demanded to be made consul. He made Rome richer.

Beginning of Christianity   37   SOTW1

During the Roman peace, Jesus was born and lived in Judea. When he turned 30, he began to travel and teach about God. He healed many and taught the people. With the help of Rome, the leaders put him to death. The Bible says that after three days, he rose from the dead.

End of the Ancient Jewish Nation 38   SOTW1

The Jews hated Roman rule, so they set fire to the home of the Roman ruler of Judea and attacked soldiers. When Rome defeated them, they burned down the Temple. Even the Temple's foundations were destroyed to get the melted gold in the cracks.

Rome and the Christians   39   SOTW1

Nero was one of the worst emperors of Rome. He blamed a fire in Rome on the Christians and persecuted them. Afraid, the Christians held their meetings in underground passages. This secrecy soon made people suspicious of them.

Review Cards